HAYEK'S SOCIAL AND ECONOMIC PHILOSOPHY

HAYEK'S SOCIAL AND ECONOMIC PHILOSOPHY

Norman P. Barry

© Norman P. Barry 1979

First published 1979 by
THE MACMILLAN PRESS LTD
London and Basingstoke
Associated companies in Delhi
Dublin Hong Kong Johannesburg Lagos
Melbourne New York Singapore Tokyo

Printed in Great Britain by
Unwin Brothers Limited
Gresham Press, Old Woking, Surrey

British Library Cataloguing in Publication Data

Barry, Norman P.
  Hayek's social and economic philosophy
  1. Hayek, Friedrich August
  300'.92'4   HB103.H3

  ISBN 0-333-25618-2

For Lynda

Contents

vii

Preface

This book is an attempt to outline and discuss the major ideas in philosophy, law, politics and economics of one of the most important social theorists of this century, Professor Friedrich August von Hayek. Professor Hayek has found academic recognition and very great world-wide respect for his contributions in a wide variety of disciplines and it is the aim of this book to present his social and economic philosophy as an integrated system of ideas in which seemingly very different subject areas can be seen as elements in a comprehensive intellectual framework. Thus, while Hayek is probably known publicly as a leading advocate of free market economics this standpoint finds its true significance only in a wider philosophical context.

This being said, I have not attempted a complete survey of all of Professor Hayek's intellectual contributions. This would be an impossible task in a book of this length, and in certain areas it would be beyond the capabilities of this author. Therefore, there will be very little discussion of *The Pure Theory of Capital*, Hayek's major contribution to formal economic theory, or some of the other primarily theoretical work of the 1930s. I have confined my discussion of economic matters to those areas which have a bearing on policy and fundamental methodological issues. I have also said little about Professor Hayek's important contributions to the history of ideas, especially his work on John Stuart Mill. While important in their own right these studies are not essential for the presentation of Professor Hayek's social philosophy. This book is, in a sense, a provisional exposition and assessment rather than a complete and systematic account.

It is also a study in ideas only and is concerned neither with biographical matters nor with the task of placing Professor Hayek's ideas in their historical context, even though many of Hayek's most important social and economic theories were formulated during the most traumatic political circumstances of this century. This again is a task for the future. Also, in the exposition of the social philosophy I have not presented an account of the development of Professor Hayek's thought from his economic writings of the 1920s to his writings on the whole range of social science disciplines today, but an exposition of the system itself. The task is made easier in Professor Hayek's case by the fact that he has maintained a remarkable consistency throughout a long and extremely productive career.

This being said, the reader may find a brief intellectual biography of Professor Hayek helpful. He was born in Vienna in 1899, the son of a professor of botany at the University. He studied law and political economy at Vienna University, the home of the famous Austrian School of Economics, which had been started by Menger and continued under Wieser, Böhm Bawerk and Mises. Hayek's work in economics is a part of this School's continuing tradition. From 1927 to 1931 he was director of the Austrian Institute of Economic Research and from 1929 to 1931 lecturer in economics at Vienna University.

In 1931 he was invited to become Tooke Professor of Economic Science and Statistics at the London School of Economics, a position which he held until 1950. During the early part of this period his main work was in economics and he published widely in the 1930s on the theories of the trade cycle, money and capital. He was involved in a dispute with Keynes over the theory of money and the causes of industrial fluctuations. In 1941 he published *The Pure Theory of Capital*, but already he was turning to wider aspects of social science. In 1944 he found some notoriety with the first statement of his social philosophy, *The Road to Serfdom*. He became a naturalised British subject in 1938.

In 1950 he became a professor at the University of Chicago, the home of American liberal political economy, although Professor Hayek was not in the economics department but held a chair in moral science. Throughout the 1950s he worked towards elaborating in a much more sophisticated form the ideas formulated in *The Road to Serfdom* and published *The Constitution of Liberty* in 1960. But earlier, in 1952, he had published a treatise in theoretical psychology, *The Sensory Order*, and a book on methodology, *The Counter-Revolution of Science*; the latter consisted mainly of essays published earlier.

Professor Hayek stayed in Chicago until 1962 when he took the Chair of Economic Policy at the University of Freiburg, West Germany. On his retirement in 1969 he returned to his native Austria and was visiting professor at the University of Salzburg. He has recently left Salzburg to return to Freiburg. During the last twelve years two important volumes of collected essays have been published and two volumes of his projected three-volume final restatement of the principles of a liberal social order, *Law, Legislation and Liberty*.

In dealing with a writer whose works, for all their scholarly detachment, have been used in political controversy, it might be advisable to declare at once my own view of the significance of his social philosophy. I think it is beyond doubt that Professor Hayek's complete works form one of the most profound political philosophies written this century. However, I have tried to present a critical appreciation of it, mainly by exploring its internal logic, and my aim has been to avoid approaching the works from any specific political, or even philosophical, position.

In the preparation of this book I have been greatly helped by the' staff of Birmingham Polytechnic library, South Centre, especially Mrs Janice Warren for quickly getting hold of some fairly obscure articles, and owe them all my thanks. I am especially grateful to Miss Barbara Abbott who typed an untidy original manuscript so expeditiously and cheerfully.

To my friend Allen Brown, of the Department of Economics, the Queen's University, Belfast, I owe a very special debt. Not only has he helped me in long hours of discussion but saved me from many a pitfall in Chapters 2, 3, 6 and 8. The errors that remain here undoubtedly stem from my stubborn refusal to take all his advice. For these, and any other mistakes and misinterpretations, I am entirely responsible.

Birmingham, May 1978 NORMAN P. BARRY

1 Introduction and Philosophical Background

1. THE RELEVANCE OF HAYEK'S SOCIAL PHILOSOPHY

The past decade has seen an important revival in political philosophy of a traditional kind where that means the intellectual discussion of substantive political principles and the critical appraisal of those normative social policies which are said to be derived from them. This is a fundamental change from the preceding era which was characterised by the notion that political philosophy was no different from any other branch of philosophy in that it was essentially an analytical activity concerned with the meaning, derived from ordinary language, of the traditional political concepts such as law, the state, sovereignty, justice and liberty. Philosophy, as a second-order discipline, had nothing to say about the substantial issues of politics and was incompetent to decide between conflicting value systems. In its extreme form, logical positivism, not only was it maintained that the universal desirability of certain ethical and political principles could not be logically demonstrated but also that principles had no special relevance to policy issues that occurred even within a particular community which might have a considerable degree of consensus over basic values.[1] All the various types of this school of thought agreed on one fundamental proposition—that philosophy is concerned with analysis only, it leaves the political world exactly as it is.

Perhaps the most significant intellectual movement in the current revival of political philosophy is economic liberalism. It is this social philosophy which has contributed most in recent times to our knowledge, for example, of the theory of democracy, and our knowledge of the conditions essential for the maintenance of a free society. A major part of the success of this doctrine has been due to its demonstration that many of the traditional economic and political disputes are not really about values but are about mistaken policies which by the normal intellectual methods can be shown to be inconsistent with the values that most people agree upon.[2] The dominant figure in this approach, F. A. Hayek, has been, and still is, laying down the intellectual foundations of the liberal order for well over forty years, initially as a pure economic theorist but latterly as a theorist of law, a social philosopher, a theoretical psychologist and a historian of ideas. Furthermore, he has maintained a remarkable consistency throughout his intellectual career and in the great variety of his works irrespective of the vagaries of intellectual fashion. In his 1967 collection of essays on political philosophy, the majority of which were written from the then dominant analytical standpoint, Anthony Quinton described Hayek's, apparently old-fashioned, *The Constitution of Liberty* as a 'magnificent dinosaur';[3] yet he did not include anything by Hayek in his book. It would be unthinkable not to include something by Hayek in a contemporary book of readings in political philosophy and highly misleading to describe his views as 'old-fashioned'.

One reason for the change of attitude is a purely intellectual one, that is, the tremendous range of Hayek's interests and published works has made him peculiarly well-equipped to study the traditional problems of political philosophy. The subject has always been a heterogeneous one and its best practitioners have been associated with a variety of disciplines. One unfortunate consequence of the purely linguistic approach to political philosophy was the detachment of the subject from the main body of the social sciences; hence the overlooking of significant contributions that had been made to the subject by other disciplines, most notably economics. Since Hayek was concerned almost entirely with pure economics for the first two decades of his professional career it is not surprising that the effects of economic science should be clearly visible in his political philosophy. But it is not just economics that has provided the source of his ideas; indeed he has constantly stressed the limitations of economic science in the study of social problems. It is economics, and all his other intellectual enquiries that add up to a complete, integrated system of ideas exhibiting a rare degree of consistency. It might well be called an 'ideology', but for the unfortunate overtones that word has acquired in the twentieth century, in that it would be possible to predict where Hayek would stand on a given range of issues purely from the knowledge one has of his fundamental philosophical ideas. Clear links can be established between, for example, basic epistemological and methodological propositions in the social sciences and such seemingly mundane matters as housing, rent control and town planning.

But there are other reasons than the purely intellectual ones which can account for the special contemporary interest in Hayek's writings. The most important of these is the apparent breakdown of the post-war consensus on economic and social policy. This consensus can be briefly summarised as follows: the near universal agreement on a positive role for the state in creating full employment, a structure of collectivised welfare services, the gradual implementation of social policies designed to bring about a greater measure of equality than would occur as a consequence of unhampered market processes, the setting of targets of economic growth and a significant measure of economic planning. The consensus view was that these aims were compatible with personal liberty, the rule of law and the maintenance of a large private enterprise market economy within a broad framework determined by the state. Above all, it was held that 'welfare societies' of this type could guarantee, if not stable prices, at least tolerable rates of inflation. It was this consensus that was being referred to in the late 1950s and early 1960s when it was suggested by many political theorists and sociologists that substantial ideological differences no longer existed in the West.[4]

It was a consensus that Hayek never joined. Throughout the post-war period he argued that Keynesian macroeconomic policies would eventually lead to runaway inflation and that the promotion of collectivised welfare policies by centralised political agencies would eventually constitute a severe threat to personal liberty and undermine the rule of law. The outcome of these processes must inevitably be the transformation of free societies into totalitarian societies. What was interesting about this prognosis, first suggested in 1944[5] before Keynesian economic policies were implemented and before the main structure of the welfare state had been set up in Britain, was the argument that totalitarianism need not come from violent, revolutionary change but may well be the long-term, unanticipated consequence of seemingly innocuous policies. In the current debate about economic policy in Britain, in which Hayek has been a vigorous participant, his role must not be seen simply as the defender of the private enterprise market economy on grounds of its superiority over Keynesianism, social democracy and communism in terms of efficiency. Of course he stresses that capitalism is more efficient than its rivals in an allocational sense; but equally important is his argument that only this form of economic organisation is consistent with personal liberty and the rule of law. Thus, one cannot pick and choose those bits and pieces of the Hayekian system which might be convenient items in a political programme, because the bits and pieces only make sense in the context of the general 'order' of ideas. For this, and other reasons, there will always be some tension between political philosophy and the practice of politics.[6]

Furthermore, the present debate on economic policy is no isolated intellectual squabble but goes back to the crucially important debate over the foundations of economics and social philosophy that took place in the 1930s. The post-war Keynesian policies of course emanate from the 1930s when the major postulate of neoclassical liberal economics, namely that unhampered market economies would automatically equilibrate at full employment, seemed to be falsified by the experience of the Great Depression. It was from this historical background that the new macroeconomics emerged which was to give the intellectual licence to later interventionist policies. As a matter of historical fact Hayek lost the great intellectual debate with Keynes in the 1930s (see Chapter 8) and in the succeeding years his own particular brand of economic thinking became exceedingly unfashionable. However, the very different problem of high inflation in recent years has undoubtedly meant that his views have received a much more sympathetic hearing. Yet, in terms of basic methodology Hayek's views have not substantially changed since his formulation of the theory of the trade cycle in the 1930s, a theory originally designed to explain the deflation and depression of that decade—a further indication of the unitary nature of his thought.

Before proceeding to enquire into the philosophical foundation of Hayek's system one particularly important problem must be raised at this early stage, if not solved. This is the problem of the relationship between science and values. The informed public are still inclined to think of Hayek as the advocate of the liberal value system[7] rather than as a neutral social scientist engaged in the objective pursuit of knowledge. This opinion is not to be unexpected in view of the fact that his most famous work *The Road to Serfdom* was a polemic and was admitted as such by its author. Hayek has regretted the fact that his name does not rest upon his scientific work in economics which he claims is *wertfrei* (value-free) in the traditional sense. The problem really arises in his later work in jurisprudence and social philosophy where he appears to be both refuting the intellectual foundations of collectivism and objecting to its moral values. In *The Constitution of Liberty* he presents individualism as a morally superior alternative to socialism where he states that his aim is to 'picture an ideal, to show how it can be achieved, and to explain what its realisation would mean in practice',[8] while in *Rules and Order*, Volume I of *Law, Legislation and Liberty*, he suggests that the differences between individualists and socialists are purely intellectual ones capable of scientific resolution.[9] In Volume II of this series, *The Mirage of Social Justice*, he would appear to be stressing both moral and intellectual differences: 'socialism is not based merely on a different system of ultimate values from that of liberalism, which one would have to respect even if one disagreed; it is based on intellectual error which makes its adherents blind to its consequences'.[10]

In fact, Hayek's procedure is indeed to concentrate more on exposing the fallacies of collectivism than on demonstrating the value of liberal individualism in his more recent work, yet this must not deceive the reader into thinking that the value differences are insignificant. Part of the task of unravelling Hayek's complex system of ideas involves separating normative statements from scientific statements. A provisional conclusion of this subject might lie in the suggestion that he is trying to demonstrate that, given certain undemanding assumptions, one and only one body of normative ideas is consistent with legitimate social science methodology. People may hold different moral values but our knowledge of social science can tell us that the consequences of certain of these values may very well be undesirable. The argument between the collectivist and the individualist would then centre on the nature, and limits, of our knowledge of the social sciences.

2. SOURCES OF HAYEK'S IDEAS

Hayek would not claim a great deal of originality for his ideas. On occasions he has said that he is merely restating in modern terms some fundamental propositions about man and society that date back to the eighteenth century; the origins of these ideas go back even further. While it is true that in restating these fundamental propositions Hayek has certainly added innovations, nevertheless it is important to know something of his intellectual forebears. In summary form it could be said that Hayek's ideas are derived from two major sources: the eighteenth century group of British social scientists and philosophers who formed a different intellectual tradition from the Enlightenment, and the Austrian School of economics, founded by Carl Menger with the publication of his revolutionary theory of subjective value in 1870.[11] In the history of economic thought Menger is credited, along with Leon Walras and William Stanley Jevons as a founder of the marginal utility school of economics which replaced the English Classical School of political economy. However, the Austrian School of marginal utility developed along significantly different lines from the standard neoclassical model and these differences became important influences on Hayek's thinking. In this section I shall be more concerned with the eighteenth-century sources as the details of Austrian economics will emerge in later chapters.

Hayek identifies an important strand of philosophical thinking about man and society in the eighteenth century which is very different from the Enlightenment. In fact this school of thought, dating approximately from Bernard Mandeville and coming to fruition in the social philosophies of David Hume, Adam Smith and Adam Ferguson, was according to Hayek well on the way to developing a genuine science of society until its influence was severely checked by the rise of European rationalism. In many ways Hayek is still fighting the old battles over the Enlightenment, especially in his theory of knowledge.

The important feature of these writers is that they developed a theory of the evolution of social institutions which was independent of design. In contrast to those theories which traced the origins of the state, society, law and so on, to deliberate acts of man (the social contract theory of government would be an example of this), this evolutionary approach stressed their almost accidental development. That is to say, nobody deliberately intended to construct a rational system of law derived from first principles but systems of rules gradually developed which survived because they were found to be convenient. The same is true of the market order, the institution of money, and of course language itself. In the famous phrase of Ferguson, which Hayek has quoted approvingly on a number of occasions, 'nations stumble upon establishments, which are indeed the result of human action but not the result of human design'.[12] This explanation avoids two falsehoods, the irrational view that institutions owe their origins to some extra-territorial source and the extreme rationalist's view that they are the deliberate product of the human mind. This latter view, constantly criticised by Hayek, has been called by him, the *anthropomorphic* explanation of social institutions.[13]

An early eighteenth-century example of the evolutionary way of thinking is Bernard Mandeville's *Fable of the Bees*.[14] Hayek is not so much interested in this work because of the celebrated paradox of virtue, even less for its somewhat elementary economics, but because Mandeville demonstrated that selfish actions of individuals produced an overall order which was clearly beneficial to individuals even though they had not, as individuals, deliberately set about producing such an order—an early example of Adam Smith's 'invisible hand' which automatically guides the self-regarding actions of individuals towards the public benefit.[15]

The important point here is that the old problem about the distinction between 'nature' and 'convention' was finally resolved.[16] Previous thinkers had great difficulty in describing institutions which were clearly not conventional or arbitrary yet which were too dependent upon human action to be called natural. The social evolution explanation, which preceded Darwin, showed that language, law and the market economy are not technically natural, since they depend on men's volitions, yet are by no means arbitrary: we cannot have any laws we please. Hume shows a similar approach when he argues thàt, although it is impossible to demonstrate a set of obligatory moral principles by the use of unaided reason, the moral order is not thereby arbitrary. He even traced an hypothetical account of the development of the rules of justice and property and called the system by the name of 'natural law' without in any way committing himself to a rationalistic natural law position.

Unfortunately, for the development of social science, in Hayek's view, this basically correct approach was almost entirely replaced by an alien methodology which in fact came to dominate the subject. It is thus as important to know the sources of Hayek's intellectual opponents as well; the confusion and error can be traced to the rationalistic natural law philosophies of the seventeenth and eighteenth centuries, the rationalistic epistemology of Descartes, and classical English utilitarianism from Bentham. The rationalistic natural law theorists presupposed that a set of moral norms could be demonstrated from first principles, and that such norms should be embodied in a legal order, independently of experience. This view is neatly summarised in Voltaire's observation that the first step in the design of a better legal system is to abolish all the existing laws, including of course all those that had developed spontaneously. This kind of thinking became associated with the idea that all law must emanate from a unique, determinate will (a sovereign) which is unlimited in extent and whose aim is some specific social purpose. This view culminated in the legal positivism of Bentham. The Cartesian rationalistic epistemology with its emphasis on the search for absolute certainty, and the elimination of that which cannot be proved to be true, by the method of geometrical reasoning, led to the development of 'scientism' in the social studies, that is, the view that economics and the political sciences should base their methodologies on the same principles as the physical sciences.[17]

The most deleterious effect of these alien approaches, according to Hayek, was that certain false ideas of individuality and freedom developed from them.[18] In the theory of social evolution individual liberty was a necessary part of spontaneous growth; individual action brought about the best use of knowledge and such action was only possible in the context of rules which had not developed for any specific social purpose but functioned as guidelines for the fulfilment of individual purposes. It is to be noted that individuals are not understood in this explanation as isolated atoms, bound together by no 'natural' rules. This is the view of the rationalists who maintained that atomised individuals could only be held together by coercive laws, issued by all-powerful sovereigns and addressed to collective ends. It is in this way that individualism quickly became collectivism and freedom was transformed from a property of individuals acting within general rules into a property of collective groups obeying particular commands.

However, the evolutionary approach was not lost to social philosophy even though utilitarianism of the Benthamite kind dominated English political philosophy for the first half of the nineteenth century. Very similar ideas returned to the mainstream of social thought, albeit in a rather different context. Carl Menger, whose place, as we have seen, in intellectual history was established by his rediscovery of the principle of marginal utility and creation of the theory of subjective value in economics, revived the explanation of the growth of institutions in terms of evolution in his later methodological work.[19] The main purpose of this work was to refute the German Historical School of economics which denied the possibility of a general, abstract non-historical economic theory; but the lasting value of this work lies not so much in its contribution to this rather exaggerated *Methodenstreit* but in its restatement of the theory that institutions develop as the unintended and unanticipated consequences of human action. A doctrine that forms one of the major foundation stones in the structure of Hayek's thought.

3. KNOWLEDGE, MIND AND REASON

Underlying all Hayek's social philosophy is a theory of knowledge. The most significant feature of this theory is Hayek's emphasis on man's *ignorance*. While he does not base his political ideas as firmly on a concept of man as does Hobbes, or Bentham, his concept of constitutionally ignorant man may well be considered something of an equivalent to Hobbes's egoistic man. Also, this view of the limits of knowledge has some affinity with Popper's stress on man's fallibility. As Popper emphasises the methods of conjecture and refutation in science to cope with fallibilism so Hayek stresses the following of rules as the only possible method for ensuring stability and continuity for individuals who can only have a very limited knowledge of the world around them.

It is not, therefore, the selfish aspect of the 'economic man' of Adam Smith that is significant, it is the fact of his ignorance.[20] Hayek concedes that the eighteenth-century political economists did speak of a universal self-love as the motivating force in human affairs but maintains that it would be wrong to see this as an expression of *mere* selfishness. Morality may well change, but what cannot change is ignorance. If a man were supremely altruistic or completely egoistic he would still only be able to comprehend the facts of a narrowly circumscribed area.

The real question for the social philosopher is whether the individual should be guided in his actions by those immediate consequences which he can know of, and influence, or 'whether he ought to be made to do what seems appropriate to somebody else who is supposed to possess a fuller comprehension of the significance of these actions to society as a whole'.[21] This has important implications for morality because this thesis of man's limited knowledge means that individuals cannot be expected to have moral obligations to society as a whole, not merely because they are incapable of the degree of altruism this would require, but because they can never know what these obligations are.

This thesis of man's limited knowledge is not merely an empirical problem, or a contingent fact about men which may be altered by some technological advance. It is a philosophical thesis about the form in which knowledge exists in the world and about the way in which the mind becomes aware of this knowledge.

The sum total of knowledge existing in any society will be fragmented and dispersed throughout the members of that society and neither economic knowledge or any other kind of knowledge can be centralised in any one mind or institution.[22] If this is true then the kind of knowledge an external observer possesses will be necessarily limited, and the possibility of objective knowledge in the social sciences, analogous to that in the physical sciences, accordingly limited (see below, Chapter 2). Since no observer can get inside the minds of those he observes, and since so much of our knowledge consists not in facts about the world but in what individuals think about the world, his ability to make accurate, quantitative predictions of future single events will be non-existent.[23] The kind of knowledge he can have will be that of general 'patterns' or 'orders' of events rather than discrete events. In economic science, for example, it is the qualitative knowledge of price systems as general economic phenomena, not quantitative data of the prices of particular commodities, that the economist can discover.[24] That this is a permanent feature of the human condition Hayek thinks is demonstrated by the fact that as our total knowledge increases, and the more complex and technological a society becomes, the proportion available to any one individual becomes less and less.[25]

Hayek has used this argument frequently to refute the *logical* possibilities of socialist planning (see below, Chapter 8). Planning is in a philosophical sense irrational because, while it obviously puts a very high premium on knowledge of tastes, technological resources, inventiveness and so on, the planner has only that knowledge which is available to him in a centralised form, and this will be clearly less than that which is available in a decentralised form throughout society.[26] The kind of knowledge an economic planner has is engineering knowledge, which is the technical knowledge limited to one input, process or purpose; whereas society is characterised by a whole variety of competing purposes. This is why Hayek attaches especial importance in economics to the knowledge of 'time and place', that is, the knowledge of merchants and traders in decentralised markets which enables them to respond to events more quickly and efficiently than a centralised planner could.[27] Hayek maintains that this thesis about the division of knowledge in society is a crucially important adjunct to Adam Smith's theory of the division of labour.[28]

He argues that those who do not pay any attention to our constitutional ignorance are victims of the 'synoptic delusion';[29] the belief in the possibility that there exists in the world knowledge of which we can be absolutely certain. This view dates from Descartes and the epistemological tradition which holds that the only knowledge worth having is that of which we can be absolutely sure. But it is because of ignorance, Hayek maintains, that we have *rules*, and such rules cannot be lightly cast aside even though we might not be able to demonstrate their absolute truth in a Cartesian sense: 'that we ought not to believe anything which has been shown to be false does not mean that we ought to believe only what has been demonstrated to be true.'[30]

It is important to ask at this stage whether Hayek's thesis of our constitutional ignorance can bear all the weight that is put on it. It is to be stressed that his objections to planning turn primarily on this philosophical argument and not on the moral claim that socialist planning produces undesirable consequences, although of course this latter argument is a striking feature of Hayek's social thought. The necessary limitation of our knowledge really proves too much because if adhered to consistently it would make *any* kind of planning beyond the level of the individual irrational and this cannot be what is meant since it would exclude all of those genuinely public activities which are permitted by the spontaneous evolution thesis. After all, certain institutions do not, for reasons to be considered later, emerge spontaneously from individual trans-actions, namely the police and protection agency and the whole system of the enforcement of general rules. No one can ever know what the appropriate level of police expenditure in a society is yet we have good reasons, irrespective of the knowledge problem, for having such institutions. It is true in a crucial sense that ignorance precludes the successful implementation of the massive centralised economic planning associated with socialist regimes; but can the doctrine by itself provide sufficient justification for Hayek's rejection of a wide range of planning policies and institutions which fall short of a socialist economy?

Given a thesis of the limits of knowledge Hayek now has to explain how we come to possess that knowledge that is indeed available to us. His theory of knowledge is based on the idea that we come to know the external world not as a series of isolated facts but as a series of 'orders' or general classification systems which have been constructed not out of the properties of the classified objects but by the process of the mind itself. As we have seen, our knowledge of the market is of an order like this, and also that of a system of law; but the most complete explanation of this is in Hayek's description of the mental world which is given in his *The Sensory Order*,[31] a book which is about the theoretical foundations of psychology but which also tells us much about Hayek's general philosophy.

Hayek's concern is with the distinction between the objective, physical world and the phenomenal world, that is the world that we perceive through our senses, and the relationship between the two. Although the physical and phenomenal orders are similar in some respects the differences are clearly important, especially in their implications for the methodologies of the various sciences.

The sensory order, the order of the phenomenal world constructed by the mind, is a unitary order the properties of which are known as a series of relations. The sensory qualities are not isolated, atomic facts but only have meaning as part of this unitary order. Particular sensations are *classified* by the mind so that our knowledge of the external world is of an *order* of events subjectively known. Although it is a subjective order, in that the sensory qualities are the properties of acting individuals and not the properties of an objective order describable in physical terms, it is not thereby useless. General statements can be made about this order because 'what appears alike or different to us usually appears alike or different to other men'.[32] Although it is not an objective order it is not thereby an order that is peculiar to the individual. Sensation and perception are acts of classification performed by the central nervous system.

The mental order can then be seen to emerge in an evolutionary manner. Through experience of the external world the central nervous system produces a 'map' of this world, a map which is produced by the mechanism of *linkages*. The concept of linkage refers to the way in which each sensory experience is only understood by its connection with a previous pre-sensory experience so that the mind's knowledge of an event in the external world consists not merely of that event but of that event as understood through previous linkages. A linkage can be understood as a learning process to enable the mind to make discriminations.[33]

From this brief and inadequate summary of a complex theory it is possible to select some features which are of importance for the general structure of Hayek's ideas. Perhaps the most important is the thoroughgoing subjectivism of his theoretical psychology. It involves a complete break with *behaviourism*, the idea that mental events can be understood as physical processes and that statements about the mental order can be reduced to statements about observable empirical phenomena. Thus sensation is an entirely subjective phenomenon which cannot be understood by the methods of experimental science. This subjectivism is of crucial importance for Hayek's methodology of the social sciences (see below, Chapter 2).

A second point which follows on from this is that the world is understood by way of theories. The classifications that the mind makes may well turn out to be false and part of the learning process is through reclassification; but the reclassification is a mental process. This means that it is not quite true to say that all we know is a result of experience; the mind is not a *tabula rasa*, but is already equipped with mental apparatus to handle new experiences, even though this apparatus is itself the product of some past experience. There are then certain general principles to which all sensory experiences must conform: knowledge of these principles constitutes our knowledge of the external world.[34]

Thirdly, while psychology is necessarily subjective there is an objective physical world which is described by physical science. In practice it is impossible to 'unify' knowledge, so that the methods of explanation will be different in the physical sciences from those in the psychological and social sciences. While an explanation is logically 'explanation of the principle', that is, explanation of phenomena in terms of a principle of classification, some types of explanation can give detailed accounts and predictions of particular events. This is true only of some aspects of physical science. It cannot be true of psychology whose subject-matter, the phenomenal world of the senses, in contrast to the physical world, is by no means *constant*. This highly variable phenomenal world can only be known subjectively, therefore the positivist's aim of a unified science involving a complete description of the world in physical terms is an impossibility.[35]

Fourthly, Hayek's *The Sensory Order* contains an argument for his thesis of the inevitable limitations on human knowledge which appears quite frequently in the main body of his work. This is the point that not only are there practical limitations on knowledge but also that there is an *absolute* limitation; namely, the general principle which holds that any apparatus of classification must possess a structure of a higher degree of complexity than is possessed by the objects which it classifies. From this Hayek claims that it follows that the brain can only explain operations of a lower order of complexity than its own: it cannot explain fully its own operations, only a higher organism can do that.[36] This argument has been further elaborated into an anti-cartesian argument about the impossibility of certain knowledge.[37] Any system of ideas, for example mathematics or a system of rules, provides meaning for all the individual elements within the system but it is impossible to demonstrate the meaning-fulness of the system itself, unless there is some higher classificatory system, in which case that higher system is faced with the same problem. Therefore, there must be some ultimate 'givens' which cannot be rationally explained. A brief discussion of H. L. A. Hart's explanation of validity in a legal system may help to clarify this point. Hart says that we validate subordinate rules in a legal system by testing them against higher rules, but there must be one ultimate rule, the rule of recognition, which although itself it is not a rule of law, confers 'rightfulness' or 'legitimacy' on all other rules.[38] It is a higher-order rule the authority of which just has to be accepted. The Hayekian view of knowledge in general is not dissimilar from this.

Before considering the above ideas in relation to the various problems of social philosophy it is advisable to make some general comments on the role of reason in human affairs. It might be thought from what has been said above that Hayek is something of an irrationalist, that he believes in the superiority of hunch and intuition over rational argument, especially as he carefully limits the realm of objective knowledge to the physical world, proclaims subjectivism in psychology and the human sciences, and is prepared to countenance that certain things which we believe to be true cannot be rationally demonstrated to be true.

Nevertheless, Hayek is very far from being a believer in any kind of irrational thought processes. He is very much in the position of David Hume who is often credited with using reason against the extreme rationalists of the Enlightenment. It is indeed the height of rationality to recognise the limits of human reason, and this is what Hayek is really doing.[39] As we shall see later, in social questions he is concerned to demonstrate the use of reason at the level of the individual, and this of course includes the notion of planning; but this is very different from saying that a society as a whole can be planned according to rational principles. That in itself is the road to unreason.

Again, what Hayek says about knowledge is not so very different from some fairly familiar ideas. The conventional distinction in the theory of knowledge between 'knowing that' and 'knowing how' is very important in Hayek's philosophy. Using this he is able to show how in the context of the development of rules of social behaviour there are many rules which are followed and understood ('internalised') yet which are impossible to state in a complete and formal manner.[40] Individuals can know how to do these things without knowing precisely why, or for what specific purpose. Many of the rules, which function as a solution to the problem of our limited knowledge, indeed cannot be understood in terms of having particular purposes. The main error in the rationalist and positivist theory of law was not only the belief that law must have a determinate author but also the idea that the sole rationale of law lay in its fulfilling a specific purpose. That being said, it still has to be shown whether these fundamental philosophical considerations do entail by themselves the complete set of social, economic and political values that constitutes Hayek's system of ideas.

2 The Methodology of the Social Sciences

Throughout his career as an economist and social philosopher Hayek has been perhaps the leading advocate of the view that the methods of the physical sciences are fundamentally different from those of the social sciences, and he has argued with great trenchancy, and not a little passion, that serious harm results from the attempt to use the same tools of explanation for these two divergent subject areas. The harm is both intellectual and political. The intellectual harm is the retarding of the growth of knowledge in the social sciences caused by the replacement of those methods which have yielded the most fruitful results of social enquiry by methods artificially transplanted from a quite different field; while the political harm has been in this century the dominance of the 'engineering' type of mind, the mind that regards a social whole as a suitable object for direct control in the same way that objects in the physical world can be directly controlled. Of course, Hayek does not claim that there is a logical connection between methodological statements and political values but he does point out the very strong non-logical connections between what he regards as mistaken methodologies and certain authoritarian and illiberal value systems. A convenient term which Hayek uses to describe the doctrine that the methods of physical science are appropriate to social science is 'scientism'.

Hayek uses two main arguments against scientism. One argument is that the major characteristic of knowledge in the social sciences is that it is *subjective*, that is, there are no observable facts of the social sciences, there are only the attitudes, beliefs and opinions of the actors in a social process and knowledge of this kind is acquired introspectively. The other argument centres on the claim that social phenomena are characterised by *complexity*. This means that in comparison with the physical sciences, which deal with essentially simple phenomena that can be isolated, observed and made explicable in terms of causal laws, the complex phenomena of society, with its greater number of variables and difficulty of observation, have to be explained by theories of much less predictive power. Now these two arguments, although they have some fairly obvious similarities, such that it is quite likely that a person holding the first will also hold the second, are by no means identical; each could provide a tenable objection to scientism on its own, and Hayek has stressed the one at the expense of the other on different occasions. In his earlier methodological writings, especially in *The Counter-Revolution of Science*,[1] it is the subjectivism that is emphasised, while in more recent work, particularly the essays in *Studies in Philosophy, Politics and Economics*,[2] and his Nobel Prize Lecture, *The Pretence of Knowledge*,[3] it is the complexity of social affairs that makes them inappropriate for treatment by methods analogous to physics.

These differences of emphasis are important because they represent some real difficulties in Hayek's philosophy of the social sciences. One is the question of its consistency with the now standard account of the philosophy of science given by Sir Karl Popper. While Popper and Hayek are in close agreement on a number of issues in social philosophy, superficially Popper's belief in the unity of method in all the sciences[4] seems to be at odds with Hayek's special claims for the social sciences. I shall deal with this general topic in a separate section but it is advisable to note at this stage that Hayek's relaxation of the strict application of the subjectivism rule for the social sciences seems to be partly a consequence of his desire to make his views as similar as possible to those of Popper. Nevertheless, I shall deal with the subjectivity thesis in some considerable detail as it is a major theme of his writings and provides a convenient bridge to link the methodology of economics proper with the rest of the social sciences.

Hayek's subjectivism in economics can be best understood in the context of the development of the Austrian School of economics. Carl Menger, the founder and source of inspiration for the many members of this School, is credited in the history of economic thought for his rediscovery, along with Jevons and Walras, of the subjectivist theory of value. Despite its many virtues, some of which Hayek has incorporated into his own system of ideas, the English Classical School of political economy, from Adam Smith onwards, broke down over a very important element in economic science, the theory of value. The Classical economists tried to explain the value of goods and services by some *objective* standard which would explain prices in the long run. Despite considerable variations between individual thinkers, the objective determinant of value was held to be *labour*, or, more strictly, command over labour. That is to say, the ultimate cause of all economic value was calculated in terms of homogeneous labour inputs. While competition in the market might make prices diverge from the 'natural' price (calculated in terms of labour inputs) the long-run tendency of the economic process was to bring about an identity between these two. The labour theory of value is properly called a cost of production theory because it attempts to explain prices entirely by supposedly objective, measurable inputs irrespective of the *demand* for goods and services which is expressed in the subjective utility they give to individual consumers. In the now classic phrase of Adam Smith: 'If among a nation of hunters . . . it usually costs twice the labour to kill a beaver which it costs to kill a deer, one beaver should naturally exchange for or be worth two deer'.[5] It is to be noted that this attempt to 'objectify' value in terms of some measurable input is an extremely good example of the kind of thinking Hayek is attacking when he writes about the recent examples of scientism.

It became clear by the mid-nineteenth century that this theory was inadequate to explain prices in market economies. The obvious question to ask was that if prices were to be explained in terms of the prices of the factors of production what explained these latter prices? The obvious answer was that the value of labour was itself determined by the value of the product and not the other way round. The value of products was thus determined by demand. Therefore a uniform theory of price was the outcome of the 'Marginalist Revolution' of the 1870s which decisively defined value in terms of the utility goods gave to consumers. Goods and services had no intrinsic value or utility, this was entirely a subjective property of individual consumers. The economic question became one of explaining resource allocation in terms of consumers' demand to the near exclusion of long-term considerations of the quantity and quality of the factors of production.

The revolution in economic theory of the 1870s enabled other problems in Classical theory to be cleared up. The Classical emphasis on macro-type variables, the returns to labour, capitalists and landlords defined as objective social classes, was replaced at the centre of the economic stage by the appearance of the utility-maximising individual. Furthermore, the old paradox of value was solved. This was the problem that, for example, although water had very great 'use value' compared with diamonds the latter had enormous value in 'exchange'. This was explained by the 'law of diminishing marginal utility.' This states that consumers will have a scale of preferences by which they order goods according to their relative significance. The more units of a want-satisfying good that are available the less valuable will be marginal additions. Consumers are never faced with a choice between the total amount of water and the total amount of diamonds but with choices at the margin. In the desert marginal increments of water will be infinitely more valuable than diamonds but in western societies the value of marginal increases is minute compared with that of diamonds; therefore the price of water is low because of its diminishing marginal utility. There is, then, no distinction between value in use and value in exchange but only differences in marginal utility.

The last point to stress in this very brief survey of perhaps the most important period in the history of economic ideas is that the theorists of subjective value did not need to assert that man is necessarily 'economic man' where that phrase means that man always behaves *economically*, in the sense of acting in a self-interested manner so as to minimise monetary costs and maximise gains. Not all utility-maximisation is economic maximisation in the theories of subjective value. This last point is especially important in the Austrian School because they broadened out their theory so that it was not exclusively an economic theory but became a theory of human action in general.

In fact the Austrian School developed along somewhat different lines from the other neoclassical traditions that emerged from the Marginalist Revolution. The divergence can largely be explained in terms of methodology. The European neoclassical tradition, especially in the system of Leon Walras, concentrated on general equilibrium economics. In this theory, given knowledge of individuals' tastes, the state of technology, prices and so on, it is possible to predict, mechanically, by the use of mathematical methods what the optimal solution to any economic problem will be. In other words, individuals are understood to be economisers, that is, they always act so as to maximise money incomes, and if knowledge is 'given', then economics as the science of choice really ceases to exist and becomes applied mathematics. The Austrians, however, were not so much concerned with general equilibrium, except as an abstract formal statement of logically possible economic relationships, but much more with the process towards an equilibrium (see below, Chapter 3). The Walrasian system was essentially concerned with the concept of a stationary equilibrium in which conditions that lead to change have been removed. In Austrian economics, however, the emphasis is on those factors that cause this tendency towards equilibrium, and thus it is how knowledge is *acquired* through the market process that is crucial.

The foremost representative of the later development of Austrian methodology was Ludwig von Mises (1881–1973), Hayek's teacher in economics. In fact, much of Hayek's early writings on methodology are elaborations of Mises's position. Mises made a clear distinction between the physical sciences and social sciences. The physical sciences are characterised by observation, quantification and testability while the social sciences consist of theories which explain purposive human behaviour, where measurement is not merely difficult but logically inadmissible. The name that Mises gave to the science of human action was praxeology. Praxeology is an entirely *a priori* science analogous to mathematics; it proceeds by deducing from self-evidently true axioms conclusions which are absolutely true regardless of time and place. It is a self-evidently true axiom of human action that human behaviour is purposive, that is, it is concerned with means–ends relationships where an end, the removal of some present state of uneasiness, is chosen and means towards this employed, in contrast with automatic, instinctive or reflexive behaviour, such as a knee-jerk. From this the entire corpus of economic theory can be deduced. Thus the time structure of production, that is the distinction between higher-order goods (producer goods) and lower-order goods (consumer goods); time-preference, that is the ratio between present and future consumption; the law of diminishing marginal utility and other economic theorems can be logically deduced from the premise of human action.[6]

It is to be noted that the axioms of praxeology are not arbitrary like those of mathematics because, unlike knowledge in the physical sciences, knowledge of human action is already given to us in our own minds. Through 'introspection', understanding the properties of our own minds, we can understand the behaviour of others. This is all we have to go on because there are no objective social facts which can be observed and measured; therefore the theorems of economics cannot be tested empirically. Thus the law of diminishing marginal utility is not a quasi-empirical statement about the saturation of wants in a psychological sense, but is a praxeological statement to the effect that an acting individual must have a scale of preferences (ordinal) by which he ranks bundles of goods. As the supply of a want-satisfying good increases its value to the individual consequently diminishes.[7] This scale is entirely subjective, it is a property only of each individual and cannot be known to an external observer and made the basis of predictions of consumer behaviour after the manner of objective science.

The praxeological approach consists in formulating elaborate theorems which cannot predict future events yet which enable us to understand the world. Menger said that it was as useless to test the ultimate, exact laws of economics by reference to empirical data as it was to test the axioms of geometry by reference to real objects.[8] Whereas economics has conventionally accumulated knowledge through the testing of hypotheses on the assumption that an objective world of social facts exists, praxeology assumes the existence of timeless generalisations which are necessarily true. Whereas false hypotheses in conventional economics are eliminated by empirical testing, a mistaken theory in praxeology can only be shown to be so by the use of logical reasoning, that is, the exposure of some contradiction in the formulation of the theory. The praxeological objection to empiricism in the construction of economic theory rests upon the claim that there are no *constants* in the social world as there are in physical world, and that statistical and econometric measurement has produced no such constants but only historical data. In fact, statistics and econometrics are parts of economic history from the point of view of praxeology.

The major problem with *a priori* theories of this type is that they maintain their certainty by eliminating all empirical content. In the Austrian theory a somewhat tenuous link with the real world is achieved by the assumption that the axioms of praxeology can be shown to be true by introspection. By understanding ourselves we can understand the behaviour of others, who have, of course, similar minds. Hayek on occasions seems very much in the *a priori* tradition and he does indeed elaborate the 'introspective' technique in subjects outside formal economics, especially in psychology; but he cannot be described as an extreme praxeologist since in his later writings he admits the criterion of 'falsifiability' as a test of a genuine scientific theory, something explicitly excluded by Mises. But before the significance of this can be considered Hayek's exposition of subjectivism must be outlined.

2. HAYEK'S SUBJECTIVISM

One difficulty with Hayek's use of the word 'subjective' in the social sciences must be cleared up immediately. This is that when Hayek maintains that knowledge in the social sciences is subjective he does not mean that the opinions and values of the social scientist cannot be removed from analysis. On the contrary, he accepts the logical distinction between facts and values and maintains that ultimate values cannot be rationally justified one way or another; although he insists that reason and social science have much to contribute to the solution of those ethical and value problems that fall short of disputes about ultimate moral ends.[9] His objection to scientism does not turn upon this but on the point that the values and opinions of individuals, and not objective fact, are the only proper objects of study for the social scientist. This very simple distinction has not, however, prevented endless confusion about the nature of subjectivism. This is partly because those who have tried to establish a science of society have spent more time refuting the argument that values cannot be eliminated from social theory than they have on meeting the very different objection that there is not a world of objective facts against which their theories can be tested.

The main reason why Hayek thinks that the social sciences are different from the natural sciences is that the mind classifies the data of the two areas of enquiry in different ways. In the latter, classification is in terms of the similar physical properties of observed objects so that the physical scientist reconstructs the external world by way of theories that describe the relationship between only physical objects.[10] The truth of such theories is independent of what men think about the world. But this objectivity is a feature of only a small number of the sciences that deal with man, for example, the study of contagious diseases, heredity, nutrition or population studies;[11] but economics, political science and sociology use, or should use, different methods. The point about these disciplines is that they deal not with the relations between things, but with the relations between men and things or the relations between men and men.[12] They have to explain human action and, most important, the unintended and undesigned results of human action. Therefore there are no natural laws of cause and effect in the social world there are only the opinions and attitudes of men about the world.[13]

To get some flavour of the unconventional nature of this subjectivism in economics it might help to compare Hayek's views with those of an economist with whom his name is somewhat uncritically linked, Professor Milton Friedman. In his celebrated essay *The Methodology of Positive Economics*[14] Friedman argues precisely the opposite view. The task of positive economics, he says, is to produce hypotheses and make predictions about unobserved events which can then be tested against the facts: 'In short, positive economics is, or can be, an "objective" science, in precisely the same sense as any of the physical sciences'.[15] For Friedman economics is a positive science precisely because it deals with phenomena which can be 'objectified' and because its predictions can be tested by statistical methods.

Hayek illustrates his theme by explaining the purposive nature of human action. Just as we cannot speak of the objective properties of a tool or instrument without saying something of the purpose for which the tool is used so we cannot speak of social institutions merely objectively. Laws, economic institutions and so on cannot be known apart from the intentions and purposes of the individuals who use them. And this knowledge is subjective in that it is the property of the individuals who participate in social activities. For example, the statement 'the crowd was in an ugly mood' is not a statement about some objective property of 'anger' which can be measured on a scale, but a statement about the values and opinions shared by the participants in this particular social process.[16] The concept of anger, in this example, is known by the observer from his own introspective experience of similar mental phenomena in a way that it could not be known to a visitor from, say, another planet. The visitor may observe all the objective phenomena but without the introspective knowledge of minds similar to those whom he is observing the events would be meaningless.

In economics when we talk of money there is no objective property inhering in the money devices used, the value of money depends entirely on the attitudes and opinions of individuals. Similarly, the theory of price has nothing to say about the prices of particular commodities, which depend upon the tastes and opinions of particular individuals, but is limited to general propositions, such as that if the demand for money falls, and the quantity of money is constant, then prices will rise. It will be impossible to predict in particular circumstances what the price rises will be, past statistical evidence is irrelevant because it is impossible to make generalisations from unique historical events, but that the general statement is true can be known absolutely.[17]

A crucial feature of this approach is the use of the compositive method. In contrast to the physical sciences which start from given observable wholes and work backwards to infer the elements of which they are composed, the social sciences start from the simple, familiar elements and reproduce the complex structures by mental reconstruction. The familiar elements are individuals and from their actions it is possible to deduce, for example, the complex structure of the market, the properties and regularities of which could not have been established by direct observation. The *empirical* facts of the social sciences are not these regularities, which are mental reconstructions, but the elements from which deduction proceeds, individual minds. Furthermore these elements, unlike those in the physical sciences, can be known beyond dispute.[18]

It is important to note here a crucial distinction between this methodology and positivism on the question of assumptions. In Friedman's positive economics the truth of the assumptions is not vital because the method depends upon predicting unobserved events which can be tested against objective facts.[19] In fact the more interesting theories, those with an increasing empirical content, may very well be based on rather unlikely assumptions. Yet Hayek, in his more emphatic subjectivist phase, has stressed that social and economic theories can never be verified or falsified by reference to facts but only tested for their consistency, and this entails that the assumptions from which deductions are made have to be correct if the conclusions of the theories are to be true.[20] Hayek concedes that we have to verify our assumptions on each occasion but is more cautious than, for example, Murray N. Rothbard, who has declared that the assumptions are absolutely true.[21] It should be apparent from this that the search for correct assumptions by the introspective method may lead to true theories but of very limited application in comparison to the positivist's theories which, despite being dependent upon statistical corroboration, have more explanatory power.

Dissatisfaction with this subjectivism has haunted economics. As long as genuine economic choice takes place it is impossible for the observer to posses the knowledge which would be essential for the making of positive predictions. As long as economists had to rely on introspective and psychological assumptions their science seemed to lag behind the natural sciences. Not surprisingly there have been attempts to purge economics of all subjective, psychological elements and construct a behavioural science of, for example, consumer choice. The most famous of these is the doctrine of revealed preference.[22] The basic idea of this theory is that an individual's preferences are revealed by his choices, and since we can observe his choices by enumerating his purchases we can indirectly observe his preferences. Thus, if a consumer buys a collection of goods A rather than available collections B, C and D, we can say that he has a revealed preference for A. With the assumption of transitivity, that is, if a consumer prefers x to y, and y to z he must prefer x to z, followers of the doctrine, by using mathematical techniques, have drawn up consumers' preference maps on the basis of hypothetically observable behaviour. Hayek briefly mentions this approach in a recent paper on Menger where he says that revealed preference was designed to avoid the reliance on introspective knowledge and, furthermore, concedes that it has shown in principle that the 'hypotheses about individual behaviour that microeconomic theory requires can be stated independently of "psychological" assumptions'.[23] This is rather surprising since the orthodox Austrian objection to the revealed preference doctrine is that if predictions are to be made about consumer behaviour then knowledge of the constancy of choices over time is required. The assumption of transitivity is merely a logical statement which has no empirical content. The theory of human action, of course, precludes statements about the constancy of human choices over time.[24]

Before going on to discuss the later development of Hayek's methodological views it might be helpful to conclude this section with some general comments on the subjectivist doctrine. Most critics have concentrated on the radical doctrine that the data of the social sciences are simply the attitudes, values and opinions of the participants, which Hayek thinks entails the idea that there cannot be true statements about social matters independent of these beliefs. This follows from Hayek's claim that there are no 'social facts' as such. But critics of subjectivism agree that people can be mistaken in their beliefs about the world and that social scientists must be able to say what is true or false about people's beliefs.

There are statements in economics about the effect, for example, of an increase in the supply of money on the price level which can be objectively demonstrated independently of any subjective beliefs. It is true that the Austrian School rejects the notion of a price level as being a classic example of objectification; they would say that quantitative statements about the price level mask important economic relationships which cannot be observed. Yet to throw out the concept of the price level would be to abandon perhaps the most useful explanatory device in economics. Protection from error in these fields is secured not by appealing to a dubious introspection but by constantly trying to refute theories, in the manner suggested by Popper.

It is undoubtedly true that *mere* observation is not adequate to explain much social phenomena. For example, Hart has shown in great detail how an external observer of a legal system would only see the visible effects of the system such as courts, sanctions, commands and so on, but he would completely miss the meaning that legal rules have as guidelines for the participants in the system.[25] Law must be understood from the 'internal' point of view. But there are clear dangers in relying only on introspection, and the related idea of empathy, because of the unconscious biases and prejudices that may influence the social scientist. At least in the objective approach constant criticism and testing of theories may eliminate these hindrances. In some areas it may simply be a practical comparison between the reliability of objective data and that of subjective knowledge. But at times Hayek simply asserts as a metaphysical dogma that there is no such thing as objective data, against which positivists might claim that their theories can at least be systematically tested.

Verstehen, as the method of introspection is sometimes called, may be a good starting point for social enquiry but surely it cannot be taken to be the sole source of knowledge. As J. W. N. Watkins said on one occasion, Hayek's philosophy implies that one must have a war-like mind to understand the behaviour of a Hitler or a Genghis Khan.[26] Outside economics and law subjectivism might reduce much of social science to uninteresting explanations. While positivists are wrong, indeed scientistic, in rejecting everything that is not quantifiable, the subjectivists are equally extravagant in their reluctance to accept the relevance, indeed the possibility, of objective data for social theory. Perhaps a realisation that extreme subjectivism was out of step with modern thinking in the philosophy of science made Hayek subtly change the emphasis of his methodology in recent years, for while he is still attacking scientism his criticism now proceeds from a different angle and it is to this newer approach that I now turn.

3. THE SOCIAL SCIENCE OF COMPLEX PHENOMENA

Hayek's latest essays on methodological topics are to be found in the collection *Studies in Philosophy, Politics and Economics* and articles on economics and economic policy. The most important of the latter works is his Nobel Prize Lecture *The Pretence of Knowledge*. The target is still the misapplication of the methods of the physical sciences to the social sciences but the emphasis now is much less on the logical differences between the disciplines and more on the misunderstandings of science by social scientists. Most important is the criticism of the belief that *quantification* is the key to a scientific understanding of society. The differences between the scientific disciplines now seem to be one of degree rather than of kind and the idea is that the difficulty of a natural science of society stems not so much from the subjective nature of our knowledge of social affairs but from the complexity of those affairs which makes it impossible for the observer to reproduce their elements in a manageable form.

Furthermore, there is greater discussion of the nature of prediction, a clear recognition of the falsifiability criterion as the hallmark of science, and an open acceptance of Sir Karl Popper's account of the basic unity of scientific method. Hayek now says the apparent difference that he once detected between the various methodologies was due to his failure to stress that the scientistic schools were mistaken over the methods of the natural sciences.[27] This is especially true of positivists who tried to show that scientific theories were based on inductive generalisation and that a purely naturalistic description of the external world was possible without the aid of any *a priori* theorising. The contemporary emphasis on the hypothetical and deductive nature of theories in the natural sciences has made the differences between those and, say, those of economics, seem less important than the structural similarities that they exhibit. Nevertheless I shall want to show later that there is perhaps a little more at work than a change in terminology and a shift in emphasis, for the acceptance of the Popperian methodology does indicate a departure from the praxeological approach characteristic of the Austrians and their followers. But I would not want to give the impression that Hayek has made drastic revisions in his social philosophy, most of the propositions that now appear in the forefront of his thought were present in his earlier writings, albeit obliquely, and there is nothing of crucial importance that he has consciously abandoned.

What makes the difference of degree now said to describe the difference between, say, physics and economics is that physics is concerned with simple phenomena while economics is about complex phenomena. In simple phenomena it is possible to identify and observe all the variables that are to be explained and it is assumed that any important factor which determines the observed event will itself be directly observable and measurable; but this is not true of social phenomena where large numbers are involved.[28] This is a crucial feature of the market which specifically requires a large number of actors for it to work at all. This distinction between simple and complex systems is most fundamental; it indicates real and lasting differences in the explanations appropriate to the subjects. Thus economics is not a backward science that will one day acquire the technical equipment to make predictions as precise as those found in physics; the truth is that economics deals with a different kind of phenomenon than physics.[29]

From this distinction it follows that although economic theories are predictive, the predictions that are derived from them are of a very special type. While not wishing to sever the link between explanation and prediction, Hayek accepts Popper's argument for their logical similarity, nevertheless he maintains that predictions in the social sciences are not of discrete events but of classes of events. Strictly speaking, Hayek maintains that all prediction is of classes of phenomena, as he must do given his epistemology, but that the class of prediction associated with complex phenomena is peculiarly wide.[30] They are explanations of the principle rather than explanations of detail. We know what general effect a change in demand will have on prices but we cannot say in detail what quantitative price changes will occur.

Another way of expressing the same thing is Hayek's use of the word 'pattern' to describe these sorts of predictions. A market order is a sort of pattern that can be predicted to emerge from the actions of individuals but the particular quantitative aspects, the relative prices of goods and services, can never be predicted because we can never get the requisite data. All social science theories are then 'algebraic' in that they arrange the elements of social phenomena in a coherent fashion but do not tell us the values of the elements in the algebraic equations.[31] The neoclassical general equilibrium theory is of this type which, since Walras, has been used to represent the general features of a competitive economic process by systems of simultaneous equations. These are so framed that 'if we were able to fill in all the blanks, i.e., if we knew all the parameters of these equations, we could calculate the prices and quantities of all commodities'.[32] But we can never get the knowledge required to fill in the blanks because in a market system it is dispersed among possibly millions of actors in the whole process.

It is not a problem of the *solution* of the millions of equations which would be required to predict future values, as was thought by some critics of socialist planning, that can be done by computers; the problem is getting hold of the knowledge.[33] Hayek illustrated this point by arguing that no economist has yet succeeded in making money by using his scientific knowledge to predict future prices, even though some have made money by selling such predictions.[34] He added, with some irony, that Keynes made his fortune by speculating in a field where his theoretical knowledge was of no use to him, in the commodity market, and lost heavily in that area where it might have been thought advantageous, namely, foreign exchange.

Such theoretical constructions as economics produces may appear to be no more than classifications, or rearrangements, of existing knowledge, in comparison with the theories of the physical sciences which are characterised by a much greater amount of empirical content. Furthermore, according to Hayek, economics does not typically proceed by framing new hypotheses in order to expand our existing knowledge but, rather, selects aspects of phenomena to be explained by well-established theories.[35] These highly general theories are not thereby useless; at least they allow us to make negative predictions. Theoretical economic science 'forbids' certain kinds of phenomena, it does not verify anything.[36] Modern economics, for example, tells us that we cannot at the same time maintain fixed rates of exchange and at will control the internal price level of a country by changing the quantity of money.[37] In more recent years Hayek has devoted much energy to showing that a continual expansion of spending power, by fiscal or monetary methods, *cannot* in the long run produce full employment. These negative theories are falsifiable in principle, although Hayek admits that falsification is a matter of degree and that high-level economic theories may be difficult to falsify in practice.[38]

It is this that leads Hayek to suggest that the proper analogy from the natural sciences to be used to describe the methodology of the social sciences is not physics but the theory of evolution in biology.[39] Darwin's law of evolution is not a scientific law in the strict sense and like the 'laws' of economics it is difficult to refute, but it has two properties of application to the social sciences. Firstly, it presents a pattern of biological phenomena, a rearrangement of familiar elements in a systematic manner, while it does not claim to predict in particular cases the specific forms that future instances of evolution may take. It is thus a clear case of an explanation of the principle rather than explanation of detail.[40] Secondly, certain prohibitions, or negative predictions follow from the theory; for example, it precludes the possibility that horses may suddenly give birth to young with wings.[41] While theories such as this, mainly the logically similar ones in economics, clearly have much less empirical content than theories that explain simple phenomena, they are no less *exact* within the ambit of their own explanatory field.[42]

While Hayek does not object to the uses of mathematics in economics, indeed he suggests that the use of mathematical language is essential for expressing some of the highly complex relationships that occur within an economic pattern or order, he certainly is a firm opponent of the use of certain quantitative techniques which aim at discovering empirically based laws in economics. What he has in mind is the statistical method. There is, of course, a difference between mathematics and statistics which is not always appreciated by the layman. For Hayek, statistics far too often are used to try to demonstrate constants in economic relationships which are not there. The method is to abstract from a large amount of data certain elements so as to discover regularities. But these regularities must not be understood as constants, or equivalent to causal laws in the physical sciences, precisely because important relationships between the variables cannot be observed. Statistics treats the individual component parts of an economic process as if they were not related.[43] Statistical methods are highly useful in dealing with complex phenomena when we already have knowledge about the variables and their inter-relationships, but it is just this knowledge that, in an economy which consists of millions of consumers, producers and economic agents, is so difficult to ascertain.

It is now possible to look at the development of Hayek's thought on methodology in more general terms. The most important feature is the stress on the differences in degree between the physical sciences and human studies and the lesser significance that is attached to the subjective aspects of the latter. The admission of the falsifiability criterion is surely an indication that there are social facts that exist independently of the observer. The praxeological approach does explicitly deny that the theorems of economics can be falsified because they are deductions from true axioms.[44]

An example might be Say's Law of Markets. This states that all markets are ultimately cleared, or supply creates its own demand. This law does not deny that in the short run particular markets may not be cleared, therefore it is not refuted by empirical evidence of such markets. It merely states that it is a necessary property of economic theory that eventually markets must clear, that there cannot be, in an unhampered market, general gluts. Hayek, in his earlier *The Counter-Revolution of Science*, gives a similar example, the law of rent. This states that if different factors of production are used in the production of a commodity and the proportion in which the factors are used can be varied, if one of the factors can be used only for the production of this commodity while the others can be used for other things, then a fall in the value of the product will affect the former more than the latter. This, as it stands, is necessarily true, irrespective of time and place because it is a 'statement about the implications of certain human attitudes towards things'.[45] However, Hayek says that it normally applies to land, that is, labour has many more uses than land therefore a fall in the value of the product will affect land more than labour. But this latter statement is empirical, and may be falsified by evidence. Indeed, Hayek gives one such example. If this is so, then, from the point of view of praxeology it does not belong properly to the laws of economics, which are in principle unfalsifiable.

In fact, the praxeological way of thinking did not become an established part of economic methodology precisely because the praxeologists were accused of uttering no more than tautologies. Mises, in fact, claimed that praxeology does give us knowledge about the real world, but the gap between the absolutely true axioms of economics and empirical economics was always difficult to bridge. The whole approach seems to put a barrier on progress in economic science because if hypotheses which can be tested empirically do not belong to economics proper, in fact Mises thought that these belonged to *history*, then economics is not an empirical science with an ever-widening content. Mises and his followers are perfectly consistent, in their view economics is not an empirical science concerned with prediction. Praxeologists, nevertheless, claim that their method is indispensable for the appraisal of economic policies. For example, it can be shown on *a priori* grounds that there are undesirable consequences of government subsidising the price of a particular good: it will only increase its consumption and hence distort the automatically-adjusting process of the market. The truth of this, however, does not depend upon empirical observation.

Hayek seems to want the best of both worlds. He does say that economic laws are difficult to refute, but he wants to avoid saying they are tautologies. In keeping with the Popperian tradition they do have empirical content, although compared to the natural sciences that content is limited. He wants to retain the logical similarity between explanation and prediction but in doing so interprets prediction in such a way that it would exclude much of the development of economic theory of the last thirty years from the status of science. This can be seen from his argument that the body of economic knowledge is not normally built up by inventing new hypotheses. Yet economics does produce new hypotheses, indeed the Chicago School, with the members of which Hayek has obvious political affinities, is constantly producing new hypotheses for testing in the manner of orthodox science. Now Hayek is clearly right in his criticisms of the attempts to 'objectify' economic phenomena that cannot be so treated, and his criticisms of Keynesianism (see below) on the grounds that it considers only that which is measurable to be scientifically significant is a classic example of his many exposures of scientism. Yet, on his own admission, the theories that he is prepared to accept explain very little. In fact a wide range of economic phenomena is consistent with that pattern type of prediction that he regards as scientifically acceptable. While the dangers of scientism must be exposed, especially when they affect policy-making, it is possible that erroneous theories will be eliminated by the rigorous attempts to falsify them according to the normal canons of scientific method. And in the process some *tentative* hypotheses may well fail to be refuted, and so add to the body of knowledge.

It is not surprising, in view of these methodological considerations, that Hayek should place strict limits on the extent to which an economy can be controlled.[46] Since, he claims, so little knowledge can be centralised and quantified, those who would direct an economy towards preconceived ends are not likely to reach their targets. Those whom he labels scientistic make the mistake of assuming that because the physical sciences have enabled men increasingly to control some aspects of their environment similar control can be achieved in social affairs. But Hayek maintains that, since we cannot acquire the knowledge required for exact prediction and control, the temptation to resort to coercion may well be irresistible.[47] The consequence of coercion in the economic sphere is likely to be the destruction of that spontaneous order of which we can have some knowledge, the market economy. In Hayek's view, a view that he has expressed consistently since his inaugural lecture at the London School of Economics, *The Trend of Economic Thinking*,[48] the kind of knowledge that we have, and of which we can be sure, is most likely to discourage dramatic demands for economic reform. The proper method is not one of control but of cultivation.

There is much to be said for the argument that governors ought to limit themselves to cultivation rather than control, to improving the workings of the economic mechanism rather than trying to steer it in some particular direction. The problems entailed by attempts at planning will be dealt with later but it is important to mention briefly here the nature of the objections to an attempt to control economic and social life. Hayek would appear to be saying that it is impossible to control any further than we can predict, that planning is somehow impossible and that the attempt to plan and direct is likely to lead to consequences undesired by the planners. But is this entailed by only his methodology? Surely, someone could believe in a different methodology and argue that it was possible to predict fairly accurately consequences of economic policies and still object to planning, either because the ability to predict does not entail the ability to control (as Hayek agrees) or because planning involves a loss of liberty. If our knowledge is as limited as Hayek says it is then we must be as ignorant of the consequences of not acting as we are of acting. One of the arguments Hayek uses for justifying the maximum individual liberty is that because we cannot know the future we may lose out in terms of progress if people are not allowed to experiment within general rules (see Chapter 4); but of course we do not apply that argument to government precisely because government action is *coercive*, and governments cannot be trusted to experiment. But this is a moral argument, indeed one of overwhelming importance; but it is not a logical argument about the philosophy of science.

4. THE ENEMIES OF SOCIAL SCIENCE

A number of important elements in Hayek's thinking on social science have not yet been discussed. These are the particular doctrines he regards as inimical to a genuine social science. They are all scientistic, although in different ways. In *The Counter-Revolution of Science* he discusses objectivism, historicism and collectivism. I shall not consider the doctrine of objectivism, the psychological theory of behaviourism which asserts that all mental states can be understood in physical terms so that all subjective statements about mind are translatable into statements about observable physical behaviour, but confine my comments to the last two doctrines plus a brief discussion of the methodological implications of Keynesianism. I have added this because it is the example of scientism that Hayek has most frequently discussed and one that goes to the heart of current methodological problems in economics, while at the same time it has a clear connection with policy matters.

(a) *Historicism*

Hayek has been, along with Popper, a persistent critic of historicism, the belief that history has a definite end or purpose the progress towards which can be understood by detecting certain laws of development. The doctrine treats history as a given 'whole', as if it were a tangible object the progress of which can be observed by an external mind by analogy with the observation of physical objects in the natural sciences.[49] The adherents of such doctrines were normally in revolt against abstract deductive systems of economics and mistook their crude empiricism for a genuine historical science.

One rather serious implication of historicism is the belief that knowledge in the social sciences is somehow merely 'relative', that is, all the propositions of social science belong to historical categories and truth is therefore relative to historical periods. Hayek, of course, does believe that the fundamental theorems of economics are universally true, because they are propositions about human attitudes towards things, and as long as there are human beings with similar minds it will be possible to construct general statements about social relationships. To an historicist, however, statements about price and monopoly are relative; a price in the twelfth century or a monopoly in the Egypt of 400 B.C. are not the same as prices and monopolies today.[50] But this is mistaken. Particular prices obviously vary from time to time and place to place but the *theory* of price is a universal statement, a mental reconstruction made out of human attitudes which can be used to explain a variety of economic phenomena. Similarly money, law and religion vary greatly throughout the world but they are essential as explanatory concepts in our understanding of social processes. The historicist mistake lies in thinking of them as names that stand for definite things rather than as mental, theoretical constructions. The most famous historicists were really trying to make the political point that the universal theorems of economics that emerged in the last century were relative to a so-called capitalist period of historical development and would cease to be valid beyond that period.

It is undoubtedly true that Hayek's attack on these doctrines is well-directed. It is not an attack on history as such but only the improper uses of history. The historian deals with unique episodes or situations which cannot form the elements in some quasi-empirical law of development, even though he will use the propositions of the theoretical social sciences, sometimes unconsciously. Hayek's views are similar to Popper's on this issue; they were formulated independently and their origins can perhaps be traced back to Menger's methodological dispute with the German Historical School over the foundations of economics in the last two decades of the last century.[51] Of course, the historicists were such poor examples of scientific thinking in social studies that a refutation of their views does not entail an acceptance of Hayek's particular views on scientific method.

(b) *Methodological Collectivism*

In the rejection of this doctrine we find Popper and Hayek again on the same side; and in their defence of methodological individualism they have pioneered one of the most dominant doctrines in modern social science. The fundamental error made by methodological collectivists is not dissimilar from the mistakes made by the historicists in supposing that collective words stand for specific entities. This belief is a systematic feature of methodological collectivism and indeed constitutes the essence of that theory of knowledge in the social sciences.

Hayek argues that there are two sorts of ideas in the social sciences, *constitutive* ideas and *explanatory* ideas.[52] Constitutive ideas are those that the phenomena that we wish to explain consist of, that is, the actions, beliefs and opinions of individuals. Explanatory ideas are the concepts that we use in the understanding of social phenomena. Now methodological collectivism rests upon the validity of popular explanatory ideas such as 'classes' or 'societies'.[53] But there are no such collective entities or facts as classes or societies. Classes do not save or consume, only individuals do these things; therefore it is fallacious to attach any significance to statements about collective entities, or to statistical generalisations about the behaviour of economic aggregates.

According to Hayek we can speak of social wholes, but only in a special sense. From his description of the compositive method it follows that social wholes do not exist in a factual sense but are constructed out of the behaviour, opinions and attitudes of individuals. Methodological individualism asserts then that all statements about collectives are logically deducible from statements about individuals. However, it does not follow from this that the social sciences are reducible to psychology.[54] Psychology is concerned with the *conscious* behaviour of individuals while the social sciences are concerned with unconscious and unintended consequences of individual action.

Obvious examples of social phenomena which are explicable in this way are market economies, languages and systems of law. Thus genuine theoretical social science consists in the explanation of these phenomena; the only social sciences that have reached any sophistication in this are economics and theoretical linguistics.[55] One method very similar to this is the method of 'conjectural history'. This is the explanation of social phenomena not by use of exact historical narrative but by an act of the imagination showing how certain institutions must have developed. Menger's explanation of the origin of money is an instance of this.[56]

One reason why the methodological individualists have achieved considerable intellectual success over their rivals is the fact that the collectivists have almost invariably been driven to saying that statements about collectives are statements about 'group minds' that exist over and above the minds of observable individuals. Indeed, it has been argued convincingly by some authorities that doctrines such as these have led to some of the inhumanities that have characterised politics in this century.[57] But although methodological individualism is probably the correct approach, given the state of our knowledge, collectivism cannot be dismissed merely because some particular collectivists have dreamt up organic theories of the state, 'superminds', group minds and other such mysticism. It is surely logically possible to exclude these notions and still not commit oneself to a thoroughgoing individualism. It is difficult to see how methodological individualism could be 'proved'; after all, it may be that in the future some collectivity may show some regularities which can be observed, and not be deducible from the behaviour of individuals. Many people, who perhaps may be sympathetic to methodological individualism, may still be uneasy at the fact that some obvious social phenomena seem not to be exhaustively described in terms of individual motivations. It would be difficult to imagine an accurate account of the behaviour of, say, a crowd, entirely in individualistic terms. The observation of large-scale behaviour in society may not be so very different from that in the physical world.[58]

In economics a move towards methodological collectivism came with the construction of macroeconomic aggregates, such as the price level, the levels of employment, investment and so on; and of course no notion of group minds is involved here. Hayek has objected to these concepts, because they are no more than statistical generalisations which mask an underlying economic reality. Yet such ideas may not be as harmful as he suggests if the traditional scientific methods of rational criticism and falsification are rigorously applied.

There are similar problems in Hayek's more general account of social science being about the study of the spontaneous evolution of practices and institutions. While it is undoubtedly true that this has been a much neglected area of social study, and while it is also true that practical policies based on rational planning that recommend the replacement of institutions that have grown and developed spontaneously by designed ones have more often produced consequences not desired by the planners, nevertheless, this form of explanation seems especially limited in some areas. This is most true of political science where the subject of *power* cannot be ignored. Since some political institutions are the product of coercion or, to be more exact, the threat of coercion, one would expect something of a science of power to emerge. This would obviously involve observation and measurement and would therefore fall foul of Hayek's methodological strictures. But can such attempts be entirely dismissed? Admittedly the results have not been very productive in the form of testable hypotheses so far, but this paucity may not be a permanent feature of political science. This having been said, it

cannot be denied that the application of some very general
economic principles to political phenomena, which is a species of
Hayek's methodology, is at the moment proving to be a more
fruitful form of social enquiry.[59]

(c) *Keynesianism*

I shall be concerned only with the methodological aspects of
Keynesianism here, the specific economic policies associated with
the doctrine will be considered later (see below, Chapter 8).
Hayek's objections should be reasonably clear from the foregoing.
He regards the Keynesian explanation of unemployment as
scientistic because it asserts that there is a simple positive correlation
between total employment and the size of aggregate demand for
goods and services.[60] The persuasiveness of this doctrine lies in the
fact that it easily lends itself to statistical treatment, and therefore
the dogma grew up that only propositions which referred to
statistically measurable elements in the real world had the dignity of
science. The Keynesian system is, then, a classic instance of
objectification in the social sciences.

Hayek's own explanation of unemployment was that there exist
'discrepancies between the distribution of demand among the
different goods and services and the allocation of labour and other
resources among the production of these outputs'.[61] In other words,
the structure of production becomes distorted through time and
there has to be a reallocation of resources, via price changes, to
bring about a new equilibrium. Unemployment is generally not
caused by a lack of demand but by distortions in the labour market
which prevent automatic adjustment. There is, he says, no
possibility that this theory can be quantified because it is impossible
to produce statistical information that would show what wage rates
would ensure a continuous sale of labour. All that can be shown is a
general theory that illustrates how an equilibrium, or a movement
towards one, emerges.

It is undoubtedly true that Keynesianism, if not the doctrines of
Keynes himself, was, and still is, heavily scientistic. It is in this
area that scientism of the extreme kind becomes positively
dangerous rather than merely academically mistaken. Hayek's
claim that a whole generation of economists trained in these
methods is somehow responsible for many of the post-war mistakes
in policy is probably exaggerated, and it must be remembered that

the greatest critics, and falsifiers, of Keynesian economics, the monetarists, are equally vulnerable to Hayek's methodological strictures.[62] But he is surely right to expose scientism when it asserts that the only phenomena that can be treated scientifically are measurable phenomena.

5. HAYEK AND POPPER

Hayek and Popper are normally bracketed together because of apparently similar views they hold on the methodology of the social sciences. They have been close allies in the intellectual battles against historicism and various forms of collectivism, and in the argument for individualism, both philosophically and politically. I have indicated earlier that there are some important differences between them. The question is whether these differences are superficial or whether they reflect a more profound divergence of opinion.

It has been suggested earlier that Hayek's emphasis on the ultimate differences beteen the sciences was based on the misunderstanding that the theories of the natural sciences were inductive. Popper, despite many interpretations to the contrary, has always been a vigorous anti-positivist where that entails a rejection of both the logical positivists' description of science as a process of verification and their distinction between meaningful and meaningless statements. In Popper's view a strict application of the positivists' epistemology would render much of modern science nonsense. The heavy emphasis on theoretical constructions is common to both Hayek and Popper. It is surprising, then, to find some modern economics textbooks that claim to be written from a Popperian standpoint and yet also profess to be in the tradition of positive science.[63] Needless to say, such books are written in a very different tradition from that of Hayek. Part of the problem is that modern writers use the word positive in contrast with normative and attempt to found an economic science independently of ethical principles and do not normally enquire into the logical status of economic knowledge beyond this. Hayek is extremely sceptical of the possibility of constructing hypotheses with much empirical content, while contemporary economists assert almost the opposite.

It is this last point that brings us to a significant difference between Hayek and Popper. The latter emphasises that the

hallmark of a scientific theory is its predictive power. Science
characterises as preferable 'the theory which tells us more; that is to
say, the theory which contains the greater amount of empirical
information or *content*'.[64] The empirical content of a theory increases
with the increasing improbability of it being true. He gives an
example from weather-forecasting; a forecast that in some time in
the future it will rain has a very high probability of being true yet
has virtually no content, while a specification of the time it is likely
to rain has a high degree of content but is quite likely to be false.[65] It
would appear to be the case that in Hayek's description economic
theories are not very scientific in that they are consistent with a wide
range of phenomena and are difficult to falsify.

A similar problem occurs on the question of subjective knowledge. Popper has consistently maintained the idea of falsifiability
in the physical sciences; theories are in no way inductively
derived from the 'facts' but nevertheless, there is an objective order
against which theories can be tested. Since he believes in the unity of
the sciences it would follow that there must be objective knowledge
also in the social sciences. In fact, Popper does say that sociology is a
theoretical and empirical science: 'the events it explains and
predicts are observable facts'.[66] He does concede an element of
subjectivity in that a physicist is not aware of the 'inside' of an atom
in the way that a social scientist may have introspective knowledge
of individuals, but insists that subjective knowledge of this kind must
be rigorously tested by normal scientific methods.[67] Furthermore,
Popper's insistence on the correspondence theory of truth, that is
the theory that the truth of a statement depends upon its
correspondence to the facts, and not upon logical coherence,[68] is
very different from the subjectivism of Hayek's earlier writings.

Against this it could be pointed out that Popper does also say that
most of the 'facts' of the social sciences are mental reconstructions,
and he also stresses the spontaneous growth of institutions and the
idea of the social sciences being about the unintended consequences
of individual action.[69] The difficulty, I think, lies in Hayek's
attempt to combine two rather different philosophies of social
science; the Austrian praxeological school with its subjectivism and
rejection of testability in favour of axiomatic reasoning, and the
hypothetico-deductive approach of contemporary science with its
emphasis on falsifiablity and empirical content. This was not really
a problem for Mises since he did not endorse the Popperian
approach but it is something of a problem for Hayek.

As I suggested earlier, despite the different emphases that I have discussed, there is a basic continuity in Hayek's writings on methodology. The uneasy relationship between praxeology and empirical science is illustrated in an early and extremely important essay, *Economics and Knowledge*,[70] published in 1937. Here Hayek's concern was to distinguish between the tautological propositions in economic theory used to describe a state of equilibrium and the economics of the process towards that position. He argues, somewhat puzzlingly, that the latter is an empirical question. That is, it is an empirical matter that, although the conditions that describe an equilibrium in Walrasian neoclassicism do not obtain in the real world, there is, nevertheless a tendency towards such an equilibrium and that economics ceases to be the 'pure logic of choice' and becomes an empirical science when this tendency is explained. This tendency is explained in terms of the manner in which the dispersed knowledge in an economy, possessed by individual agents, is coordinated through the market process. This, on the face of it, is a slightly different enterprise from explaining the world with the basic concepts of praxeology, human action and purpose—although he doubts that the enterprise opens up a wide field of research from which we will learn much that is new.[71] This, of course, involves the important question of the theory of competition as a market process, and it is to this that I now turn.

3 The Market Order and Competition

As we know from Hayek's epistemology our understanding of the world consists of explanations in terms of 'orders', explanations of the principle rather than explanation of detail. This is a necessary consequence of the incurable limitations on the human mind. In the social sciences our knowledge is therefore the knowledge of an order of events and the order of which we have most knowledge in economic theory is the competitive market order. However, it is in this basic area of economics that the Austrian School in general, and Hayek in particular, have made some of their most significant departures from orthodoxy. The departures concern the meaning of such key concepts as 'equilibrium', 'competition' and 'economy'. The differences, in substance, reflect methodological differences of a fundamental kind.

The orthodox tradition holds that a market economy is best. understood in terms of a general equilibrium consisting of the timeless tautologies of pure economic theory. Given knowledge of tastes, technology and resources it would be possible to predict the solution to any economic problem on the assumption that individuals behave economically. As has often been pointed out,[1] in an important sense, there is no real 'choice' in this process since choice, if genuine, is unpredictable precisely because it is subjective. In the neoclassical general equilibrium model the observing economist, however, in principle can mechanically predict the outcome of an economic process. Lord Robbins's famous definition of economic science as the 'study of the disposal of scarce means towards the realisation of given ends' fits this approach accurately.[2] The activity of economising in the general equilibrium model consists of so arranging resources that a position is reached where it is impossible to switch a resource from one use to another and receive a net benefit; put more technically, the marginal rates of substitution between any two factors of production must be identical in all their different uses.[3] In principle, if individuals do act so as to maximise their economic gains, and the existing state of knowledge is available, then an equilibrium state could be 'objectified', that is, translated into quantitative terms by the observing economist. Hayek's objection to this approach has centred on its inapplicability to the real economic problem that faces society, and its distortion of the correct meaning of competition.

It is to be noted, however, that Hayek does not reject the notion of equilibrium entirely. After all a tendency to equilibrium in the real world, the observation of some regularities in the relationship between prices and costs, was the beginning of an abstract science of economics.[4] But this must be distinguished from the equilibrium of a stationary state where all incentives to change have been removed. A theory in which all adjustments in economic activity have come to an end is not very useful. Therefore Hayek talks of a dynamic equilibrium concept which, although fictitious, describes the hypothetical movement of the economic process through time, and is consistent with change.

Hayek says that we can only speak of the traditional concept of equilibrium in relation to the individual and his plans. It is possible to deduce an equilibrium position for one actor simply by using the tautological propositions of pure economic theory. An actor is in an equilibrium position when his actions are consistent with his plans. In fact this whole idea is no more than a way of attributing the notion of 'rationality' to individual action.[5]

But when we move from the actions of an individual to society as a whole we cannot speak so easily of equilibrium in the traditional sense because it is not possible to objectify the data of all the participating actors in the economic process. There is a difference between the knowledge that can be quantified by the economist and the knowledge that exists in an economic system which is not explained in the traditional theory.[6] It would follow from Hayek's subjectivism that we can never know in terms of measurable prices and costs whether an economy is in equilibrium according to the allocational view explicit in objectivist neoclassical theory. The requisite knowledge is not given to the observer but exists in a dispersed form throughout the economy. All that can be said, according to Hayek, is that there is a tendency towards equilibrium in a market process, where this means that the plans of the acting individuals are made compatible and expectations are not disappointed.[7] But a precise quantifiable equilibrium cannot be known in advance of a market process.

This rather obscure argument became important in the 1930s in the methodological disputes about the possibility of a rational socialist economic order. If it could be predicted mechanically what the optimal solution to an economic problem is then it would follow that an economy could be deliberately adjusted, from the logic of static equilibrium theory, to bring this about. Thus a socialist economy might be designed without a market or decentralised planning by individuals. But it is precisely this objective solution that Hayek denied on the grounds that the requisite knowledge was not given to the central planner.[8] The knowledge of prices and costs required in order to achieve an efficient allocation of resources can only be acquired by the *operation of a market process itself*. In fact, for the Austrian economists, cost is an entirely subjective phenomenon; it is not the observable money expenditure required to produce a commodity but the value of foregone output from an alternative use of the same resources. But obviously this alternative use can be known *only* to the actors in the process. The best way, then, to serve the interests of all in an economy is to allow producers to make the best use of decentralised knowledge through competition itself and give them the freedom to find out what it is that consumers desire.

There is, therefore, an order in a market economy and this order does make the best use of existing knowledge; and economics is in essence the study of how the dispersed, fragmented knowledge is transmitted to the individual participants. It produces results that if they were brought about by a single directing mind, that mind would have to possess knowledge which, in fact, no single mind could possess.[9] A socialist planner could never get the information for a rational direction of the economy.[10]

It is important not to forget that if economic *behaviour* is not mechanical and predictable as the general equilibrium model might imply there is nevertheless an economic *order* which is predictable. There is a tendency towards equilibrium but it is not a static one which removes all the determinants of change, it is essentially a *process* towards equilibrium which is constantly being disturbed by changes in data. The static equilibrium assumes away all the interesting features of the market as a process, especially that of competition.

2. ECONOMIES AND CATALLAXIES

To emphasise the differences between market processes and the neoclassical equilibrium system Hayek has recently started to use a different term. His argument is that the word 'economy' is used to describe two very different states of affairs. The word economy proper ought to be used only to describe a social practice defined in terms of a 'unitary hierarchy of ends', where knowledge of how to achieve these ends is 'given'.[11] A household or a firm is an economy in this sense. The economic calculus, what Hayek calls the Pure Logic of Choice, is the appropriate method of study for these phenomena, and the operations of the social practices so studied can be evaluated for their success in achieving their ends. An economy is a deliberate organisation designed to bring about common ends, and it can be evaluated, by traditional economic methods to see whether, for example, it is performing 'efficiently' in a technical sense.[12]

In contrast there is what Hayek calls a *catallaxy*, which is not defined at all in terms of a unitary hierarchy of ends.[13] In fact a *catallaxy* is a network of many economies, firms, households etc. but it has no specific common purpose itself; and it is not a deliberately made organisation but is a product of spontaneous growth. The market order or *catallaxy*, because it has no common purpose of its own, enables a great variety of individual purposes to be fulfilled: 'the order of the market rests not on common purposes but on reciprocity; that is, on the reconciliation of different purposes for the mutual benefit of the participants'.[14] In this conception of economic order a better word to describe the activities of the participants might be 'exchange' rather than choice; and in fact Hayek does tend to reserve the latter word to describe the activity of participants in economies where the apparatus of the 'pure logic of choice' applies.[15] Through the process of exchange individuals, by pursuing their own purposes contribute, without being aware of it, to the overall order of the *catallaxy*. The ends of a *catallaxy*, and the dispersed knowledge within it, are not given in their totality to anyone in the process, nor are they given to the observing economist. In a sense there are no 'ends' at all, beyond the maintenance of the apparatus itself.

It follows from this last point that, unlike an economy, a *catallaxy* cannot be evaluated for its success in fulfilling common purposes in the way that an economy can. One of the mistakes of modern economics, Hayek argues, is the attempt to treat a *catallaxy* as if it were an economy. This can be seen in some versions of welfare economics where an economic system is condemned as 'inefficient' because of the presence of some market imperfection, and policies are recommended to reproduce the outcome that would have occurred but for the presence of the imperfection. But according to the logic of a *catallaxy* it is impossible for any observer to have the knowledge which would enable him to predict the outcome of a market process, nor to know what an 'efficient' allocation would be.[16] The particular example, however, that Hayek picks out to illustrate the attempt to make a *catallaxy* serve some unitary purpose is that of distributive justice. In this a particular distributive pattern is imposed upon the outcome of a spontaneous process (see below, Chapter 7).

All this is not to say that *catallactic* processes are not intimately bound up with economic action. They most certainly are, and Hayek is critical of those who deride the economic nexus. In a *catallaxy* people are generally held together by 'vulgar' economic relationships, and the process of exchange enables individuals to improve their economic positions.[17] But, nevertheless, a *catallaxy* can encompass narrowly selfish or altruistic actions precisely because no common ends are presupposed towards which action has to be geared.

3. MARKET PROCESS

Since knowledge in any economic system is never given to a single mind the market system as described by general equilibrium economics is very different from that described by the science of *catallactics*. In a very important essay, 'The Use of Knowledge in Society', first published in 1945,[18] Hayek described succinctly the role of the market as a discovery procedure and a coordinating device.

The mistaken impression that economics is the problem of allocating 'given' resources to known ends arose, he claims out of the attempt to treat knowledge in the way that the natural sciences treat knowledge. Scientific knowledge can be put in the form of concrete information which can be then handled by experts to produce generally desired outcomes; but much knowledge in economics is not like this. It is the knowledge that is known only by particular individuals in particular places. The knowledge of the estate agent, or foreign currency dealer is of this type. And in a market process individuals only have to know the bits of knowledge that affect them. The function of the price mechanism is to integrate these dispersed fragments of information (knowledge of time and place) to produce an overall order which was intended by nobody. Hayek is not the only economist to 'marvel' at the process and to suggest that if such a system had been designed by a single mind it would have been acclaimed as one of the greatest inventions of mankind;[19] indeed it is the peculiar discovery of economics that a coherent social order is possible in the absence of central direction. One of the problems the economist has is convincing his fellow social scientists that not all order is 'made' order, that is, the product of political will.

Even those socialists who have thought seriously about the economics of a planned society have often availed themselves of the price mechanism. In principle the market system is an information device which transmits knowledge automatically through the signals sent out by prices. The important point about high wages and high profits is that these attract labour and capital to their most productive sources, and in doing so produce a greater net output for the society as a whole than would otherwise be the case. In the absence of such a system a socialist economy would have to *design* some other procedure to utilise resources and obtain the best use of knowledge.

It is crucial to distinguish competition in a *catallaxy* from the abstract model of perfect competition, as so often the case for market economics is erroneously made to rest on the perfect competition assumed by general equilibrium theory.[20] In fact, none of the defining charcteristics of *competition* are present in the description of perfect competition because that state of affairs assumes to exist the very things competition is supposed to bring about. For example, perfect competition assumes perfect knowledge while the process of competition is, as we have seen, the mechanism by which necessarily imperfect and fragmented knowledge is coordinated and integrated. Again, perfect competition of the stationary state concept of equilibrium precludes the idea of *entrepreneurship*, since this involves the possibility of individuals seeing a possible difference between product prices and factor prices which constitutes profit. Israel Kirzner[21] has shown in considerable detail how entreprene-urial *alertness*, that is, an awareness of new commercial opportunities, characterises a market process, and constantly moves an economy away from the imaginary state of rest described by perfect competition.

It would of course be foolish for defenders of the market order to rely upon the abstract concept of perfect competition as an argument against centralised planning and intervention. The conditions of perfect competition, that is, an homogeneous commodity bought and sold by large numbers of buyers and sellers all unable to influence price, free entry into the market, and complete knowledge on the part of all economic agents, are highly unreal and, as has just been indicated, likely to preclude further competition and distract attention from the true virtue of the market process. The real comparison ought to be between situations characterised by some competition, in which goods have a tendency to be produced at minimum cost, and the *dirigiste* alternatives, in which true costs are likely to be unknown precisely because of the absence of any competition at all. Even where the market throws up natural monopolies it may still be advisable to avoid the kind of intervention that tries to create competition as the monopoly may not be necessarily harmful. It may reflect superior efficiency, and if it does not, as long as no barriers are put in the way of new entrants, it is likely to disappear. As defenders of the free market have often pointed out, natural monopolies are extremely rare. Most monopolies are the product of misguided government intervention. Hayek stresses that we should be less intolerant of market imperfections and concentrate attention in those areas in which competition is suppressed.[22]

It should be evident that Hayek, and the general Austrian approach, is very different from the orthodox discussion of market economics. The differences are fundamentally methodological and philosophical. The general equilibrium—perfect competition approach is in principle addressed to the problem of prediction. If tastes are known in advance, along with technology and resources, then behaviour of 'Robbinsian economisers' can be predicted by mechanical methods. But with the Austrian concept of human action, behaviour cannot be predicted because economic agents are not omniscient and they face a world of uncertainty in which, through the exchange process, they use the little bits of knowledge that they have for their individual purposes. In this context it is odd to speak of economic action being about the efficient realising of a common hierarchy of ends. The market order is then not to be understood crudely as a means towards any end, it is simply the process of exchange which allows individuals to act reasonably predictably towards each other in an ever-changing and uncertain world.

Positivist economists are not so much interested in understanding and explaining an economic order or pattern in the way Hayek describes as in formulating hypotheses from which predictions may be derived and tested by quantitative techniques. The positivists would maintain that the concept of perfect competition can be retained, not because it is a descriptively accurate account of the real world, but because better predictions can be inferred from theories that assume it than from theories that involve different assumptions. Indeed, some Austrians have objected to economic theories of general equilibrium that assume perfect competition precisely because the assumptions of these theories are unrealistic.[23] But the objections to the positivists do not really turn on this; if the positivists can make accurate predictions of unobserved events from their theories they will meet their own standards of an economic science, after the manner of physics, irrespective of the 'realism' of their assumptions.[24] The real objection, and one that Hayek has constantly raised, is more philosophical. It is addressed to the orthodox view of market behaviour as entirely predictive, mechanical behaviour, and it is argued that a science of economics based solely on these premises is highly misleading. The study of *catallactics*, or the science of exchange, because it is not concerned with purely allocational problems in the sense described by Robbins, is not therefore burdened with the problem of explaining how men rationally use given knowledge to secure 'given' ends, but explains how, by individuals making the best use of existing, fragmented knowledge, an overall order is produced.

4. THE DEFENCE OF THE MARKET ORDER

A *catallaxy*, that purposeless and end-independent form of economic organisation that emerges spontaneously from the voluntary transactions of individuals, is a clear example of the evolutionary growth of institutions which Hayek regards as the proper study of the social scientist. But the description of a *catallaxy* alone is not enough to account for social and economic organisations. Exchanges can take place only within the context of rules and the development of a legal order is a logical and empirical counterpart to the development of a market order, and this will be considered in detail later (see below, Chapter 5). However, at this stage some problems of the market order must be discussed.

The major problem is the intellectual defence of this order. It is a system that is unlikely to secure automatic support, especially as its reliance on spontaneity and adaptive evolution seems strangely out of tune with modern thinking which sees virtually all political and economic order as a result of conscious direction and control. Also, undeniably, the *catallactic* process seems to throw up phenomena which, superficially at least, appear to be in conflict with the main tenets of the liberal credo. Obvious examples are monopoly, collusion and price-fixing on the part of employers; and other forms of monopoly, including the use of coercion against fellow-workers, on the part of labour. The interesting question is then, how far should the state act coercively to, in a sense, re-create the conditions of a competitive order? There is an important strain in libertarian thinking, and it is present in parts of Hayek's social philosophy, which regards state activity with such distrust that even that directed towards the highly desirable aim, from the libertarian's point of view, of establishing a competitive order is to be rejected. Most of these problems turn upon the criteria for adjudging the legitimacy of state action and will be considered in detail in succeeding chapters (especially Chapter 6) but some general comments are appropriate at this stage.

In his essays relevant to this field published in *Individualism and Economic Order* Hayek was of the opinion that if any success was to be achieved in removing the monopoly of trade unions there would have to be positive action against monopolies on the side of capital but in *The Constitution of Liberty*, and in other essays, he took the view that labour monopolies not only are the greater threat to the smooth functioning of the competitive market order but also that the two cases are not the same. It would appear that the monopoly power of unions is a product of discriminatory laws granting unions special privileges, used mainly against the workers themselves, while that of employers, as well as being much exaggerated, does not pose the same threat to liberty.

What constitutes the special privileges of trade unions is the complex of laws which has converted the right of free association, which was unjustly denied to labour unions in earlier times, into a form of compulsion.[25] The most significant piece of legislation in

Britain in this respect is the 1906 Trade Disputes Act which effectively exempts unions from legal liability for wrongs committed in the course of an industrial dispute. Furthermore, tolerant picketing laws enable unions to coerce and intimidate workers so as to prevent the free movement of labour bringing down the wage to that level which would prevail on a free market. This, of course, benefits workers who remain in employment. Because of union creation of a monopoly in the supply of labour the wage rate exceeds the market-clearing price, producing involuntary unemployment in that the higher wages paid mean that employers will hire fewer workers than they would in an automatically adjusting *catallaxy*.[26] A further stimulus to union power, which will be examined in great detail in later chapters, is mistaken monetary policy. The idea that it is the responsibility of governments to create additional spending power to mop up unemployment, most often caused by the actions of unions themselves, simply hands over to the unions massive economic power that could not possibly have occurred from the voluntary transactions of individuals in a *catallaxy*.[27]

In regard to monopolies on the side of employers Hayek has consistently denied the thesis that they are inevitable consequences of *catallactic* activities.[28] This has often been the justification for interventionism by those totally opposed to a market economy who maintain that economies of scale brought about by large operations make the case for decentralised competition redundant. On the contrary, Hayek argues that the very complexity of a modern industrial economy make the possibility of a centralised planner comprehending all the knowledge necessary for efficient management less likely than in smaller and simpler systems.[29]

But Hayek also finds himself in opposition to what might be termed that 'rationalistic' type of liberal who wishes to deliberately plan a competitive order by breaking up large-scale industrial organisations by coercive legislation. This is a denial of the possibility of a self-generating, self-correcting and evolving *catallaxy*. Against this Hayek has shown considerable distrust of anti-trust legislation because it rarely works to the benefit of consumers at large.[30] Often large firms are deterred from competition because a consequence of this may be a reduction of the number of firms in the industry so making the larger concerns liable for anti-trust suits.[31] Furthermore, the existence of 'natural' monopolies, for example a telephone system, may be beneficial to consumers where the artificial fostering of competition may be wasteful.

The trouble with government intervention is always that the side-effects of government activity may be worse than the defect in the competitive system that it is designed to cure; and Hayek has no difficulty in pointing out that, historically, the emergence of monopoly on a wide scale is a product of government sponsorship.[32] Nevertheless, Hayek is prepared to countenance some action, beyond the enforcement of general rules of law, to improve the working of the *catallaxy*. The most important question is not the fact of the size of enterprises but the possibility of free entry into the activity and governments have a responsibility to ensure this.[33] Also, and this is a little more surprising, Hayek believes that producers ought to be made to treat all customers alike. Hence Hayek's consideration of the desirability of outlawing the practice of price discrimination, the case where a producer finds it profitable to charge different prices for the same product to different consumers.[34] Many libertarians, including Mises, do not regard this as sufficient justification for government intervention.[35] But once again Hayek accompanies this recommendation with some scepticism about the reliability of governments in this and other matters.

From these rather conservative comments about the possibility of improving the working of a *catallaxy* it should not be inferred that they betray an uncritical acceptance of things as they are. Hayek has frequently indicated that those who defend the market order are often those in receipt of government privileges.[36] He makes an important distinction between 'ordered competition' and the competitive order proper.[37] The former refers to the type of competition that exists under conservative planners where competition is allowed to function only within guidelines set by centralised authorities. It is this kind of competition that has been favoured, for example, by Conservative governments in post-war Britain. In those approaches the market is not allowed to operate spontaneously but is geared towards meeting centrally-determined goals. Also, Conservative governments have been as persistent as their rivals in assiduously protecting favoured groups from the full effect of market forces, while at the same time proclaiming the virtues of free enterprise.

The point of this slight digression is not merely to criticise the failure of political authorities to meet the intellectual standards set by social thinkers but to illustrate a very important feature of Hayek's philosophy. That is, a system of ideas must be pursued rigorously and dogmatically even if in a particular case a relaxation of standards might produce some immediate, discernible benefit. A market system then, like a system of rules, must be applied impartially to all cases because the benefits are all long-term and cannot be assessed from particular cases.[38] In this sense the market order is properly a 'discipline' that imposes standards on future unknown cases. If the market order is not to be associated with a particular class or group in society, as it so often is, it must be seen to apply to all.

An essential complement of the market order is of course the legal order. No *catallaxy* can work at all without a general system of rules. The latter part of Hayek's career has been largely concerned with elaborating the structure of principles that describe a legal system appropriate for an ongoing *catallaxy*. Before this can be considered, however, some analysis must be made of two concepts that underlie all aspects of his social philosophy—liberty and coercion.

4 Liberty and Coercion

I. THE IMPORTANCE OF LIBERTY IN HAYEK'S SOCIAL PHILOSOPHY

It would be difficult to exaggerate the significance that the concept of liberty or freedom (Hayek uses the two words interchangeably) has for his system of thought. This in itself may sound trivial, since almost all social philosophers have been at pains to stress that their systems of ideas are designed to advance liberty, but what distinguishes Hayek is his ideological, and that is his word,[1] insistence on the priority of freedom over other ideals and his obvious intellectual and moral disquiet at the attraction other values, especially those of equality and social justice, have had for other social thinkers in this century. Freedom can be properly said to be at the centre of gravity of his thought in that both his philosophy of social science and his system of morality find their places around this crucial idea. It was this dogmatic commitment to liberty that found him notoriety, first in *The Road to Serfdom* and later in *The Constitution of Liberty*, primarily because the conclusions in matters of social policy that he drew from a rigorous, not to say rigid, application of the principle were so much at variance with what had become the consensus of opinion in these matters. It is important, therefore, to distinguish liberty in his philosophy of social science from liberty in his idea of morality. This is a distinction of analytical convenience only because there is in Hayek's system the aim of finding harmony between all the superficially differing elements. For example, not only is coercion an evil in a moral sense, and it should be the aim of participants in an organised society to reduce it to a minimum, but also it is maintained that the more coercion is used to control individual actions the less use will be made of knowledge in a scientific sense.

In Hayek's social science liberty stands as a kind of necessary postulate in a proper explanation of social affairs. Since an abstract science of society is concerned with the spontaneous evolution of

54

undesigned and unplanned institutions such as *catallaxies*, languages and systems of rules then it follows that the appropriate disciplines are limited to theories that explain the consequences of free actions of individuals.[2] The economist is limited to analysing that kind of order, or regular pattern of behaviour, known as the market order, that emerges from the uncoerced transactions of individuals. Of course, the regularities are not observed 'facts' in a crude inductive sense, but mental reconstructions on the part of the economist which explain the phenomena in question. Thus explanation is a kind of imaginative act; the economist deduces what *would* happen if one or more elements in his abstract model of the real world were to be changed; it can be imagined, for example, what new pattern of economic activity would emerge if a tax on a good were imposed. These kinds of theoretical explanations depend for their validity on the possibility of transactions freely taking place. In a perfectly planned economy where predetermined economic targets are met by coercion there could not be a proper explanatory science, only a collection of 'facts'. Hayek has maintained consistently that there could not be an abstract, deductive science of economics under socialism.[3]

In the context of morality Hayek stresses that not only is liberty the supreme value but it is also the condition for other values.[4] This means that a society is to be evaluated in accordance with freedom and not in accordance with some trade-off between, for example, freedom and social justice, or by a criterion of 'economic efficiency' in a technological or engineering sense, and that the other values which individuals may wish to promote through their voluntary exchanges depend ultimately on the institutions of a free society. This latter point means that a genuine altruism, which is not only conceivable but indeed only possible in a free society, is quite inconsistent with the promotion of a 'social morality' by coercive law.[5]

This last question is of particular importance in the context of the welfare state. This is because this type of society, according to Hayek, has done much to undermine the notion of personal responsibility which is essential for liberty. Freedom would be meaningless if agents were not thought to be responsible for their actions where that means that they are capable of responding to certain sorts of pressures. If people cannot help what they do, in the sense of not being able to conduct their actions in the light of consequences that can be known to them, then it would be absurd to put forward the ideal of freedom.[6] This does not require the notion of the self as an independent entity standing outside the normal chain of cause and effect, a metaphysical proposition which, if true, would make freedom an impossibility, but only the idea that individuals can in the future, because of their possibility of learning from the past, act differently. The current sociological theories of behaviour which see individuals responding mechanically to certain causal environmental factors are, in Hayek's view, destructive of personal responsibility.

What is quite inconsistent with this idea of responsibility is the claim that individuals can be made responsible for states of affairs that are remote from their personal circumstances. This is the moral philosophy that makes a kind of 'general altruism' morally obligatory. The whole idea of a social morality which transcends personal responsibility for actions the consequences of which can be known to individuals is anathema to Hayek.[7] Not only is it the perversion of a genuine personal morality, on which the free society depends, but it is likely to lead to the suppression of individual liberty in the name of 'society'.

There is much to be said for Hayek's salutary observations on the way ideas of morality have developed under the institutions of the welfare state. The paternalist aspects of social welfare have to some extent undermined personal responsibility while at the same time they have not been accompanied by any noticeable increase in genuine socially-oriented actions. Furthermore, these supposedly social feelings that individuals ought to have according to collectivist thinking, have in the last resort been imposed by the officials of the organised state. In which case they are not genuine social values at all but the individual values of the officials. For Hayek, the best way of serving society is by pursuing one's own interests since this leads to the more efficient use of knowledge and therefore increases the net social product.

In what follows below I shall describe in some detail Hayek's account of the meanings of liberty and coercion and indicate their significance for social policy. Many of the important problems, however, cannot be properly understood without an appreciation of his philosophy of law. Therefore some of the crucial, and indeed difficult, questions concerning the relationship between liberty, coercion and the law will be reserved for the next chapter.

2. DEFINITION AND MEANING

While Hayek clearly does not belong to that school of political philosophy that limits the discipline to the exhaustive analysis of political terms he nevertheless prefaces his substantive account of the principle of liberty with an important exercise in clarification. This is undoubtedly an essential prerequisite in the case of liberty because so great are the emotive overtones of the word, indeed it has very little descriptive content outside the context of particular restraints, that many people of quite different political persuasions justify their recommendations by an appeal to it. It would be claimed by many libertarians that the word has been 'hijacked' by those whose political philosophies, if implemented, would mean the end of liberty as commonly understood. This would seem to be true of many contemporary 'liberation' movements, the practical policies of which imply considerable measures of coercion.

As a first approximation to Hayek's definition of freedom it could be said that it falls in the tradition of 'negative' liberty. That is the tradition that an individual is free to the extent that his actions are not restrained by external obstacles; in most cases this means law.[8] What makes an action free is not the content of the action but whether a person is restrained or not in the performance of it. In contrast, 'positive' liberty refers more to the content of an act. A person is free when he is pursuing worthy, or morally desirable ends. Other versions locate freedom in terms of an individual's self-mastery; he is free when his actions proceed from his rational will rather than from momentary impulses which make him a slave of his irrational desires.

Hayek defines freedom in *The Constitution of Liberty* as that 'state in which a man is not subject to coercion by the arbitrary will of another'.[9] This clearly locates freedom in the context of the relationship between men and men. To have one's ends decided by others, to be a tool in their plans, is not to be free. In *Rules and Order* he makes the same point in a slightly different form: freedom is a 'state in which each can use his own knowledge for his own purposes'.[10] It is important to note that for Hayek liberty is absent when an individual is subject to the will of another and that this is a slightly different formulation from that of the orthodox theory of negative liberty which normally locates lack of freedom in any restraint (except for natural obstacles), including laws. As I shall show, Hayek in a very important sense, does not necessarily regard laws as constituting restraints. Thus freedom does not depend upon the range of choice open to the individual[11] (the orthodox view does measure liberty in terms of the absence of law) but in whether the restraint is of human origin. Under a rightly constituted legal order the notions of law and liberty are consistent.

Hayek contrasts his view of liberty with other, he thinks mistaken, ideas, namely, political liberty, liberty as power and 'inner freedom'. Political freedom normally means the freedom to participate in government, the right to vote, form political parties and so on.[12] In orthodox accounts of democracy it is automatically assumed that these political rights are conceptually a part of freedom. In fact, one influential contemporary writer on politics, Professor Bernard Crick, in a critique of Sir Isaiah Berlin's concept of negative liberty, somewhat extravagantly claimed that political activity is freedom itself and that not to countenance politics as an essential part of free activity was the liberal's typically timid retreat from the public into the private world.[13] It is to this concept of a private world as a necessary feature of a civilised society that Hayek is determined to give intellectual support. He regards political liberty as an illegitimate extension of freedom from the individual to the collective sphere.[14] Against this Hayek suggests that as long as each individual is guaranteed equality under the law, freedom from arbitrary arrest, the right to own property, freedom of movement and free choice of occupation then the conditions of a free society exist.[15] It follows that these conditions could be met in a regime characterised by the absence of at least some of the conventional political liberties.

Many of Hayek's criticisms of the association of political freedom with freedom itself are peculiarly apt in western democracies where, since the last war, whole areas of economic and social life which were formerly governed by individual choice are now decided by collective decision. It would be difficult to maintain that the replacement of individual choice by the political machinery of elections and accountability of ministers and officials, even if operated effectively, is a net addition to liberty. The continuous 'politicisation' of economics in Great Britain has hardly, *pace* Crick, contributed to liberty in Hayek's sense. But nevertheless it may still be legitimate to ask whether Hayek can exclude entirely the concept of political rights from the rubric of liberty by a kind of verbal fiat? Surely Lord Robbins is correct in suggesting that it would be difficult to describe a society as a liberal society if it did not include political rights among the rights of its subjects.[16] This in itself would not preclude the setting of limits by general rules to the range of concerns that may be handled politically.

It might be suggested that there is a trade-off between political liberty and other principles of liberty, that individuals may regard themselves as making a net gain in liberty if they sacrifice a little of one for a gain in another; but it is just this sort of conceptual deal to which Hayek objects.[17] He concedes that it would not be irrational, in a technical sense, to prefer other values to liberty,[18] but denies that there can be any gain in *freedom* if political liberty is preferred to, say, economic liberty. It does seem to be little more than an assertion that certain sorts of activity which a long tradition of liberal thought has regarded as free should be regarded as not worthy of the title. This is, to repeat, not to deny the serious economic and moral objections to the intrusion of politics into affairs that should be decided by individual choice but only to suggest that these are, indeed, economic and moral objections rather than questions about linguistic propriety. One problem, to be considered later in this section, is that of the cases where individuals *freely choose* to have their affairs handled politically. The outcomes of such choices would not resemble a free society in Hayek's sense but the choices could still be free in an analytical sense.

The second view of liberty which Hayek rejects is that which associates freedom with the power, faculty or ability to do certain things.[19] This is a normal feature of socialist thought; it is frequently claimed that the negative account of liberty is vacuous because, although a person may be free in a formal sense to act in certain ways, he cannot be said to be free in a substantive sense if he lacks the means, normally financial means, to act. The upshot of the argument is to identify liberty with wealth. Hayek is not alone in regarding this as a particularly dangerous argument. The concept is quite fallacious. Freedom is not power or wealth, it is not being coerced; a slave would not be free, no matter how economically well-off, if he were at the mercy of his master, while another person might be economically worse off but if he lived in a free society he would still be at liberty to choose and decide for himself. But it is also a threat to the institutions of a liberal order. Taken literally the doctrine puts no limits on the extent to which centralised authorities can intervene in order to increase the 'powers' of citizens, in the mistaken belief that their freedom is also being increased.[20] Of course it may be legitimate to argue, although Hayek would deny this, that centralised authorities ought to intervene on other moral grounds, such as equality, but it is a mistake to suppose that such intervention increases personal liberty.

The other mistaken concept of liberty is that which understands it in terms of 'inner freedom'.[21] This is an ideal of liberty associated with the theorists of positive liberty mentioned earlier in this section and describes a person's freedom in terms of the extent to which he acts according to his rational will. Very often the personality is bifurcated, and an individual is said to be free insofar as his 'higher' self, the source of his rational decisions, is in command of his 'lower' self, the source of his ephemeral and irrational desires. Hayek argues that the extent to which a person acts as he ought to act is a different question from that of whether he is being coerced by another agent. The latter question is certainly a question about freedom but the former is a matter of psychology. He concedes that there may be a connection between the two issues in that things which may count only as minor obstacles to be got over by some individuals may constitute coercive forces to others. The idea of 'rational' freedom that underlies the notion of 'inner freedom' has been thoroughly discredited and the ease with which an obscure metaphysical doctrine can be turned into a political instrument of totalitarianism has been effectively demonstrated by Cranston and Berlin.[22] Yet there might be a kernel of truth in some of these ideas. It is possible to speak of a lack of freedom because of some psychological constraint, and the case of brainwashing clearly shows this. Obviously Hayek would regard someone who willingly obeyed the will of another because of some psychological pressure as a case of coercion, and it clearly is. But an interesting question might be whether there is a logical distinction between being coerced psychologically and acting freely in Hayek's sense, or whether there is a distinction of degree only? It might be maintained that there is a spectrum ranging from genuine psychological coercion through to free choice but which includes perhaps some of the more subtler forms of persuasion about which it is difficult to say whether they effect a genuine loss of liberty or merely adversely affect those individuals of weak will or emotional vulnerability.

Since Hayek understands liberty in the sense of not being coerced by other men it follows that his social philosophy will emphasise the importance of the private world for the preservation of a genuine individualism. This distinction between private and public is crucial because it illustrates his distinction between two concepts of law—the law of an organisation with specific purposes and the rules of a purposeless spontaneous society. The private world is not characterised by the absence of rules, as crude libertarians sometimes imply, but by rules which do not direct the individual towards centrally determined ends and which provide the framework of reasonable security within which he can pursue his ends. The public world, however, operates through commands addressed to officials for the fulfilment of specific collective purposes. The private sphere is what Hayek calls the 'protected domain'.[23]

The protected domain, the essential condition of a liberal social order, includes property; law, liberty and property are regarded as inseparable. That property precedes civilisation, and is a prerequisite of a rule-governed society, Hayek maintains is a scientific truth.[24] By property he does not mean the possession of physical goods only. Quoting Locke, he maintains that a person possesses property in his person to the extent that he is free to exchange his labour with another and to move without hindrance within a system of general rules.[25] Property guarantees freedom but a person can still be free though he might possess very little property in a material sense. As long as the means which enable him to pursue a course of action are not in the exclusive control of another then he may enjoy liberty. The important point is that it is not the amount of property that individuals possess that determines their freedom, but its dispersal throughout society at large.[26]

This, however, is only the beginning of the problems of property for what is to count as property in terms of legal provisions is very much a matter of dispute. The controversies about property have become important recently because of the interest shown by economists in 'neighbourhood' effects of the economic activities of individual agents. Individual producers may impose costs on the community at large through, for example, pollution, and these are costs which the producers do not pay. In many cases individual property rights are affected but the costs in such cases are not so easily assessable as in the traditional examples of damage to property. Do house-owners living near airports have property rights in the quiet atmosphere disturbed by the noise of aeroplanes, and if so, how could their losses be calculated? Equally important for Hayek is the question of whether in any meaningful sense the public can be said to 'own' property collectively, for example, electricity? These problems will be considered in more detail later (see below, Chapter 6) but it can be said at this stage that the stressing of the importance of the abstract concept of property is only the first step towards understanding the problems of property in the liberal order.

There are also problems in the question of the relationship between socialism and property. Hayek has frequently suggested that a socialist system of ideas challenges the conceptual connection between law, liberty and property; the implication being that a socialist order would attempt to abolish property.[27] Since he claims that the argument that property precedes civilisation is a scientific truth, the further implication is that of necessity socialism must lead to barbarism. But it is not clear that this argument supports all he wants to say, for what he is really trying to demonstrate is the pre-eminence of *private* property. But the concept of property does not entail the pre-eminence of private property, all that it entails is that *rules* should govern the transmission and management of things that people come to regard as property.[28] Conceptually, nothing is implied about what the public – private mix should be. Also, given Hayek's own argument that an individual's freedom does not depend upon the amount of property he has, in the sense of personal belongings, it might be possible for freedom to obtain in a socialist regime as long as property was dispersed among a number of public authorities and subject to strict rules. I do not, in fact, think that this is at all likely, although it is conceptually possible, and in practice freedom is almost certainly best preserved by a wide dispersal of private property. But the question is, in view of the importance of neighbourhood effects, partially an empirical one. What particular mix of public and private property is appropriate for a liberal society? It is a question which cannot be answered from Hayek's own methodology.

Property is not the only feature of the protected domain. It goes almost without saying that economic freedom in general is an indispensable condition of all other freedoms and free enterprise is both a genuine expression of liberty and necessary for all other personal liberties.[29] This has to be stressed since contemporary intellectual opinion is not favourable to the idea of economic freedom as being a genuine case of liberty; at best it is regarded as a means to an end of superior liberty. Since Mill's *On Liberty* the value of liberty of expression has been greater than that of free enterprise in the eyes of the intellectuals.

Hayek is equally insistent on the importance of freedom to choose one's own moral standards in personal matters within the protected domain. The law has no business in imposing a set of moral values on individuals to restrain their actions within the private sphere. Whether Hayek's description of the legal order is sufficient to generate the protection of the freedom to pursue one's own moral standards inside the protected domain will be discussed in the next chapter. What must be remembered at this stage is that Hayek's conception of liberty precludes any specific content being given to the protected domain. Freedom consists in not being coerced by other men; it does not consist in doing any particular thing. It is the mistaken rationalist view of liberty that links it to certain activities.

The mistaken philosophies of liberty are of mainly continental origin and Hayek's objections to them are a part of his general objections to the false individualism that he traces to the Enlightment. He contrasts the rationalist conception of liberty, which, he claims, mistakenly associates liberty with design and social institutions with contrivance and deliberation, with the empirical tradition which connects freedom with tradition.[30] In the latter conception free institutions were not deliberately planned but emerged accidentally from individual interaction. They were not designed to bring about specific benefits to men; but once it became apparent that limitations on government were to the advantage of men then this was a reason for maintaining them.

What has surprised, and indeed disheartened, some critics of Hayek's thought is not so much his distinction between a true and a false liberty, although it has been suggested that he has a rather precious, metaphysical conception of liberty and individualism which only a few thinkers have been able to grasp,[31] but his rejection of so many thinkers who might have been thought well-qualified for admission to a somewhat exclusive circle. It is the categorising of Bentham as a false liberal that has caused most of the dissent. Hayek is particularly critical of Bentham's oft-quoted phrase that 'every law is an infraction of liberty'. In fact, it is this comment that entitles Bentham to be included in the category of negative liberty according to the standard accounts of the subject. Hayek's objection to this is that it says that all laws restrict liberty when it is his view that only laws of a certain type do this, and that it implies that freedom has to be justified *pragmatically* every time on the grounds of some other principle.[32] As I shall show in the next section of this chapter, Hayek maintains that liberty cannot be satisfactorily justified in this way.

It is certainly true that there are many collectivist overtones in traditional utilitarianism, and that liberty was always subordinate to utility; but the critics have a point in criticising Hayek for somewhat dogmatically consigning Bentham to the same intellectual category as, for example, Rousseau. The utilitarians did take the individual as their unit of analysis, and although they failed to derive statements about social utility from the preferences of individuals, they were in the forefront against a certain kind of mystical, conservative collectivism on behalf of liberty during the first half of the nineteenth century.

Similar reasoning leads to Hayek's rejection of the doctrine of *laissez-faire*, which he claims is not the same thing as economic liberty.[33] The doctrine of *laissez-faire* is singled out as a specific example of rationalism. It would appear to be the case that Hayek's objection centres on the fact that the *laissez-faire* doctrine holds that a society is necessarily better to the extent that its laws are reduced; any decrease in law must entail an increase in liberty. Against this Hayek maintains that a genuinely free society spontaneously develops those rules which liberty requires. There is not a natural goodness in man which makes it possible to dispense with rules; on the contrary, men have developed rules for coping with the antisocial consequences that emerge from the excessive pursuit of self-interest by some individuals.[34] Hayek claims that anarchy is the logical implication of an extreme *laissez-faire* stance. This is again rather surprising since no continental, rationalist philosopher of *laissez-faire* believed that the functions of government could be dispensed with entirely. What they did believe was that rational principles could be demonstrated to show where the dividing line between the individual and *organised* society should fall; and this may be at a different point than that which emerges from spontaneous evolution. There is a long tradition of political economy, a tradition which is experiencing something of a revival in America,[35] which is explicitly concerned with the justification on rational grounds of the minimal state.

The puzzling thing is that Hayek himself is a part of two traditions. Sometimes he writes in the style of a libertarian rationalist intent upon justifying limited government on the grounds of an abstract principle; yet at other times he writes in the manner of a Burkean conservative, suspicious of any kind of change. And of course Burke is a writer for whom he has very great respect. There may be no contradiction between the two intellectual procedures. Perhaps by the use of the method of 'conjectural history' it is possible to describe the institutions of a free society that would emerge from the spontaneous actions of individuals. This is the way that Menger explained the origins of money and the way that Professor Nozick has more recently explained the emergence of the state.[36] But there does seem to be a difference between the acceptance of things because they can be explained in this way and the acceptance of them merely because they are there. Hayek would deny that his social philosophy had anything to do with the latter view but his reverence for Burke and his criticism of doctrinal *laissez-faire* sometimes give that impression. The issue is a little confusing because, as I shall show later, some of the reforms that Hayek has suggested for the monetary system and for parliamentary forms of government are quite radical in their implications and seem a long way from Burkean conservatism.

There is a further important aspect of the problem of the meaning of liberty to be considered before I go on to the question of the justification of liberty. The word liberty (or freedom) seems to be used in two subtly different senses throughout Hayek's work, and these different usages are apparent in the work of other libertarian thinkers, although the distinction is rarely made explicit. Liberty is said to characterise voluntary, uncoerced actions of individuals such as exchange in an economic market, or exchange in the sense of the interplay of ideas in the intellectual world; yet the concept is also used to describe, favourably, a society that exhibits those very features. However, as a matter of logic, it is not necessarily the case that a liberal society, a society described in terms of freely contracting individuals, will result from the free contracts of individuals. Individuals may very well freely agree to impose restraints upon themselves of a kind severe enough to warrant the outcome being called 'illiberal' even though each individual may regard himself as better off as a result of the prior exchanges. In most practical cases the distinction is probably not that important. It tends to be assumed in Hayek's system that the free transactions of individuals are consistent with the spontaneous growth of free institutions; but there is a theoretical difference that does have policy implications. Critics of the private enterprise market economy presumably have the distinction in mind when they claim that the outcomes of market transactions often result in phenomena quite alien to liberal ideals, for example, monopoly, cartels and the customary market imperfections.

The distinction does in fact lead to two theoretically different types of liberalism: one that sees a role for law to reproduce the features of an ideal liberal society where market exchanges may be said to have failed, and another that accepts *any outcome* of individual transactions where these are free and uncoerced. Hayek is not unaware of the distinction and discusses it implicitly in connection with the problem of individuals *freely contracting* themselves into slavery.[37] The case of pure slavery is rather too good an example; the real, and much more likely, problems occur in situations short of this where people contract themselves into terms of employment which turn out to be particularly onerous or which put them in conditions of servility towards an employer. Hayek, optimistically I think, tends to regard these possible voluntary renunciations of liberty as occurring only in the context of the exercise of political or collective liberty. As he points out, there have been examples this century of communities voting themselvs into servitude; and the citizens of underdeveloped countries appear to prefer the tyrannical government of their own race to relatively liberal regimes of colonial rulers.[38] But it is possible for individuals, through non-collective transactions, to produce illiberal orders.

Normally Hayek speaks of liberty in an 'instrumental' sense, and actually says on one occasion that what people do with it is their own affair.[39] This would be consistent with his view that no content can be put into the individual's protected domain. But he is not entirely consistent, and I shall discuss one example, the case of the voluntary closed shop in industrial relations, where he seems to favour coercive laws to produce a liberal outcome, in the last section of this chapter.

An extreme libertarian would oppose any attempt by legislators to create a particular social order, no matter how desirable that may be. But such a standpoint does turn out to have at least one peculiar virtue. It is capable of accommodating almost any social order that emanates from consent. Thus Nozick has shown that socialist regimes logically could emerge from the condition of the enforcement of voluntary contracts that characterises instrumental liberty.[40] Hayek claims to have scientifically refuted socialism, on the grounds that it produces inefficient outcomes and that it negates individual liberty; but individuals could accept freely such a system and its consequences within the framework of the minimal state. It is merely a contingent fact that all the socialist systems of which we have experience have involved severe restrictions on liberty. This is, of course, a crucially important fact, and important enough to settle most arguments about the desirability of a socialist order; but it does not provide a conceptual portcullis against the admission of socialist ideas.

3. THE JUSTIFICATION OF FREEDOM

Many of the arguments that Hayek uses in support of liberty are implicit in what has been said already, but the topic is of such importance that it requires separate treatment. Hayek claims that the arguments in favour of liberty are of an empirical kind, in fact he repeatedly contrasts his cautious, tentative approach with the *a priori* reasoning of the rationalist philosophers. Readers may find this puzzling, and possibly in contradiction with the generally anti-empirical tenor of his methodological writings. But this would be to misunderstand his position. Although his justification of liberty certainly depends upon the long-term benefits it brings to a society, this must not be mistaken for a piecemeal, pragmatic justification in which each particular free act is appraised according to the amount of quantifiable benefit it brings. I shall show that his procedure is the opposite of this.

The first point to consider is whether liberty is a value in itself or whether its worth depends upon other things. Hayek holds both these views. But although he does say that freedom is an important moral value irrespective of its consequences his main emphasis is on it being essential for his theory of progress and his theory of the acquisition of knowledge. He has been criticised for this apparent lack of interest in proclaiming the value of liberty itself; but it is difficult to see how else he could have approached the subject. Very little in the way of criticism of mistaken ideologies comes from a *mere* passionate and emotional defence of liberty compared with the quite formidable critical weapon that can be forged when this principle is related to a general system of ideas.

Despite his criticism of the Enlightenment Hayek shares at least one thing with that intellectual movement—a belief in human progress, not a naive belief in some law of inevitable progression but a conviction that the institutions of a free society do tend to produce discernible benefits for mankind.[41] It is, of course, to the threat to human progress that comes from mistaken social philosophies that his thought is addressed.

His argument for the benefits of liberty rest upon his familiar thesis of the unpredictability of human knowledge. It is because we cannot know the future or predict the growth of knowledge that we allow each individual the freedom to experiment within the framework of general rules. Hayek's comment that omniscient men would not need liberty[42] is an accurate summary of his view on the relationship between freedom and ignorance. His main objection to the rationalist theory of liberty on this score is that the rationalist associates the growth of knowledge with control and predictability while those phenomena that are controllable and predictable constitute only a small part of human and social experience.[43] The evolutionary approach to freedom and knowledge allows for the accidental, the unexpected and the spontaneous. A major feature of this argument is the epistemological proposition that it is impossible for the mind to stand outside the process of social evolution and predict its future course.[44] This assumption, and the Cartesian proposition that we ought only to believe that of which we can be absolutely sure, Hayek maintains, form a kind of philosophical background within which systems that try and organise knowledge and deliberately control the environment are formulated.[45] But since much of human knowledge cannot be specifically organised, the knowledge of time and place in decentralised market economies is an example of unorganised knowledge, individuals in society require considerable freedom of action if it is to be utilised. This argument is closely linked to a point I have mentioned before in describing Hayek's theory of knowledge. That is, so much more knowledge is available to a free society than a planned society because in the former all individuals, by using their knowledge for their purposes, maximise the use of fragmented knowledge, while in the latter only the knowledge possessed by the centralised planner is used, which must necessarily be much less.

An argument frequently used against individual liberty and on behalf of planning is that because of the complexity of modern society its various operations have to be directed by some mastermind, supposedly fully cognisant of these operations. The argument would appear to be that there is a 'given' amount of complex knowledge which can only be utilised through central planning. Hayek rather neatly reverses the logic of the argument. It is because of freedom and spontaneity that societies develop to a great degree of complexity. Free societies are necessarily more complex than planned societies, through greater specialisation and extension of the division of labour, and therefore it cannot be the case that it is the complexity of modern society that negates the case for liberty.[46]

Perhaps the most decisive argument that Hayek uses for the advantages of free experimentation in the growth and acquisition of knowledge is that in an open society such knowledge is made available freely to all.[47] Whereas land and material resources are necessarily scarce, ideas and techniques can be used by others. This enables rapid progress to be made by less advanced societies because they can avail themselves of the discoveries of others. It is for this reason that on a number of occasions Hayek has expressed disquiet at the creation of monopolies through the extension of patent rights.[48] There is of course a problem here in that the growth of knowledge may very well be retarded if potential inventors and pioneers of new knowledge cannot profit from their contributions, just as much as the fact that some groups will make little progress if the access to new methods of production is arbitrarily blocked.

The most important feature of Hayek's defence of liberty is its deliberately dogmatic approach, not dogmatic in the pejorative sense of the word but in the sense of a general defence of liberty rather than *particular* cases of it. It is this that makes his claim that his justification for liberty is empiricist appear somewhat dubious. The claim for freedom does not depend upon its observable and quantifiable consequences (and he insists that people ought to be allowed to act freely within general rules even though we may disapprove of the consequences of their actions), but upon freedom being consistently pursued.[49] The benefits may not be immediately observable but in the long run the advantages of the system of liberty are obvious.

It is true that the tactical argument for liberty must take the form of a general justification for freedom as a kind of 'system' because if one were to take the particular freedoms one by one it would be fairly easy to produce empirical justifications for restricting them. This is especially true of justifications of particular freedoms that turn upon majority consent. It goes almost without saying that Hayek's case for freedom does not depend on the approval of the majority. Nevertheless, however convincing these arguments for freedom may be, it would be difficult to categorise them as 'empirical' in any strict sense of the word, and Hayek would presumably deny that they were technically empirical. He uses the word in contrast with rationalist theories of liberty rather than as a means of placing his work in the conventional empirical tradition. The benefits of liberty are not strictly observable and the 'harm' that liberty may cause in particular cases can never refute the general case for liberty. Indeed it is difficult to see how the case for liberty in terms of spontaneous evolution could ever be refuted.

In fact Hayek's justification for freedom is in a sense not theoretical at all. Men did not think up a libertarian value system and deduce the necessary institutions from the values. It is rather the case that by accident men discovered the advantages of limiting the powers of their rulers and chose to extend, and indeed universalise the benefits of so doing.[50] This is not to say that a liberal society proceeds without a profound belief in the *principle* of liberty, quite the contrary, and Hayek maintains that the so-called 'muddling through' and commonsense approach to human and social affairs characteristic of the English tradition concealed a profound commitment to the principle of freedom.[51] What Hayek is objecting to is not principles but the approach to principles in which the limits of liberty are deduced axiomatically from first principles.

There is little doubt that Hayek's defence of freedom is the most eloquent, persuasive and closely-reasoned since Mill's *On Liberty*. Of course, with its stress on spontaneity and unpredictability it lacks Mill's rationalism and intentionalist utilitarianism. Hayek does not think that *a priori* moral principles can determine the limits of liberty and would be sceptical of Mill's contempt for custom and tradition. As I shall show in the next chapter, Hayek's main concern is to indicate how liberty can be made compatible with general rules while Mill seems to want to determine the relationship between liberty and rules, which for him always seem to be coercive, by reference to some other principle, that is, utility. It is for these and other reasons that Hayek is reluctant to accept Mill into the fellowship of true interpreters of the liberal tradition. While many of Mill's other writings do display a typical utilitarian approach this is much less true of *On Liberty*, which, as has often been pointed out, sits rather uneasily by the side of his general philosophy. For this reason alone it would be more than a little arbitrary to exclude Mill from the liberal individualist tradition.

Perhaps a more fundamental objection that might be made to Hayek's defence of liberty centres on its dogmatism. Is it the supreme value that ought never to be given up for another principle? Certainly Hayek concedes that liberty is not always to our liking, and that certain individuals may be unhappy with their freedom and may wish to trade it for something more comforting and less demanding, but he is adamant that under a genuine liberal philosophy a government is not entitled to use force to bring about, say, a greater measure of equality. A contemporary, and popular, approach to political philosophy holds that in matters of public policy trade-offs can be made between principles, that marginal amounts of liberty may be given up for marginal increases in equality.[52] This is precluded by Hayek's system; the commitment to liberty must be dogmatic, and some critics have winced at this. Does it not entail that massive inequalities are to be tolerated because to do anything to alleviate them would involve the use of coercion? This would appear to follow because in Hayek's thought there is no quantifiable relationship between liberty and other principles. This important topic is dealt with more fully later (see below, Chapter 7) but it is worth noting at this point that the acceptability of a system of ideas that permits the persistence of undesirable outcomes even when it would be possible to prevent them without too much coercion is not likely to be great. Of course, the question of the truth and coherence of Hayek's system has nothing to do with its acceptability in a political sense.

4. COERCION

Freedom is always contrasted with coercion by Hayek. Normally, it is not laws that coerce, at least not laws cast in the form of general rules equally applicable to all, it is men who, by their actions, make others their tools. The kind of laws that do involve coercion are those that authorise officials to issue explicit directions to individuals to do particular things. But the definition of coercion, Hayek admits, is almost as tricky as that of freedom.

Coercion does not involve the absence of choice. A person who is coerced still chooses to act in certain ways.[53] If an individual is faced with an agent who can dispose of overwhelming force and decides to obey that will then he has still made a rational choice. But what, according to Hayek, constitutes a conceptual difference between decisions made under coercive threats and decisions made for other reasons is that in the former case the presence of a coercing agent puts the individual in a situation where he cannot choose what he wants to do but has to choose that which the coercer wants.[54] The individual cannot use his own knowledge for his own purposes but is himself used as a means to the ends of his coercer. It is clear that Hayek wants to reserve the use of the word coercion to describe very special situations and avoid its use in situations where an individual merely has some choice in a range of rather unpleasant options. There is a difference between having to work for low wages in a competitive capitalist economy and being directed to work at specific tasks in a completely planned economy.

It is the aim of a free society to reduce coercion to a minimum, although it is impossible to eliminate it entirely. The main justification for the use of coercion by centralised authority is to prevent coercion by others. Therefore it will use coercive instruments to prevent violence, fraud, blackmail and so on.[55] The exercise of coercion in these fields is not a threat to the individual who keeps within the rules. These rules do not direct him to do anything and he can so plan his life that he avoids them. There are, however, some coercive activities of government that cannot be avoided, for example, taxation and conscription. But Hayek claims that the coercive features of these acts are mitigated to the extent that they are predictable, and if they operate through general rules and are equally binding on government as well as citizens.[56]

In any society there will be a range of coercive activities and all that government can do is try and eliminate their most severe manifestations. Coercion may occur in domestic situations but Hayek maintains that it is very difficult for government to do anything about this. In factory situations there is the likelihood of coercion because individuals in most cases have to do the bidding of their superiors with no possibility of their using their own knowledge for all their own purposes. Here Hayek claims that to the extent that factory production operates under general standing orders, with gaps being filled in by individuals lower down the hierarchy, coercion does not really exist.[57]

The two important disputed issues in Hayek's account of coercion are whether general rules impartially applied are a sufficient protection of individual freedom, and whether his restrictive definition of coercion leaves out certain sorts of activities which may be regarded as coercive on other, equally plausible, definitions. The former problem will be discussed in some detail in the next chapter, the latter can be touched upon now.

The question is whether the free enterprise market economy may not produce coercion at least as equivalent in its effects to that exercised by centralised authorities. Do not cases of monopsony in employment, a single employer and a large number of workers such as may occur in a one-firm town, constitute examples of coercion which may in their effect be much worse than a particular direction from a political authority? On the whole Hayek thinks that the kind of monopolies that the market may throw up are not coercive. In periods of severe unemployment employers may be able to impose conditions of service equivalent to coercion, and even in circumstances of less than widespread unemployment they may be able to cause pain.[58] But in a normal competitive market economy the most an employer can do to an individual is to cut off one source of employment only; cases of monopsony are extremely rare.

While it is true that the opportunities for coercion on the part of employers in a market economy have been grossly exaggerated by collectivist critics, and certainly they do not compare to that exercised by the officials of the state in a planned economy, nevertheless one or two points can be raised. Firstly, since Hayek concedes that there is a *range* of coercive activities, this in principle would allow the inclusion of more employer/employee relationships in the coercive category than appear there as odd exceptions, such as monopsony, in an otherwise open economy. Secondly, he is able to exclude certain candidates for coercion virtually by definition. Since coercion exists only when an individual is under the control and direction of another agent, the meaning of the concept does not turn upon the severity of the act of the coercer. This means that it is possible that the effects of, say, the action of an employer over an employee would not be coercive, even if they were particularly severe, since the employee could have technically gone elsewhere, while fairly mild directions from political officials would count as coercive orders.

Hayek also considers under what conditions the actions of a monopoly seller of services can be considered as coercive. A monopolist rarely acts coercively towards his customers. This would only be the case if a monopolist fixed the price of a commodity which was crucial to the existence of the individual, otherwise coercion is not implicit in the terms on which people exchange. The most Hayek concedes is that there is a case for making monopolists charge the same price to all their customers; but, this seems to me to be a clear case of discriminatory, coercive law. The kinds of examples of coercion occurring in market situations that Hayek gives are the owner of an oasis in the desert or the supplier of essential medical services in certain situations.[59]

Hayek has made it clear, in a reply to a critic, that coercion does not take place whenever a change is brought about which benefits one person more than another: 'to constitute coercion it is also necessary that the action of the coercer should put the coerced in a position which he regards as worse than that in which he would have been without that action'.[60] Thus, if an individual freely transacts with another, even if the deal should greatly advantage one, it cannot be coercive if the disadvantaged is still better off than he otherwise would have been. This puts Hayek into the category of an extreme libertarian, that is, as long as actions are free and voluntary all transactions are compatible with liberal principles whatever their outcome. This corresponds to the instrumental interpretation of liberty I gave earlier in this chapter and Hayek often writes in this vein—as he must do, since to give content to free actions would bring him perilously close to the position of the rationalistic liberals. Yet he is clearly worried by the fact that a free society will not always develop desirable values and that it may maintain values which are not compatible with the preservation of freedom. On at least one important public issue, the question of the closed shop in industrial relations, Hayek is, in a sense, not libertarian enough. I shall explore this problem in a little more detail to get at the internal logic of Hayek's liberal views.

Hayek maintains that the most pervasive and dangerous example of monopoly in modern industrial society is that on the side of labour.[61] The aim of unions is to comprehensively organise labour so that employers have to accept the terms of the union leaders. But the most important coercion exercised by unions is that over their fellow-workers who are frequently bullied into unions through fear of losing their jobs. Hayek claims that unions can exercise coercion for two major reasons. Firstly, tolerant picketing laws enable unions, by threat of violence, to prevent workers from taking employment at rates lower than those demanded by unions and, secondly, the institution of the closed shop enables employers and employees to agree that only union men shall be hired. Clearly, in those cases where the activity of picketing puts certain groups outside the common law system there is coercion; but it is less clear that this is also true of closed-shop agreements.

Hayek claims that closed-shop agreements are contracts in restraint of trade and should not therefore be enforced at law.[62] But not all libertarians would agree with this argument. After all, almost any contract can be interpreted as a restraint of trade and, furthermore, any law that specifically banned voluntarily made closed-shop agreements would be, as a matter of logic, as discriminatory and coercive as a law which made them obligatory. If an employer freely makes a closed-shop agreement with a union then he is quite likely to be imposing costs upon himself; but it is for the competitive market to impose its impersonal discipline on such activities, not the coercive law of the state. Under Hayek's own definition, if an employer is not forced to make a closed-shop agreement he cannot be said to be coerced. If he makes it freely, then although it may cause him disadvantages, he is clearly in a preferred position to that of not making it. A strict libertarian might well argue that as long as the normal rules of law obtain the competitive market economy is a better protection of liberty than the coercive laws of the state, which might not always be used in such desirable directions.[63] Under such conditions a situation equivalent to the oasis in the desert example is hardly likely to arise. It is the other legal privileges, mainly to do with picketing, which are the real cases of coercion, and without these, libertarians maintain, examples of the closed shop would be extremely rare.

Strict libertarians might also maintain that, on the side of labour, as long as there is an open economy with a variety of firms and employment prospects, freedom will be maintained. In a sense, the condition that a worker must join a union to get the job is not different from any other condition that an employer might impose, and most of these would not count as coercive under Hayek's own definition. There are special problems in economies, such as that of Great Britain, with large public sector monopolies; but is not the correct libertarian response to attack these monopolies rather than invest governments with yet more coercive powers? None of this implies any approval of the closed shop on the part of libertarians, it merely indicates a strict instrumental view of freedom. On this issue at least Hayek appears to view liberty in terms of the characteristics of a 'free society' and is prepared to countenance legislation to bring it about should it not emerge spontaneously.

5 The Theory of Law

The bulk of Hayek's work in social philosophy over the past twenty years has been in the theory of law. He has given accounts of the nature of law, as formal treatises in the science of jurisprudence, and has also linked legal philosophy with other aspects of his thought; notably the methodology of social science and the theory of justice. The final aim of those enquiries has been to place legal phenomena correctly in the context of the necessary conditions for the existence of a free society. As in other aspects of Hayek's work there is the dual aim of formulating the correct scientific procedures in the field and inferring from these important points for longer-term, ultimately ethical, considerations. Hayek has stressed, on a number of occasions, the necessity of understanding the whole range of academic disciplines for a proper appreciation of the forces that determine social phenomena. While economics is clearly the most advanced of the social science disciplines a knowledge of economics alone is not enough. Indeed, he has said that many of the policy mistakes and wrong turnings taken by free societies can be traced to the influence on governments of economists who know only economics, and often defective economics at that. The deleterious effects of mistaken economic policies are not only felt in the economic sphere, which has been characterised by unrealised potential, but in the whole structure of freedom.

The theory of law then finds its place in the general account of the impersonal forces that govern social relationships. The progress of free societies, Hayek maintains, depends upon there being impersonal rules to guide the conduct of individuals just as much as it depends upon the allocation of resources by the impersonal forces of the market. The goal of maximising liberty depends upon the reduction to a minimum of that area of an individual's life which is controlled by personalised central authorities. Thus law, properly understood, is not a barrier to individual liberty but a necessary condition of it. Law is not the creature of political authority, as some versions of legal positivism from Hobbes onwards have maintained, but is prior to it.

Hayek's theory of law cannot be divorced from his theory of knowledge in general. Our knowledge of the world is knowledge of classes of events and we can have knowledge of a class or order without having detailed knowledge of the elements that compose it. All knowledge consists of classifications made by the mind of orders of events by a process of abstraction and reconstruction. Just as the observing economist abstracts from the economic world an order known as the *catallaxy* the legal theorist abstracts from legal phenomena its defining elements and reproduces, by a process of mental reconstruction, the legal order. The common law system, for example, can never be understood merely as a collection of observable legal decisions but only as an abstract system of rules.

Hayek's general approach to law is difficult to place in contemporary schools of jurisprudence. It is customary to divide schools of jurisprudence into two basic categories: natural law and positive law. The distinction between the two turns upon the question of the nature of law, or more precisely, what determines validity in a legal system. Traditionally natural law theorists have made the validity of rules within a legal system turn upon their consistency with a set of external, objective moral norms. Usually it is argued that the truth of these moral norms can be determined by reason; they are not, in other words, the subjective values of the theorists of law but are universal in application. This last point means that they apply to all men independently of time and place. A rule is not merely said to be good or bad in accordance with objective morality, but its status as a law depends on this. Bad laws are, in effect, not entitled to the dignity and status of law and with all that that entails for obligation and authority. Such an extreme view is rarely held today, partly because of the rise of non-cognitivism in formal ethics, and partly because such an approach makes nonsense of our normal usage of the word law. Nevertheless, some notion of objective moral standards must lie behind any natural law theory; although contemporary versions tend to concentrate on the procedures of fairness and equality that rules must meet if they are to be considered as lawful, rather than on their content. The point that unites all natural law thinkers is that not everything which is valid in a formal sense counts as law in the wider sense.

Positive lawyers believe in a set of doctrines almost the exact opposite of those described above. There are a number of different schools of positive law but they are at one in the belief that questions of legal validity are logically separate from questions of moral worth. There must be, it is claimed, a criterion, or set of criteria, which conclusively determines lawfulness and this cannot be a moral one. Since the primary aim of positive law theory, or analytical jurisprudence as it is frequently called, is to find *certainty* in the law, it is said that this can never be found in the constantly shifting, and ultimately subjective, standards put forward by moral philosophers. Positive lawyers are then engaged in a scientific enterprise but they might also claim some practical advantage in their approach. If judges, and individuals, have the authority to regard laws as not being proper laws on the grounds of morality, and therefore not obligatory, then the essential elements of predictability and continuity would be absent from a legal system.

Historically the most famous positive law theory is that of the English Command school. This theory, associated with Bentham and Austin but ultimately deriving from Hobbes, defined law in terms of a command emanating from a determinate sovereign. The sovereign could secure obedience by the use of sanctions while he owed obedience to no-one and was in a technical sense above the law. But not all positive law theories are of this type and the most formidable critic of the command theory, and the doctrine of sovereignty, Professor H. L. A. Hart, is also insistent on the necessity of separating law from morals.[1] What makes Hayek's exposition of the theory of law a little confusing is that he tends to treat all positive law theories as if they were disguised versions of the command theory.

On the whole Hayek tries to steer a delicate course between the extremes of natural law and positive law. Obviously he cannot accept the rationalism of some versions of natural law with their proclamation of abstract ethical principles as the determinants of validity as these may license the overturning of stable systems that have developed spontaneously. Nevertheless, principles play a crucial role in his legal theory, but they are principles immanent in an ongoing system of rules. They provide grounds for validating purported legal rules but they do not emanate from the minds of theorists of law. His main objection to positive law is that law must not be seen exclusively as a product of the *will* of the legislator. It is not will that determines lawfulness but *opinion*;[2] rightfulness, and indeed effectiveness, in an ongoing system depends upon the opinions of men in the system, and this precedes the process by which rules are fully articulated. There is clearly a connection between Hayek's rejection of both positive law and positive economics. A legal system cannot be subjected to the engineering type of treatment, where goals are set and institutions constructed so as to achieve these goals mechanically, any more than an economic system can.

At the heart of Hayek's legal philosophy lie the concepts of rules and rule-following. Rules are distinct from commands and the gradual replacement of rules by commands, he thinks, has been responsible for the erosion of liberty. It is to the idea of rules, therefore, that I turn first.

2. RULES

In contrast with the rationalist tradition which sees social behaviour almost exclusively in terms of deliberate behaviour, Hayek understands this as rule-governed behaviour. This means that the explanation of human conduct is a matter of reconstructing the rules that govern that conduct rather than observing deliberate, specific events. He has on more than one occasion quoted A. N. Whitehead's celebrated observation: 'Civilisation advances by extending the number of important operations which we can perform without thinking about them',[3] a phrase which nicely illustrates the importance he attaches to *regularised* behaviour for the understanding of society. The fact that people's actions may not strictly conform to the deliberative, conscious model does not mean they are irrational or have no discernible pattern. In fact, the opposite is the case.

The notion of human behaviour as rule-governed behaviour is a good illustration of the use that Hayek makes of the distinction between 'knowing that' and 'knowing how'.[4] People may know how to do things, and exhibit this knowledge in regularised behaviour, yet may not be able to state explicitly the rules that govern their conduct. The classic instance of this is, of course, language. Children learn very quickly to construct sentences of considerable complexity, and may even be able to spot grammatical errors in others, yet they cannot possibly state the rules of grammar that govern a language.

Similarly, perception is a matter of the mind understanding the world through rules, or regularities. The mind perceives the external world in terms of patterns rather than discrete events without it being aware of the elements of which they are composed. Hayek is very sceptical of the widely-held belief that all recognition of abstract forms (classifications) is derived from a prior conception of concrete forms. That is to say, it is not necessarily the case that our theoretical understanding of the world follows on from our perception of particular events.[5] It is more likely to be the case that the mind is already equipped with rules of perception to understand the world. Thus understanding of complex phenomena is achieved through what Hayek calls 'master moulds', mental abstract patterns of rules which enable us to understand diverse events.[6] This notion of understanding through rules is clearly a long way from the behaviourist view of understanding through experience alone.

The rules that govern social behaviour are transmitted both genetically and culturally. Rules transmitted genetically are 'innate', as if the organism were already equipped with a set of rules; while rules that are culturally transmitted are 'learnt'. It is by these rules that an order of events is communicated even though it is not possible to specify them all; there will always be more rules that are followed than can possibly be stated.[7] One important method of communicating rules which Hayek stresses is imitation. The capacity for imitating does not depend upon the capacity to describe the imitated action in words but such actions certainly have 'meaning' to participants in a social process.[8]

To act according to a rule is to be disposed to act in a regular manner within the confines of custom or practice. Hayek makes a very important distinction between articulated and non-articulated rules.[9] A non-articulated rule is a descriptive rule, a pattern of regularised behaviour which has not been specifically expressed in language, while articulated rules are formalised normative rules that do not merely describe behaviour but govern that behaviour in terms of setting appropriate standards. This distinction is important for the understanding of a legal system because judicial activity in difficult cases involves articulating and making explicit hitherto non-articulated rules. It is because of this point that legal reasoning is not syllogistic, that is, it does not consist in the making of deductive inferences from explicit premises because non-articulated rules cannot form explicit premises of syllogisms.[10] A good example of what Hayek calls non-articulated rules is that of the 'sense of justice' – which means that although people's behaviour can be described in terms of rules of fair play it may be difficult to formulate these precisely into normative rules.[11] This distinction between articulated and non-articulated rules is more fundamental than that between unwritten and written law because although unwritten law is not found in authoritative codes it is nevertheless fully articulated into a body of normative rules.[12]

The crucial feature of systems of rules is that they are 'abstract'. This means that a body of rules is not understood in terms of the specific elements of which it is composed, but in terms of the order of events which it serves. We do not, for example, understand the common law as a list of cases, but as a body of general rules abstracted from the particular cases which we can apply to future unknown cases. The abstract rules of a society do not themselves fulfil a specific purpose, they are the framework within which concrete individual purposes are fulfilled. The Great Society (Hayek's name for Popper's Open Society) is characterised by a very high level of abstraction of its rules, in comparison with the rules of a primitive society which are specific and concrete.[13]

The following of *some* rules does produce an overall order, but Hayek notes that the overall order of a society is not the same thing as the order of individual conduct. The regularised behaviour of individuals is not the same thing as the regularity of the social order because no individual in his action aims at producing an overall order. This is a by-product, an unplanned outcome of the actions of individuals.[14] As societies develop they retain those rules which experience proves to be expedient, though the rules were not specifically designed with expediency in mind. The overall order is not reducible to the actions of individuals because social behaviour is not merely individual behaviour—it consists of the interactions between individuals and the interactions between individuals and their environment. In this very limited sense the whole may be said to be greater than the sum of the parts,[15] although the whole has no 'purpose', in the traditional teleological sense, other than the purposes of the individuals. Furthermore, not *all* rule-governed behaviour leads to stability or overall order. The following of certain rules may lead to disorder and chaos, and Hayek claims that the successful societies are those that have adopted and retained those rules that are conducive to order.[16]

Of course, Hayek is fully aware of the fact that the following of rules is not the only way that overall order may be produced. He distinguishes between orders produced by spontaneous regular actions and orders produced by central direction—by analogy with a central organ in the body such as the brain.[17] Perhaps a command system of law could produce stability, but Hayek is obviously keen to demonstrate that free societies operate on different principles to command-directed organisations and to show why a society that is transformed from a rule-governed process to a command-directed organisation will lose all the advantages that come from freedom.

Before I discuss these issues in the following sections I want to briefly mention one aspect of Hayek's account of rules which illustrates the limitations of his approach. Hayek says that overall order does not necessarily result from individuals following rules: 'individual responses to particular circumstances will result in overall order only if the individuals obey such rules *as will produce an order*'[18] (my italics). But we can never know in advance what rules will produce order. Hayek says that those groups that survive and adapt to their environment better than others have done so precisely because they have adopted the most appropriate set of rules.[19] It would appear that we can only know this after the event; we can only know which rules are conducive to survival by looking at those groups that have survived. But we cannot know which particular rules are most conducive to survival, and which may be copied by others, because clearly some rules survive in any system even though they serve no useful purpose. Only the most extreme conservative holds that rules are useful merely because they are there. Hayek is not a conservative, in the commonly-understood sense, but he does not give us a criterion for evaluating rules beyond their contribution to the survival of groups. This is of course an essential antidote to the mindless social engineering that wishes to dispense with all rules. But such a negative approach runs into difficulties when the issue of the creation and enforcement of those rules which do not normally emerge spontaneously, and yet which are essential for survival of a society, arises. I am thinking here of the rules of even a limited government, and those rules which it is in the interests of us all to obey but which from a private point of view we have an interest in not obeying.

3. THE NATURE OF LAW

Hayek has given two substantial accounts of law, one in *The Constitution of Liberty* and the other in *Rules and Order*. There are no significant differences in the two accounts except that in the latter Hayek is more concerned to stress the undesirable consequences of an inappropriate mixing of two equally valid types of law: that based on the concept of a rule and that based on command. In the former he is more concerned to describe the abstract properties that a rule must have if it is to count as a law. Most important in the earlier work is the detailed description of that concept of the rule of law which functions as a replacement of the rationalistic natural law theories as a device for evaluating legal systems.

In the formulation of Hayek's concept of law the most important distinction he makes is that between *law* and *command*. It would appear that the distinction is not a logical one because he says that both laws and commands are in the same logical category in contrast with facts,[20] and that laws gradually shade into commands the less general they become. A law is distinguished from a command on the criterion of the level of abstraction. A command is an instruction emanating from a determinate source and addressed to a specific purpose while a law is highly general in form, does not presuppose a definite source, and does not specify a particular action but merely forbids a range of actions.[21] Since the word law normally covers both types of utterance it is perhaps better to use the word rule to cover what has been above termed law and retain the word command for specific instructions. The point about following rules is that in doing so we do not follow another person's will. The fact that a rule merely forbids certain courses of action means that these courses are closed to the individual, it does not mean that he is coerced into performing a specific action. Thus rules shade into commands as the range of permitted actions is reduced.

Hayek is able to contrast a primitive society where rules are specific and concrete, thereby resembling commands, with a Great Society where the rules are abstract and general. In a primitive society it is possible to conceive of a head directing operations precisely because in such a closed or intimate community there is likely to be a common hierarchy of ends which the rules serve.[22] In a Great Society, however, where there is not a unified hierarchy of ends, but on the contrary a variety of possibly conflicting ends, the rules function more as guidelines within which individual behaviour can be reasonably predictable. Stability is therefore possible without central direction. Hence Hayek's claim that laws properly so called are more like 'laws of nature' to be planned for and avoided. While the state has to use coercive laws, to prevent coercion being used by private individuals, if that coercion operates through general injunctions forbidding certain courses of action no individual has reason to fear them.[23]

It is only through general rules that the dispersed knowledge in a society can be effectively coordinated. When an individual obeys a command from a superior he is not using his knowledge for his purposes but is subject to the plans of the superior. Since ideal rules of law are entirely general and presuppose no specific commander they enable the maximum amount of knowledge to be used and the maximum number of ends to be pursued. In a Great Society the important feature is that men can live under, and order their lives by, rules not of their own making.[24] If general rules are created then continuity, stability and predictability can be ensured because, to the extent that the rules are general, the legislator does not know to whom the rules will apply. It is this which constitutes abstraction in an ongoing legal system.

Furthermore, as long as the rules are interpreted by an independent judiciary, discretion is limited since judges will have no choice in the conclusions that they draw.[25] In fact, judges do not exercise discretion in the way that politicians may do, if and when the latter act above the law, since they have to work within general rules and their decisions are subject to an appeal procedure. If we add the notion of *equality*, meaning that laws should be applied 'blindly' and impartially to all manner of persons, the idea that laws should not be *retrospective* in their application, and the goal of *certainty*, we have an outline of a doctrine of the rule of law, to be considered in more detail in the next section. It is sufficient to note at this stage a distinction between mere legality (and even constitutionalism) and the rule of law proper. Rules that emanate legitimately from a legislature may still not be consistent with the ideal of the rule of law.[26] This ideal does not put any necessary content into the rules, it merely imposes procedural standards to which they ought to conform.

Hayek has elaborated these basic ideas and blended them into his general theory of society. In recent years he has stressed two important conceptual distinctions. He uses the word *cosmos*[27] to describe a spontaneous social order characterised by the absence of a common hierarchy of ends and by the presence of individual purposes and ends made compatible by general rules. The law associated with this form of society is *nomos*.[28] This is the kind of political arrangement within which *catallactic* or exchange activities take place. The form of organisation characterised by specific purposes he now calls a *taxis*,[29] and the rules appropriate to this he calls *theses*.[30] In fact, they are more like commands precisely because they are directed towards collective goals. He says that both *nomos* and *thesis* are legitimately called law, and that a spontaneous society could not survive without some structure of commands, but stresses that they cannot be mixed in any manner we please without threatening the fabric of a spontaneous order. The difference between *nomos* and *thesis* corresponds largely to the more familiar distinction between private and public law. Private law consists of the rules that govern individual transactions while public law consists of the orders given to officials to carry out collective plans.[31] However, Hayek is slightly sceptical of this wording as it gives the impression that only individual, self-regarding benefits accrue from private law when the opposite is the case. The whole system of private law is not just for the benefit of private individuals but advances the genuine interests of society as a whole.[32] The danger is that too great an extension of the public law system will not lead to the promotion of genuine public interests but to the dominance of group interests.

The structure of an abstract system of rules, *nomos*, is not logically dissimilar from the structure of a *catallaxy*. It is not the product of a design or deliberate plan but the outcome of spontaneous growth. The tradition of the English common law, which at one time provided a good empirical example of the idea of *nomos*,[33] is characterised by unplanned growth yet it nevertheless provides a coherent framework of rules within which individuals may behave reasonably predictably toward one another. The essential point is that the total structure is not the product of will.

The command theorists of law, and their successors, sought a uniform theory of law which ultimately explained all law by the same principle. In most theories the existence of a determinate source explained the validity of all law. In fact, Bentham thought that a special kind of logic, 'the logic of the will', explained the process of validation within a legal system in which *all* law was a species of command that issued from an observable source. But models of law such as these could not be used so easily to explain the common law, the law that is in a sense created by judges in a case by case manner through their interpretation of the existing law. The usual answer of the positivists was that while the legislator could not frame statutes to deal with all cases, though of course it was the aim of the extreme, rationalistic utilitarians to so devise statutes that all future hypothetical cases could be covered, there would be the need for a judiciary to interpret law and deal with the uncertainties that are bound to arise in any legal system and which cannot be handled by the sovereign. But the validity of the common law nevertheless depended upon the tacit consent of the sovereign. This means that since the existence of the common law depended upon the authority of the legislator this law could be said, by analogy, to emanate from the same source as statute law, thus preserving the essential unity of the theory.[34]

Hayek has persistently opposed this line of reasoning. While it is true, he concedes, that the existence and continuing operation of the common law may be said to depend upon the will of the legislator it does not at all follow that he commands the content of that law.[35] The content of the law is not a product of any particular will but is the outcome of the interpretation of judges, perhaps going back hundreds of years, an outcome which emerges through the judges working entirely within a given structure of rules. The law is thus not a set of particular facts but a pattern of general rules.

It is important to say something here about the nature of judicial reasoning. Judicial activity is an intellectual activity, a kind of puzzle-solving in which the judge tries to find the appropriate rule to apply in a particular case.[36] It is not the function of the judge to bring about some desirable state of affairs, but to find the objectively right decision within the general system of rules. This may be contrasted with the method of the administrator who is entirely concerned with policy; therefore, the idea of the binding nature of general rules will appear as a hindrance and an obstacle in the way of his implementation of policy. Hayek describes the conclusions of the judge as objectively right, not because they are in any way designed to satisfy particular interests, or even the 'general interest' in an immediate sense, although the whole system of rules survives because it brings long-term benefits to the participants in a rule-governed process, but because they are consistent with the general structure of rules.

It is at this point that the distinction between articulated and non-articulated rules becomes important. When cases come before a private law judge they are obviously in dispute, each party will have a set of expectations which demand to be satisfied by rules, but the judge may well have to draw upon a non-articulated rule to settle the dispute and in doing so a new articulated rule will be made available for future expectations.[37] In these situations the judge will not be guided by considerations of policy or by prevailing views about social aims or purposes. What makes his rule valid is whether it can be universalised within the total complex of rules. In a *cosmos* law is 'discovered' through the process of exploration of what the system implies, and the rule must be enforced even though in a particular case more benefit may result from not enforcing the rule.[38] It is this process of discovery which marks off an evolving system of law, a system that used to be exemplified by the English common law, from a system of 'made' law that emanates from a legislature. The greater the extent to which men are governed by rules which are discovered the greater they are governed by laws rather than other men.

It is perhaps this stress on the discovery of law through the invocation of non-articulated rules that would cause most concern to legal positivists. Orthodox legal positivism is familiar with uncertainty in the law. Hart has called that area of doubt about the application of a rule in a particular case the 'penumbral' aspect of law.[39] The formalist approach to law, deductive reasoning from explicit premises, is inadequate because no legislator can foresee all the cases to which his rules will apply, and law is necessarily 'open-textured', or has a penumbra of doubt and uncertainty. In some cases, therefore, judges do indeed make law and may very well take account of wider social purposes, and even satisfy particular interests, in the creation of new rules. While it does not at all follow from this that the Realists are right in their extreme claim that rules are irrelevant to the understanding of law,[40] it does follow that judges are doing a lot more than merely discovering the law.

One objection to the distinction between articulated rules and non-articulated rules is that the claim that the latter are somehow a part of law must inevitably increase the uncertainty of law. A whole number of different rules may be consistent with the total structure of rules and there will be no way of knowing which is the most appropriate rule in any objective sense. Hayek has claimed, with some justice, that the number of disputed cases is no indication of the uncertainty of law because there are obviously innumerable cases where the rules prove satisfactory and thus never reach the courts.[41] What is more surprising is his claim, in *Rules and Order*, that a system in which judges draw upon non-articulated rules, as in the common law, is likely to be more predictable than a system based largely upon formal statutes because in the latter the *only* law is that which is in the statute. In his earlier work, *The Constitution of Liberty*, he suggested that a spontaneous order might well emerge from a system based either on common law principles or one consisting of formalised codes.[42]

It is also significant that Hayek himself concedes that the common law does not necessarily develop in the direction of the ideal rules of just conduct which are required for the functioning of an ongoing, end-independent *cosmos*. In a remarkable passage in *Rules and Order* he says, in a manner reminiscent of collectivist and sociological interpretations of the common law, that the gradual development of a system of rules may produce quite unsatisfactory outcomes and even result in laws favouring class interests. An example he gives is that of landlord and tenant law of the last century which clearly favoured the interests of property-holders as a class.[43] In such phenomena the continual application of existing rules may just produce legal dead-ends, and legislation will have to be introduced to establish a spontaneous order to harmonise expectations which are frustrated by the existing rules. This of course implies that there are principles that lie outside the structure of existing rules and which act as standards to which the law ought to conform.

The obvious question that springs to mind is, how rare are the examples that Hayek mentions? It is surely quite common for legal systems to develop spontaneously in undesired directions. For all Hayek's criticisms of the rationalism of the utilitarians they were faced with not merely a number of untidy elements in the system of law at the beginning of the nineteenth century but a welter of conflicting and confusing laws which required restructuring on more or less rational principles. The system could hardly be said to provide a model of the rules of just conduct available indiscriminately to all; and the legal profession, upon whose expertise and intellectual qualities Hayek relies to maintain the ongoing body of rules, had a vested interest, perhaps even a class interest, in preserving its complexity and needless technicality.

To complete this discussion of the nature of law it is essential to discuss the other claimant to the title of law—the law of *thesis*, the set of rules appropriate to the functioning of a *taxis*, or as it is more commonly known, an organisation. Hayek admits that it would be impossible to imagine a society without laws of this kind. The type of organisation which is primarily concerned with the law of *thesis* is, of course, government itself. There will always be a minimum role for government if only to provide the framework for the operation of the whole system.[44] Orders have to be issued to officials to enforce the rules of just conduct. Furthermore, there are some rules which, although it is in the interests of all members of society that they be obeyed, it may not be in the interest of each individual, taken separately, to obey. The whole apparatus of compulsory taxation, which is required for the financing of those public goods and services that are not provided spontaneously by the market, comes into this category.

Hayek argues that, historically, it was not the role of parliaments to make laws of the *nomos* type but to issue commands to officials to carry out specific functions.[45] Unlike rules proper, which provide a range of permitted actions, the commands of an organisation are specific and compulsory. While they are addressed to the enforcement of the rules of just conduct and to the provision of government services they need not necessarily undermine the structure of a free society. Freedom will be maintained if the officials of government, in implementing the law of *thesis*, do not arbitrarily use the person and property of the individual for the ends of government itself.[46] There is a private domain which must be protected by the rules of just conduct from invasion from the commands of government. Hayek allows full legislative supremacy of the body making the law of *thesis*, as long as that body itself is limited by the rules of just conduct.

The problem in the modern world, however, is that the same body which makes the rules of just conduct also makes the laws of organisation.[47] It is this which, Hayek claims, poses a major threat to the survival of a free society. It is this that has allowed public law, the law concerned with the direction of government activities, to take over the area of social life previously occupied by private law. He gives two reasons for this. Firstly, the rise of majoritarian democracy has contributed to the gradual elimination of the restraints on legislatures.[48] Hayek is clearly correct in identifying the adverse consequences of the contemporary practice of regarding 'will' as the only source of authority. While it is not the view of current analytical jurisprudence that the existence of a law presupposes a determinate commander, it would appear to be a view prevalent in political circles. It may indeed be the case that in Britain people are no longer familiar with the idea of living under laws not of their own making and expect centralised legislative action in every sphere of life.

The second reason for the takeover of private law by public law is a little more curious. He suggests that the legal profession has become increasingly dominated by public lawyers who have little experience of the spontaneous development of a legal system and whose only knowledge is knowledge of legislation.[49] Furthermore, Hayek claims that collectivist economists have persuaded lawyers that the market cannot be relied upon to work efficiently and that economies should be run as organisations within the framework of public rules. I say this is a curious argument because it is difficult to know how much significance to attach to it. In which direction is causation being said to operate? Are lawyers merely responding to politically-determined events or do legal and economic ideas exert some independent force in the determination of events? Often Hayek stresses the latter, and perhaps places too much emphasis on the importance of ideas, but he also stresses institutional factors. Especially important here is the fact that the making of the general rules of just conduct and the making of specific commands is in the same hands, since Hayek claims that a legislator is hardly likely to be as concerned for the principles of the rule of law as is a judge. A final point on Hayek's argument about the intellectual errors of contemporary lawyers and economists is this. How is it that the two intellectual disciplines, law and economics, that have most adequately explained the emergence and development of spontaneous orders should also in some way be responsible for their disintegration? Economists and lawyers appear as both heroes and villains in Hayek's social philosophy.

4. THE RULE OF LAW

The concept of the rule of law plays a crucial role in Hayek's legal theory. In a sense it operates as a principle for evaluating laws equivalent to the traditional natural law doctrine; but whereas that doctrine evaluated laws according to their consistency with a set of objective moral truths, expressions that were not consistent with these truths were not proper laws, Hayek's doctrine evaluates claims to law in terms of their general characteristics. In other words the rule of law doctrine does not evaluate the content of a law, but purported laws are assessed in terms of their general attributes. This exemplifies the algebraic approach to the study of social institutions; a law is understood in terms of general properties and its acceptability or otherwise turns upon this and not upon the particular elements a general law might consist of. A law must not be understood in terms of the particular elements because it would follow from Hayek's theory of knowledge that no legislator could possibly design the content of a law which is appropriate for *all* future occasions. The evaluation of law in terms of its general features means that Hayek does not have to evoke abstract principles, this would be the approach of the rationalist, but can criticise particular laws in the context of an evolving system of rules.

The elements of the rule of law doctrine are implicit in what has been discussed so far. Hayek identifies its main properties in the English common law system, although he has frequently stressed that that system no longer obtains in its original form because of the almost inexorable rise of public law, but the ideal of the rule of law is not confined to this. Similar ideas appear in the German idea of the *Rechtsstaat*, which flowered briefly in the nineteenth century, in the continental administrative law systems, and of course any constitutional structure that exhibits a fundamental and rigorous separation of powers.[50]

The main elements of the rule of law can be briefly described. Laws should be perfectly general, that is, they should name no-one and should not discriminate for or against any person or identifiable group. They should embody equality where that means only that they should apply equally to all. Since men are unequal the attempt to make them equal by law would involve treating them unequally, which would be inconsistent with the rule of law. All egalitarian laws, as distinct from laws that affect people equally, are therefore inconsistent with the rule of law. Laws should not be retrospective in application since if they were no individual could reasonably predict how they would affect him. The essential element of certainty would therefore be undermined. It is an essential feature of the *Rechtsstaat*, or rule of law state, that everybody, including governments should be bound by general rules.[51]

The doctrine of the rule of law is a 'meta-legal' doctrine.[52] This means that it is not intrinsically a part of a legal system, the rule of law is not itself a legal rule like, for example, the law of contract is, but is a concept to be used to understand the whole legal system. It is a political ideal which depends for its efficacy on the opinion of the members of the community to whom the general rules are to apply.[53] It is to be noticed that the doctrine could be seen to be both too expansive for some and too restrictive for others. Orthodox legal positivists might well claim that Hayek's account of the rule of law would outlaw many laws which on any other criteria would be perfectly valid. They would say that Hayek's distinction between legislative validity and consistency with the rule of law allows moral notions to creep into the account of the *meaning* of the word law. The positivists would insist that a more accurate description of the properties of the rule of law would nevertheless be consistent with great iniquity but that such iniquity would have to be condemned on general moral grounds, and not simply excluded as unlawful on definitional grounds.[54]

Those who consider the account of the rule of law too restrictive are obviously the more radical lawyers who wish the law to reflect a deeper moral purpose than that described by Hayek. Radicals might claim that the law ought to create a more substantial equality than that contained in the definition of general rules. Laws that enforce non-discrimination, for example, in matters of race and sex are claimed by some to be consistent with general theories of law and 'liberal' ideals. But such laws would be quite inconsistent with Hayek's conception of the rule of law. That the law should treat people equally and impartially does not entail that a particular goal of 'social equality' be promoted by coercive rules. If employers discriminate on grounds of colour or sex then it is not the business of law to intervene. A free market is a much better protector of employment opportunities than coercive laws. While Hayek has not explicitly discussed the contemporary issues of discrimination the above points seem to me to follow from his algebraic conception of the rule of law, and his general distrust of giving the state coercive powers that go beyond the enforcement of the rules of just conduct.

But apart from the question of whether the account of the rule of law is too restrictive or too expansive there is the additional problem of whether Hayek's theory of law is adequate for his own purposes. One example should illustrate this point. Hayek does not want laws to name individuals or groups, or to discriminate in favour of individuals or groups, but some critics have wondered if the requirement that laws be perfectly general is sufficient to guarantee this. It is logically possible to construct general rules that do, in effect, pick out particular people without actually naming them. For example, in a predominantly Protestant country a perfectly general rule which prohibited playing sport on a Sunday would not have to name the Catholic minority but its members would clearly be adversely affected by the law. Is not the concept of the 'patrial' in

British immigration law, whereby citizens of Commonwealth countries whose grandparents were born in Britain are allowed unrestricted entry into Britain, in effect discriminating against non-whites although they are not formally named? The possibility of examples such as these follows from Hayek's algebraic conception of law. We understand laws by their general attributes, not by asking whether they are consistent with an external criterion of morality, but sometimes the appeal to such a criterion is unavoidable.

Hayek is aware that some laws will inevitably have to name people and so breach his non-discrimination rule. He gives the example of laws that clearly affect only women. In cases such as this he adds the proviso that discriminatory laws are consistent with the rule of law if they are approved of by both a majority of those affected by them and a majority of those not.[55] J. W. N. Watkins has suggested that these principles may be satisfactory in some cases; for example, apartheid laws would be ruled out because they are obviously not equally acceptable to non-whites and whites, while third-party motor insurance would not be since that law is presumably equally acceptable to both motorists and non-motorists. But in other cases he thinks not; for example, are laws against sexual assault equally acceptable to a majority affected by them and a majority not?[56] There seems to be a consensus among critics that under Hayek's rules a minority could legitimately prevent the implementation of legislation that might be desirable on other grounds. Both Watkins and Samuel Brittan agree that the objection to steeply progressive income tax cannot merely be the fact of the opposition of the rich.[57] I think, however, that the difficult cases are fewer than they think because the double-majority principle would seem to apply only to those cases where the law has to discriminate. This is not to deny, though, that grievances might easily occur. An ardent feminist might well object to laws that forebade women working in coalmines even if they were approved of by a majority of men and women.

It is of course difficult to frame general rules without some specific moral content and there is a natural tendency to evaluate laws in terms of their content rather than their general attributes. If Hayek cannot be said to have completely succeeded in this enterprise his theory of the rule of law is nevertheless a powerful intellectual weapon in the general struggle between the ideals of traditional liberalism and centralised authority. In two areas his arguments have a lasting significance; in the dispute over the place of the concept of sovereignty in jurisprudence and in the problem of the control of officials by general rules.

It is an essential feature of the command version of the doctrine of positive law, though not all versions of legal positivism, that all law must emanate from a determinate will that is above the law. If it were true that a legal system required a sovereign of this type then the case for the rule of law would fall to the ground. Hayek refutes this doctrine by an important distinction between *will* and *opinion*. Following Hume, Hayek argues that in any ongoing legal system the effectiveness of the will of that which we may wish to call sovereign depends upon the opinion as to its rightness. This is as true of a dictatorship as of a limited government of a liberal democracy. The rightness of a purported law will depend upon whether its general properties and attributes satisfy the opinion of the bulk of the community to whom the law is addressed.[58] All claims to sovereignty, then, ultimately depend upon opinion not will. It does not follow from this that the prevailing opinion will represent the main features of the ideal rule of law but it does demonstrate the inadequacy of the simple command model of law that sharply bifurcates society into all-powerful lawgivers who determine what is 'right' and passive, obedient subjects.

The problem of sovereignty is becoming particularly important in the context of the British constitution today. The British system, which did seem to fit the command theory, with its unlimited parliament, is coming under increasing strain precisely because of doubts about the consistency of sovereignty with the rule of law. For centuries the formal absoluteness of parliament was limited by conventions and informal rules which were generally adhered to by successive governments, but the rise of activist political parties, of which socialists are merely the most prominent examples, has undermined the informal rules. It is this that has led to the demand for stricter limitations on the activities of government, of whatever political persuasion, and the establishment of a proper constitutional procedure.[59]

Similarly, the demand for the legal control of the administration entails the demand for the establishment of the rule of law. In the British system dispute has centred on the fact that the actions of ministers and officials are not normally subject to review by the ordinary courts of the land if they are within the ambit of authority conferred by the appropriate statute. While Hayek is not opposed to government taking powers needed for the efficient carrying out of its functions, and is not even opposed to government being delegated powers, he has been a consistent advocate of the view that *all* the activities of officials be subject to general rules.[60] It is most important for the protection of the lives and property of individuals that officials not be delegated powers to act outside general rules. It is probably somewhat utopian to think that it would be feasible to eliminate the discretion of officials entirely and subject all the actions of government to general rules; nevertheless, Hayek is, and has been, in the forefront of a growing movement which aims at limiting the discretion of public officials by general rules.

5. VALIDITY AND MORALITY

At the heart of any theory of law must lie an explanation of validity. This means that there must be some criteria for distinguishing genuine law from bogus law. At the beginning of this chapter I mentioned the important distinction between natural law and positive law on this very point. Now Hayek unfortunately tends to use the phrase positive law as a label to describe those theories that make validity turn upon the 'sovereign will' model. But, of course, not all positivists accept the command theory of law, and the most eminent of contemporary positivists, H. L. A. Hart, has also provided the most elegant refutation of the necessity of sovereignty thesis.[61] The defining characteristic of positive law for Hart is the fact that in this theory the validity of law does not depend upon its moral qualities. The separation of law and morality in Hart's approach in no way commits the theorist to a lack of interest in moral questions, and Hart points to the fact that the classical positivists, Bentham and Austin, both held very strong moral views as to what qualities laws should possess. But for purposes of intellectual rigour and clarity Hart argues that the two questions, which are logically distinct, should be kept distinct. One of the unfortunate consequences of neglecting the distinction is the loss of certainty. And uncertainty is further compounded if courts have the authority to dispense with laws that fail to meet with abstract standards of morality.[62]

Hayek maintains that his theory of law does not depend upon a fusion of law and abstract moral standards. Not only does he explicitly agree with Hart on this point[63] but also he has often criticised rationalistic natural lawyers on similar grounds. The question is, however, whether he has an adequate theory of validity which exists independently of morality, or whether moral notions, having been formally excluded at the front door of his legal structure, nevertheless creep in through the back. The answer to this question requires further consideration of his account of validity.

To an orthodox positivist Hayek's theory of the rule of law would appear to be a somewhat diluted version of a moral theory. Clearly many laws are passed which are inconsistent with the ideal rule of law yet are valid by the tenets of the legal system. It is to be noted that Hayek does not say that the commands of government have no claim to law. General coercive orders are lawful, and if they are certain and predictable, can be consistent with his somewhat rarefied notion of legality. The real problems occur when rules and commands are improperly mixed. A system ceases to be properly lawful when the law of *thesis* takes over from the law of *nomos*. Unfortunately, we are never told what the precise mix should be if legality is to be preserved, and it follows from Hayek's theory of knowledge that we can never know this in detail. Furthermore, a positivist would maintain that legal validity could obtain even if virtually all the law was of the *thesis* type. He might still deny the sovereignty thesis by saying that some fundamental rule underlay the whole structure, but that rule might be a highly permissive rule that authorised legislation that would be invalid by Hayek's strict rule of law.

When Hayek deals with validity in an ongoing legal order he wishes to demonstrate that not all law is created by specific legislation, a large part of law spontaneously emerges through the development of the system itself. This is undoubtedly true but there is still the question of what makes it valid. Clearly there can be no appeal to external criteria, validity must come from the system itself, and Hayek's main emphasis here is on the fact that judges, in the activity of puzzle-solving, draw upon non-articulated rules. He says that what makes a purported rule valid law is whether it can be universalised within the system. A rule can be universalised if it is consistent with the whole body of rules and whether it is a suitable abstract rule which can be applied to future unknown cases. But many different rules can be universalised within a system of rules with the consequence that universalisability cannot provide certainty in law. Furthermore, universalisability seems to have an uncertain relationship with the spontaneous evolution thesis. In Rousseau's theory, for example, the only proper laws are those which are of universal application, yet they can hardly be said to be the product of spontaneous evolution, they emanate from a collective will.[64]

It is useful to compare Hayek's theory of law with a rather different one, that of Professor R. Dworkin,[65] but one which rests on not-dissimilar foundations. Dworkin, in a critique of Hart's positivism, makes a distinction between principles and rules and accounts for the existence of law in terms, ultimately, of binding principles. When judges are faced with 'hard cases', cases where the existing body of rules give no clear answer, they apply principles. Now, although, principles are vaguer than rules, for example, it would be possible to enumerate all the applications of a rule whereas this is not possible with principles, nevertheless, they are not the subjective opinions of judges and must be considered as part of law.[66] Furthermore, Dworkin distinguishes between principles and policies, arguments about principles are about ultimate rights that individuals have as members of a legal system whereas arguments about policies are about the advancement of certain collective goals, and maintains that it is principles that judges are invoking when they decide in hard cases.[67] Although principles are necessarily imprecise they constitute limitations on the discretion of judges so that judges are not, as the positivists would have it, creating new legislation in hard cases but are trying to find what is right within the body of law as principles and rules.

There seems to be some similarity here between Hayek's notion of non-articulated rules and Dworkin's notion of principles. Indeed, Hayek explicitly acknowledges his agreement with the substance of Dworkin's argument, although not entirely agreeing with his terminology.[68] But the disturbing thing is that Dworkin manages to come up with a radical package of legal principles, including reverse discrimination, egalitarianism, and a fairly permissive right to disobedience, which he claims are entailed by his jurisprudence and are not therefore personal or subjective.[69] The full implications of Dworkin's legal philosophy appear in his full-scale work, *Taking Rights Seriously*, while Hayek's agreement is with an earlier paper only. Clearly, the kind of principles Dworkin has in mind would be anathema to Hayek.

The similarity is really only superficial. Hayek's concept of non-articulated rules is meant to limit severely the extent to which the law may give effect to a set of moral principles. The ideal of a system of *nomos* is to protect each individual's private domain and enforce the transactions that individuals make. If it limits itself to this task a variety of moral ideals may be accommodated within the *cosmos*. It is this that constitutes the difference between the Great Society, in which people who do not know each other are governed by rules not of their own making, and the primitive or intimate society, in which harmony and coherence is maintained because of an agreement over a common hierarchy of ends. Dworkin, by attaching a particularly strong conception of rights, perhaps ultimately a rationalistic one, to his theory of law seems to be trying to make the law reflect a particular morality.

That such different social philosophies should have even a superficial resemblance is perhaps surprising. But it is less so when one considers that they both suffer from a weakness in comparison with the orthodox positive lawyers in that Dworkin's invocation of principles, and Hayek's invocation of non-articulated rules, widens the area of uncertainty in the law. This is particularly unfortunate for Hayek as he is concerned to demonstrate the certainty that a system of general rules will have in comparison with the discretion of officials. Positivists would not claim that complete certainty is possible in law, the penumbral or open-textured aspect of rules prevents this, but they would deny that judges are merely discovering the law when they decide hard cases. They are making new rules and in doing so will take account of social aims, purposes and policies.

Orthodox positivists, who are not command theorists, demand a rigorous account of validity in a legal system. Hart's theory of law as a combination of primary and secondary rules is in many ways not dissimilar to Hayek's, especially in the clear distinction they both make between commands and rules and in their rejection of the sovereignty argument, but they part company on the question of validity. For Hart the 'rule of recognition', the ultimate secondary rule in a general system of rules, confers validity on subordinate rules.[70] The rule that what parliament wills is law is an example of a simple rule of recognition, the American Constitution is an example of a particularly complicated one. In any legal system a hierarchy of rules will determine who has authority to make law and what is to count as a law. This doctrine is quite consistent with the idea that courts play a crucial role in determining the meaning of rules, and their authority will even extend to the interpretation of the rule of recognition itself. This does not imply, however, that somehow the courts are not limited by rules or that their authority is not the product of rules.

Hart's concept of the rule of recognition bears only the slightest resemblance to Hayek's concept of the rule of law. It is not itself a rule of law but it determinates the legal validity of subordinate rules. The rule of recognition cannot itself be a rule of law because if it were it could still be asked—what makes *this rule* a genuine rule? The answer to this question would require the invocation of some further rule, and so on indefinitely. Therefore, in any legal system there has to be an ultimate rule, the rule of recognition, which is simply accepted. Now it is clear that a rule of recognition does not have to satisfy the requirements of Hayek's ideal rule of law to be a genuine rule. This follows from the separation between law as it is and law as it ought to be. But Hayek explicitly says that a rule may have all the force of law yet may not be valid.[71] This might happen when a judge makes a false decision, a decision inconsistent with the general system of rules, even though his decision is authoritative in a formal sense.

Hayek does not regard validity in a legal system as being a product of constitutions.[72] Constitutions are really part of public law, or the rules of the organisation of government. A constitution is said to be a kind of 'superstructure erected over a pre-existing system of law to organise the enforcement of that law'.[73] The constitutional rules and the highest constitutional rule, the rule of recognition, may limit government, and Hayek certainly thinks that they should, but they do not, he says, make the law valid. Validity is a consequence of consistency within a pre-existing system of private law, and constitutional law may very well be ephemeral while private law is understood as a permanent, ongoing system of rules.

It would appear then that Hayek's ideas on validity in the law are not of the traditional natural law variety. Consistency with a surviving and evolving system of rules is not the same thing as consistency with a set of external moral principles. Nevertheless, the standards set by his concept of the ideal rule of law would probably be regarded by orthodox positivists as moral standards. His theory produces the paradox that a rule may be valid by the canons of the rule of recognition but invalid according to the criterion of universalisability within a pre-existing system. Thus, it cannot be said that this provides the kind of certainty and predictability that Hayek wants. One virtue of the positivist approach to law is that the consistent separation of law and morality does produce a clarity in intellectual argument about law and a greater approach to certainty in the practice of law.

One reason why Hayek is so critical of positivism is that he tends to blame the influence of the doctrine in European law schools for the collapse of legal standards before the last war.[74] There are really two claims implicit in the argument. Firstly, the suggestion that there is some causal link between legal positivism and tyranny, and secondly, the claim that positivists were indifferent to morality.

Both arguments are difficult to evaluate. The first is a familiar claim made by natural lawyers, of a rather different persuasion from Hayek; but no-one can ever know what influence political and legal doctrines have on practical events. Certainly the English command law tradition, from Bentham, has no connection at all with the collapse of legal standards. The second point, that legal positivists are indifferent to morality, is equally contentious. It is true that some positivists, notably Hans Kelsen and his followers, were both non-cognitivists in ethics, that is, they believed that ethical statements convey no information but are merely expressions of emotion, and advocates of the idea of law as emanating from will. But indifference to morality is not a general characteristic of positive lawyers. They would say that they were making a purely logical distinction, and they might also add that the cause of morality is actually harmed by needlessly confusing it with law. The nineteenth-century utilitarians clearly separated law from morals but were critical of existing laws and in the vanguard of an humanitarian movement for legal reform. Hayek, of course, would reject the social philosophy of utilitarianism but this would be an argument about ethics, not an argument about jurisprudence. Hayek would also claim that he even accepts the distinction between law and morality as long as that does not entail acceptance of the theory that all valid law is a species of command and a product of will. But this confuses the issue, the acceptance of the idea of a rule of recognition as a validating device does not imply agreement with any set of moral values while Hayek's use of the ideal rule of law concept would seem to, though these are very different from those found in traditional natural law doctrines.

6. LAW AND LIBERTY

It is important to link the discussion of Hayek's theory of law with the earlier discussion of liberty because the two ideas are intimately connected. I mentioned in the preceding chapter the fact that, unlike many negative theorists of liberty, Hayek does not necessarily see an antagonism between law and liberty. Bentham, of course, did regard every law as an infraction of liberty, but argued that a law was justified only if it brought about a net benefit to individuals and society; if the loss of liberty that the implementation of a law entails is compensated for by an increase in utility that it brings. This route is closed to Hayek because if liberty is the supreme principle then it cannot be made to serve some supposedly higher end such as utility. The justification for legal restraints must then lie in the claim that they in fact *advance* liberty rather than restrain it. And this is indeed the claim that Hayek does advance. That is, there is a causal connection between laws which are properly constructed and individual liberty. Not all laws are so consistent because, as Hayek stresses, the laws of an organisation which are directed towards the achievement of specific purposes have a genuine claim to the title of law, yet they may not be compatible with liberty. I emphasise that Hayek thinks there is a causal connection between laws as general rules and liberty rather than a logical connection because it does seem to be Hayek's position that the existence of a general rule may involve a diminution of liberty, even though critics have noted that he occasionally writes as if the connection is a necessary one. If the connection should be logical, then Hayek's argument would be uninteresting. If general rules are by definition consistent with liberty then the link between law and liberty is tautological only.

Hayek's claim is that an individual is not free only when he has to obey commands to do specific things, for he is then made to serve another's will. When laws are cast in the form of perfectly general rules which do not require specific actions, then to that extent he is free. Rules then merely prohibit certain actions and he can therefore avoid them. It is this feature of general rules that leads him to assimilate them to laws of nature of the physical world in that they merely put essential boundaries to individual action. A man can follow his own will since, like laws of nature, these general rules do not emanate from a particular will. This is true of overtly coercive laws of taxation and conscription, as long as they are predictable and non-discriminatory.

It is this relationship between law and liberty that has not satisfied Hayek's critics who are in general unhappy with the idea that freedom should not depend necessarily on the range of choice open to the individual. In an extremely perceptive criticism J. W. N. Watkins has commented that, although general rules do allow alternative courses of action to those forbidden they may very well be much worse for the individual than the action which is forbidden.[75] Hayek is, of course, aware that general rules do impose restraints but thinks that, if the restraints apply equally to rulers as to the ruled, people have little to fear. He thinks the main problem occurs usually when the general rules are of a religious kind.[76] Again, Lord Robbins's observation, that while discriminatory laws are probably more oppressive than general rules, nevertheless the latter can be a much greater threat to liberty than Hayek suggests, is surely correct.[77] It would appear that a proper protection for individual liberty requires a more substantive limitation on what a government can do than that contained in the requirement that rules be perfectly general and non-discriminatory.

In *Rules and Order* Hayek meets some of these criticisms with the suggestion that the existence of the protected domain ensures that general rules constitute an adequate protection of liberty.[78] The argument is that general rules cannot be concerned with what a man does within his own four walls. This is within the libertarian tradition but does point to a different range of considerations than that indicated by the original formulation. It still does not supply a satisfactory answer to the problems for libertarians raised by the questions of the use of drugs or unconventional sexual behaviour. These questions may have to be argued through on their merits irrespective of the formal structure of the rules of a society. Even an appeal to a carefully formulated principle of utility may have to be made. It is also not inconceivable that a justification for a general rule to be formulated which does invade the private sphere, for example, in a society with a particularly strong religious or moral tradition which regards certain modes of self-regarding behaviour as essential for its survival, might be made consistent with Hayek's philosophy.

In fact the strict libertarian's view on the legitimacy of a law turns not upon the form in which it is cast but on whether or not it invades the personal and property rights of the individual. Any laws which prohibit free exchanges, including those that forbid the sale and consumption of narcotics, would therefore be illegitimate. In recent years libertarians in America have concentrated mainly upon, in their view, the immorality of conscription laws.

6 The Agenda of Government

1. THE PROBLEM OF THE STATE

It would be no exaggeration to say that the problem that has exercised the mind of Hayek, and all others of the traditional liberal philosophical outlook, over the last thirty years has been that of containing the seemingly ineluctable growth in the activity of the state or government (the two words can be used interchangeably). Since the advent of the welfare state in western countries there has been the constant fear that the benevolent aims of centralised authorities in the fields of health, welfare and income redistribution may conceal malevolent longer-term effects. Hayek first found notoriety in 1944 with his claim, which then appeared to be somewhat extravagant, that even mild attempts to control the economy, and improve the general welfare by collective measures, would bring into being consequences not at all intended by the authors of the original schemes. The original sceptics of 'welfarism' were doubtful that increased state activity could combine efficiency and freedom in the delivery of welfare services and the more honest of the original advocates of interventionism were prepared to accept a loss of individual liberty on grounds of expediency. Hayek, of course, has always maintained that freedom cannot simply be exchanged for efficiency and that a diminution of liberty and choice will always frustrate the use that can be made of our necessarily decentralised knowledge and hence retard human progress.

Early critics of the introduction of the mild socialist schemes in Britain were mainly concerned, however, with the loss of efficiency that they suspected would ensue. The nationalisation programmes of the Labour Party were criticised precisely because the placing of industries outside the competitive market process would remove all incentives to economic efficiency. Experience of those industries that had been nationalised seemed to bear this out. But less criticism was directed against the introduction of more comprehensive welfare services, especially socialised medicine. In these areas the strict liberals were very much in a minority, as there did seem to be wide agreement that some things were just too important to be left to market forces.[1] Although the arguments for socialised health and welfare were not often well-formulated, and frequently relied quite overtly on the paternalist argument that individuals could not be trusted to spend their own money on these services so that the state had to do it for them, nevertheless, the consensus on the desirability of collective provision of those services could well be described as overwhelming.

One problem the liberal faced was that of working out a convincing set of criteria to determine that area of social and economic life which should be left to individual choice and that which should be governed by collective decision. The problem of the 'agenda' of government has been a recurring one since the foundations of liberalism were laid by Adam Smith, but only in recent years have satisfactory answers begun to be formulated. But during this century two intellectual forces have constantly upset the rather fine distinctions between the public and private spheres made by liberals and political economists. Firstly, the belief that the democratic process itself, where that normally means majoritarianism, legitimises all political activity and that no further limits need be put on centralised political authorities; and secondly, the separation made between politics and economics by reformers has underestimated the contribution made by economic science to the understanding of society as a whole and resulted in targets being set for state activity which just cannot be fulfilled. To the latter point it must be added that the proponents of a wide sphere of authority for the state have sometimes had a naive belief in the benevolence of state officials and have assumed that the state somehow represents the 'public interest' while the actors in a market process merely pursue their 'private interests'. It is one of the major achievements of the 'Virginia School' of political economists that they have shown convincingly that the officials of the state can be understood in terms of the same motives that influence private actors and that therefore the utility-maximising apparatus of orthodox microeconomics can be applied to their behaviour.[2] It is not necessarily the case that, even under a democratic system, the officials of government, elected or not, will pursue the public interest.

Hayek has addressed himself to these problems in a variety of ways. The rule of law thesis itself implies that the actions of government be limited by general and predictable rules and the decentralisation of knowledge thesis implies that a market process in which each individual uses his own knowledge for his own purposes is likely to produce a more complex and efficient order than that produced by central command. But an evolving *cosmos* will of course produce at least one compulsory order, the order of government, precisely because, although there are some rules which it is in our interests as members of the public to obey, it will not be in our interests so to do as private persons or as members of collective groups within the *cosmos*. While some compulsory rules will therefore guarantee security and predictability, there is, nevertheless, the danger that the organisation that enforces those rules may become the source of a new form of enslavement. The new slavery, according to Hayek, is just as likely to come from those anxious to promote 'social welfare' as those with more malevolent intentions. It is the impatience of those radicals and politicians who believe that state direction and control can achieve better results than a spontaneously evolving *catallaxy* that has primarily concerned him.

2. REJECTED CRITERIA FOR STATE ACTION

As is often the case with Hayek's social philosophy, more criticism seems to be directed at the supposed friends of liberty and capitalism than its professed enemies. It is not surprising that *laissez-faire* should be rejected as a philosophy of government. I discussed this point briefly in the chapter on liberty but it must be explained more fully in the context of economic policy. It is not state inactivity as such that Hayek wishes to see but a proper set of principles to determine what state activity there should be. The state is not excluded *a priori* from economic activity itself but its participation here depends upon certain conditions being fulfilled. Indeed Hayek has consistently argued that there is much the state can do to improve the workings of competition where this is restricted to the improvement of the ground-rules of the *catallaxy*, and has even suggested, albeit somewhat obliquely, that the conditions for a spontaneous order may actually be created, or designed.[3] He does not, therefore, evaluate government activity by reference to its volume but to its character and form. A government may have a very small role in an economy, for example, it may own very little in the way of productive resources, but if its activity is founded upon erroneous principles the outcome for liberty may be much worse than in a society in which the government, although playing a much bigger part in its economic life, nevertheless conducts its activities in a manner conducive to the evolution of a spontaneous order.[4] One example Hayek gives in which government inactivity has proved to be disastrous is in industrial relations where failure to enforce existing picket laws, and failure to design more appropriate ones, has done much to undermine the conditions of a competitive order.

It should be clear from the exposition of Hayek's thought so far that the limits of a government's authority must not be determined by considerations of expediency. The idea that each proposed act should be judged according to whether it produces measurable benefits is completely alien to his whole way of thinking. In fact this seemingly innocuous *pragmatism*,[5] an approach beloved of moderate politicians, has been emphasised frequently by Hayek as one of the principal causes of the slide into collectivism this century. The idea that the boundaries of government action should be determined by expediency is quite consistent with the scientistic, quantificationist approach to social and economic affairs. It is for this, and related, reasons that Hayek rejects much of what is today called welfare economics, where this has been concerned with the problem of defining a social optimum by which the rationality of economic policy can be judged.

The earliest example of this approach is Benthamite utilitarianism. While this social philosophy is often associated with free enterprise economics, Hayek has been at pains to stress that the association was based on pragmatic, instrumental grounds. The utilitarians supposed that all questions of economic policy could be settled by reference to an objective standard, utility. On the assumption that a measurable quantity of satisfaction attaches to every human action then a government's strategy ought to be directed to promoting policies that maximise aggregate satisfactions. Thus classical utilitarianism assumes that there exists the common measuring rod of pleasure by which differing policies may be compared, rather in the way that weight, volume and length are used to classify different physical objects, and that interpersonal comparisons of utility can be made, so that losses in pleasure of some individuals caused by certain policies could be compensated by the gains of others, and a net balance, in terms of utility for society as a whole, struck. Hayek has always taken the orthodox view that there is no measuring rod of utility and that interpersonal comparisons of utility cannot be scientifically made so that aggregative judgements about the desirability of a proposed economic policy are highly subjective and rest on intuition and not observation.[6]

Hayek's original contribution to the critique of utilitarianism as a justification of government policy is to draw out the connection between law and economics in the doctrine. Since Bentham, and his followers, made no distinction between rules and commands, and reduced all types of law to that of command emanating from a sovereign will, then there are no limits on the authority of a government implementing what can only be a set of subjective preferences under the guise of an alleged objective standard of social utility. If it turned out that social utility could be better promoted by central direction of the economy then it would follow that the market should be replaced by coercive orders. The connection between utilitarianism and market economics is, therefore, a purely instrumental one.

In fact, Hayek rejects all attempts of modern welfare economics to devise conditions for an optimal economic policy which presuppose the possibility of maximising aggregate real social income.[7] He argues that attempts to objectify or measure social welfare are doomed to failure because they ultimately depend upon illegitimate comparisons of utilities that economic policies bring to different persons. His own version of an optimal economic policy is typically qualitative. An economic policy is optimal if it is directed towards 'increasing the chances of any member of society taken at random of having a high income'.[8] This means that government activity should be concerned with ensuring that the rules of the game do not favour any groups or individuals and that access to economic opportunities should not be closed to groups or individuals by the coercive actions of others. If these conditions are met then the operation of a *catallaxy* will mean that goods will be produced at the lowest possible cost. That is all that can be said about efficiency.

3. THE LIMITS OF GOVERNMENT

In the discussion of one or two of the inappropriate approaches to the problem of the agenda of government Hayek reveals the basic elements of his own approach. It is already clear that it is not what governments do that is important, although Hayek does believe that most western governments do far too much, but the methods they employ in whatever it is that they do. The principle, therefore, that determines the legitimacy of state action is the principle of the rule of law. If whatever it is that governments wish to do can be done by general, predictable and impersonal rules, then it is to that extent legitimate.[9] Government activity is not limited to coercion, it may provide services which are purely economic. The only coercive role of government is to enforce the rules of just conduct so as to prevent coercion by private individuals. Questions of expediency do not arise here; the government must have a monopoly of the use of coercion and because of this it can have no discretion. Its actions must be as predictable as possible if freedom is to be made consistent with law. However, in government's non-coercive activities, providing that the proposed course of action is consistent with the rule of law, questions of expediency may be asked.[10] If a proposed course of action is highly expedient for the government to undertake, even if the desirable aim could not be achieved other than by government action, but it cannot be brought about within the rules of just conduct, then it ought not to be pursued.[11] In the government's non-coercive activities, provided they are consistent with the rule of law, it may exercise considerable discretion.

It may be helpful to dwell upon this point a little further. The legitimacy of state action turns essentially on a philosophical conception of the rule of law; it is not a question of empirical evidence. This is unusual since most of the work done by economists in this field has not been overtly philosophical, although it may have philosophical implications. Typical questions asked have been about the efficiency of providing services collectively or privately, and what particular mix of public and private services makes individuals better off. One of the pioneers in this field, Professor Gordon Tullock, has stated that the answers to these questions very much depend upon empirical evidence.[12] For Hayek, however, these matters, although important, are secondary to the more general question of the consistency of the government's action with the rule of law.

A government's action in the economic field would be contrary to the rule of law if it discriminated between individuals. If a government enterprise sold the same goods at different prices to different individuals, arbitrarily restricted access to a trade to a favoured group, or set up a monopoly in a particular activity, its actions would be illegitimate. In general, it can be said that, according to Hayek's thesis, the actions of government must not be made to serve particular ends. Where there has to be government discretion in non-coercive activities, such discretion must be within general rules, from which appeals to the courts can be made.

Hayek argues that socialism is unacceptable, irrespective of considerations of efficiency, precisely because the direction of production according to a collective plan must be in breach of the rule of law in that the implementation of such a plan would involve the invasion of the individual's protected domain. Governments would have to proceed by commands rather than general rules and establish monopolies in almost every part of the economy.[13]

But Hayek argues that some government intervention which falls short of socialism would also breach the rule of law. In discussing the case of controls over prices, including those over the price of labour by way of an incomes policy, he directly assimilates the working of the *catallaxy* to the doctrine of the rule of law.[14] He argues that it is impossible to regulate a *catallaxy* by specific orders because market conditions are constantly changing; as prices change according to supply and demand so would the rules the government make to govern those prices. The only way this could be done is by arbitrary command. Now if prices are fixed differently from those that would form in a free market then markets will not clear and central authorities will have to distribute the economic product by decree. If, for example, the government fixed the price of a good below the price that would clear the market the government has to decide who is to buy or sell. Incomes policies, by fixing the price of labour differently from its market price, must lead to the direction of labour to ends deemed desirable by the government. In fact, what is likely to happen in these cases is the emergence of black markets, though Hayek does not explicitly discuss this. In all this the point to stress is that Hayek's objection to socialism and to lesser forms of economic interventionism turns primarily on the qualitative test of the rule of law and only secondarily on the test of efficiency.

This identification of the rule of law with the free market economy, while fully consistent with Hayek's social philosophy, may appear to some as a little unsatisfactory—not because it describes a full-blooded socialist society as 'lawless', a view which is likely to attract support from a wide variety of views, but because it also encompasses social and economic policies which fall some way short of this. It is true that the kind of intervention of which Hayek is so critical, namely controls over prices and incomes, is likely to be highly *inefficient*, in that it distorts the economic system and prevents the price mechanism from allocating resources to their most productive uses; but even within Hayek's account of the rule of law it might be possible to lay down general rules to govern prices which were predictable and by which individuals could manage their affairs. If the resulting outcome proved to be economically unsatisfactory, as it would and, indeed, has in those countries that have so experimented, it might very well lead to rationing and allocation by centralised authorities. But this action would presumably be in pursuit of efficiency. The authorities would be trying to find an optimal use of resources in the absence of the signals of the market. However, if the authorities were not concerned with efficiency it would be possible to maintain an order based upon general rules, albeit somewhat precariously.

I make this point not to dispute Hayek's general distrust of state interventionism but to question the line of reasoning that puts a prohibition on a great variety of economic policies by a set of integrated definitions. It seems to be not the case that socialism and planning *mean* the absence of the rule of law but that if this goal is to be combined with another desired end, the efficient use of productive resources, there is likely to be a gradual diminution in the predictability of the rules that govern individuals' lives. Furthermore, critics might also say that Hayek's account of the rule of law is too demanding anyway, and suggest that slight relaxations, for example, lessening the emphasis on economic liberty within the protected domain, might make more active government possible while preserving the main elements of legality.

It is also noticeable that certain interventions that Hayek does regard as desirable, and which go beyond the enforcement of the rules of just conduct, are interpreted as being consistent with the rule of law. One interesting example comes from the much-discussed question of licensure, the practice of permitting only those with the prescribed qualifications to enter into certain occupations.[15] This, on the face of it, seems to imply a discrimination in law between individuals and extreme libertarians have opposed it for that very reason. They claim that the public are better protected from frauds and charlatans in the professions by impersonal market forces and that the practice of licensure merely grants a monopoly to those that meet the arbitrarily determined standards. Hayek claims that licensure is consistent with the rule of law if the conditions required are laid down in the form of general rules and if everybody possessing the necessary qualifications has the right to practise the trade in question. But this illustrates the general problem of Hayek's formulation of the rule of law, for it is possible to effectively restrict entry to a profession by general rules. In Great Britain the legal profession is coming under severe attack because of its effective monopoly in certain types of legal transaction.

Hayek is able to make many of the non-coercive functions of the modern state consistent with his rule of law doctrine. It must be stressed that these functions relate to the conditions that make a *catallaxy* work more effectively. They are obviously not designed to move the *catallaxy* in any *particular* direction. Thus we find health and safety regulations, and rules governing safety in housing and factory conditions, controls on the use of poisons and firearms, the public provision of roads, parks and civic amenities.[16] There is even the concession that subsidies to producers are acceptable, provided that they do not impede access to the market by non-subsidised enterprises, and that the subsidies do not directly benefit those engaged in the production of the goods in question but the public at large.[17] It must be stressed here that Hayek is very much aware of the dangers inherent in the non-coercive activities of the state. It may very well become coercive and discriminatory, as when governments claim a monopoly in certain enterprises and engage in unfair practices which disadvantage private enterprise, although the situation may fall short of monopoly.

Nevertheless, the contents of Hayek's agenda of government do seem a little arbitrary and would not be accepted by all liberals. The rule of law criteria seem capable of a number of interpretations. Hayek's principles would allow subsidies to the arts, the provision of parks and other civic amenities.[18] These might well be objected to by strict libertarians as they involve the political authorities deliberately favouring the consumers of these services against other consumers. The fact that access to these services is not restricted would not be considered a good enough condition. The problem that lies behind the whole question of the state's non-coercive activities is that these normally have to be paid for by taxation, which is collected coercively. And Hayek really has no answer to this problem beyond saying, somewhat unconvincingly, that most people find it expedient to contribute towards the purposes of other individuals on the understanding that they will gain from similar contributions towards their ends.[19]

Perhaps one of Hayek's most convincing arguments against too great an involvement by the state is contained in *The Road to Serfdom* but is not used specifically in this connection in later writings, although it does appear strongly as an argument against government pursuing a policy of distributive or social justice. This is the point that state intervention is likely to be disadvantageous in a market society precisely because this kind of society is characterised by a lack of agreement about concrete ends.[20] The state ought therefore to be limited to those few areas where there is general agreement. If they go beyond this there is likely to be a loss of liberty and a steady erosion of the market economy. It is one of the disturbing features of modern democracies, especially in the case of Britain with its sovereign parliament, that wide extensions of the state's authority have occurred which, although they are technically legitimate, often do not have widespread support.

One area of economic life in which Hayek allows some state intervention has attracted the attention of economists in recent years. This is the field of externalities, of which public goods are a special case. Externalities, or 'spillover' effects as they are sometimes called, are the effects on the general public caused by the actions of private individuals and which are not priced by the normal market process.[21] There can be external 'bads' and external 'goods'. Examples of the former are the familiar ones of pollution, congestion and damage to the environment. A producer when using the least-cost method of production will be operating efficiently but in doing so may impose social costs by emitting noxious fumes from his factory, or destroying the fish in a stream into which he discharges the waste products of his process. External goods, those products of individual action which benefit the public generally may be exemplified by the side-effects produced by scientific research or the enjoyment by the general public of some individual's attractive house and well-kept garden.[22]

The problem is that externalities are numerous and various. Almost any private action can produce an effect, adverse or otherwise, to others not directly involved in the transaction. Even the choice of one's clothes has an effect on others and one writer, in an attempt to justify censorship of obscene literature without recourse to moral argument, has claimed that the sight of others reading such material imposes a negative externality on him which calls for correction.[23] It is logically possible for externalities to be 'internalised' by voluntary agreement between individuals, for the losers to bribe the gainers; but the presence of an externality is normally used as justification for the state to intervene. The danger is, however, that the externality argument may be used to smuggle in a vast range of government actions under the guise of a market philosophy.

Hayek, in *The Constitution of Liberty*, agreed that there was a need for some government action to correct market failure and to supply goods which, although desired by all individuals, it would not be in the interest of any one to produce. However, such action must be consistent with the rule of law, and questions of efficiency are subordinate to this fundamental criterion. He also pointed out that economists had contributed very little in the area of spillover effects (this statement would not be true today) and that the customary legal rules of private property and freedom of contract do not provide a ready-made answer to these problems.[24] In fact, it is doubtful whether the Hayekian system can provide an answer. He obviously cannot use a traditional argument from welfare economics to the effect that government intervention ought to take the form of corrective measures to produce the particular outcomes which would have occured but for the presence of the externality. This sort of objectification, and attempt to quantify welfare losses, is explicitly precluded by his epistemology.[25] It is in the nature of a *catallactic* process that we cannot know what pattern of goods and services people desire in advance of their choosing it. Since, for example, we cannot ever know just how much output people may be prepared to sacrifice for a reduction in pollution, how can we evaluate a proposed pollution tax? On the whole Hayek thinks that the exact form the legal rules should take within which competition operates should be left to evolution and experience.[26]

I mentioned earlier in this section the kinds of government activity Hayek permits in the area where competition does not produce things which are generally desired. These are the traditional public goods, defence, law and order and so on. A public good is normally defined as one that can be consumed by one person without any diminution in the amount available to others. Public goods are extreme cases of externality, and, while it is not logically necessary that they be produced by the state, they are the primary justification for the existence of the state by liberals. Contemporary economists are concerned almost solely with efficiency in this area, with trying to find what mix of private and public provision makes individuals better off. As I have said before, Hayek is almost entirely concerned with qualitative considerations, his main concern is the

threat to liberty and the rule of law that state action involves. Where
things have to be produced by central authorities it is better that
they be produced by authorities below the level of the central state
so as to prevent a concentration of authority at any one point.[27]

I have said nothing about Hayek's views on the government's role
in the management of the economy. These will be discussed in
Chapter 8 but it is worth mentioning at this stage a very important
change in his views on one issue. Until very recently he had always
believed that governments should have a monopoly of the supply of
money,[28] but the post-war inflation and the misuse that governments have made of their discretionary powers has led him to
believe that a better monetary system would emerge if governments
lost their monopoly of money and were forced to compete with other
issuers of currency in the market.[29]

Before I leave the question of the agenda of government there are
one or two areas which have posed special problems for liberals in
the past thirty years which must be considered in more detail. These
are the welfare state, conservation and planning.

4. THE WELFARE STATE

It would be quite false to say that liberals in general, and Hayek in
particular, are opposed to the idea of a welfare state. It would also
be quite false to suggest that the doctrine of spontaneous evolution
has anything to do with Social Darwinism or the survival of the
fittest in human terms, or that the state and its officials ought to have
no responsibility for those who, for one reason or another, cannot
secure an adequate living in the *catallaxy*.[30] Indeed, Hayek has
frequently claimed that the division of labour and the division of
knowledge enables the market economy to function at a high
enough level of productivity for sufficient payments to be made
outside the market to those individuals. In *The Constitution of Liberty*
he was mainly concerned with the threats to liberty that may occur
if some of the aims of the welfare state are pursued by governments.[31] The problem is that the demonstration that some welfare
aims are legitimate may lead governments to pursue them by means
that will destroy freedom. So once again it is the means employed to
achieve generally desirable ends that are important.

The general concern is that the machinery of the welfare state
may be used to smuggle in a more comprehensive socialism not

desired by the original designers of welfare schemes. At the time that Hayek wrote *The Constitution of Liberty* he felt that the threat of overt socialism had receded, that particular collectivist economic theories had been refuted, but that the same ends might well be brought about by other means.[32] What he regarded as the difficulty with the welfarist ideology was that since its aims were diffuse and difficult to precisely categorise, it was that much more difficult to conclusively reject by comparison with the more traditional socialist doctrines. However, the one aim of welfarism Hayek has consistently and emphatically opposed is the attempt to use the legitimate argument that the state ought to provide some absolute level of security against deprivation for its citizens as a general argument for a more egalitarian distribution of incomes. I shall deal with this last point more fully in the next chapter, which deals with Hayek's theory of justice.

The kind of welfare state that Hayek objects to is that in which individuals are deprived of the opportunity of attending to their own arrangements for such things as old-age pensions, health and housing. In these fields there has been a great deal of state activity, some of which involves compulsion, in post-war Britain. While Hayek does not object to some form of compulsory insurance against unemployment, sickness and other aspects of social security, and even sees a role for the state in the establishment of such schemes, he has constantly warned of the dangers of a tendency towards a state monopoly. What has happened in the field of social security is that the principle of insurance has gradually been eroded.[33] Social security payments are not financed from contributions but from general taxation so that the system has become a tool of politicians. Instead of individuals receiving what they are entitled to in accordance with their contributions the tendency is for them to be given what they 'need', as if there were some objective criterion of need. The effect of this is to put great power in the hands of the officials who administer the system as well as the politicians who determine its ends.

A further important effect of the state playing a dominant role in welfare is the emergence of a vast bureaucracy the members of which, in some cases, may have great discretionary power over individuals.[34] But they also constitute a body of persons whose careers depend very much on the continued expansion of state services. Hayek has on occasions commented, pessimistically, that it may prove politically impossible to get rid of the apparatus of the welfare state.[35] One problem is that because of the proliferation of welfare services the whole system has become extremely complex and is often only understood by those who work in it. Hence government committees that are set up to enquire into the system are invariably staffed by 'insiders' who have a vested interest in its expansion.[36] Economists, who would have something to say about the efficiency of the various methods of delivering the welfare good, and lawyers, who would be interested in whether the various agencies operate within general rules of law, are rarely consulted because they are not experts in the bureaucratic intricacies of the system itself.

One of the particular services of the modern welfare state which is of particular interest is the health service. This was at one time thought to be the ark of the socialist covenant, and still is in some circles. It was claimed that the provision of a comprehensive health service which was free at the point of consumption would always be superior to private provision based on insurance principles. The claims made for this system have always been doubted by economic liberals. Hayek has stressed the fact that there is no objective measure of health care—this must change not merely with the state of medical knowledge but with changes in the attitudes people have towards the importance of health. When the state decides the level of health care it is making a political, indeed arbitrary, decision about how the people's money is to be spent.[37] In fact, what has tended to happen is that the state has spent less on health than would be spent by individuals through private insurance schemes.[38] The oft-quoted complaints in the British system about lengthy waiting periods for operations might well be justified by this line of reasoning. At the heart of Hayek's objections is the argument that political methods, whether by democratic voting procedures or pressure group activity, are much less effective than market choice in transmitting information about what individuals want in the way of welfare services.

Hayek's arguments against certain aspects of the welfare state rest upon considerations to do with the rule of law and questions of efficiency. The rule of law is breached when statutes give officials power to discriminate between individuals, often on quite subjective grounds of need, and from such decisions appeal is extremely difficult. In fact, the whole system of administrative tribunals which has grown up to govern the relationship between officials and clients has been severely, and repeatedly, criticised for developing outside the normal tradition of the common law. The efficiency argument is that people do not get what they want out of the welfare system, that it does not really help those it was originally designed for, the poor, and that it has spawned a vast army of administrators. One tendency has been a redistributive one, services delivered on grounds of need have been really used to bring about egalitarianism. But even here the redistribution has not helped the poor. As Hayek and others have repeatedly pointed out, progressive income tax has been used to exploit the rich for the benefit of the middle incomes, the largest voting group, rather than the poor.[39]

In the last twenty years there has been growing dissatisfaction with the welfare state, especially in Great Britain, and Hayek's comments, which were written during what might be called the heyday of the system, are echoed frequently, and not only by fellow economic liberals. Much research done over the past ten years has indeed confirmed some of his fears. One point is always worth stressing, that is the tendency towards state monopoly in welfare means that experiments and new ideas in welfare are less likely to get a hearing.[40] Bureaucracies become resistant to change. This is especially true in health and education in Great Britain where radical schemes for new ways of financing these services, and maximising consumer choice, have not made much headway with those who actually run the services.

Nevertheless, one or two cautionary comments may be made. Firstly, Hayek's thesis about the welfare state is the strong one that not only is it likely to promote inefficiency and breaches of the rule of law but that it may bring about a completely socialist society by stealth. He even goes so far as to suggest that public relations exercises promoted by welfare agencies to extend their services are equivalent to the power over minds that is exercised by a totalitarian state with a monopoly of the supply of information.[41] This seems more than a little extravagant. There are many other good explanations of the rise of extreme socialism and totalitarianism and it is impossible to assess the causal effect of the institution of certain welfare services. The main danger is still inefficiency, caused mainly by the bringing of welfare services too far into the arena of politics.

Secondly, there is a danger that Hayek's comments about welfare may sound partisan rather than analytical. This is because he stresses always the defects of the state system and rarely the defects of the private market system. One example is in health where he does not consider the importance of the nature of knowledge in medicine. Unlike in the purchase of other goods, the patient is at the mercy of the doctor as he is not in a position to dispute his judgement, except by going to another doctor. This, plus the virtual monopoly over the supply of doctors that medical associations have, means that the medical profession can, in a market system, earn high salaries, a significant percentage of which is economic rent. There is clearly a role for the state here which would not breach liberal principles yet it is not considered by Hayek.

Another example is in the field of housing where he quite rightly criticises rent control and governments subsidising council rents,[42] yet he does not mention tax concessions to owner-occupiers which are discriminatory in his sense and cause distortions in the housing market.[43] I am quite sure he would be equally opposed to these privileges but he does not always drive home as effectively as some liberals economic arguments against privileges enjoyed by the middle classes.

5. CONSERVATION

A recent candidate for state intervention is the whole field of conservation of natural resources. The criticism of the market here is that it allows a very rapid run-down of exhaustible resources. The argument also is that the relentless pursuit of economic growth which, it is claimed, is a product of liberal individualism, produces unacceptable externalities in the form of congestion, pollution and general damage to the environment in addition to the problem of the using up of scarce natural resources. It is possible to deal with the costs of economic growth in terms of market economics, and many of the anti-growth economists would claim that they belong to the individualist tradition, but the problems raised in this area have been used to justify a more collective approach and to invest the government with more powers to plan the use of scarce resources and place direct controls over production methods.

Economic liberals have always been sceptical of the claims of some of the extreme conservationists. Since they believe that the price mechanism itself provides the best instrument for regulating the use of natural resources, (for example, in a free market as fossil fuels become more scarce their prices will rise so that automatically individuals will be encouraged to conserve them), they argue that state action is unnecessary. Furthermore, attempts by governments to control directly the use of natural resources will inhibit the search for substitutes which occurs spontaneously in a free market. Economic liberals are in any case sceptical of the figures produced which forecast the exhaustion of sources of energy in predictable time periods. Hayek has long been critical of the placing of too much reliance on the evidence of the physical facts of exhaustion of the world's resources and in 1960 said that industrial development would have been held back if warnings about the threatened exhaustion of coal supplies had been heeded earlier in this century.[44]

Hayek believes that an obsessive concern with conservation is based on the unreasoned prejudice that steps should be taken to maintain the present yield of a given resource. He sees no necessary harm resulting from the working of a particular resource and then abandoning it when it is no longer profitable, and argues that to prevent the spontaneous process of the market operating through deliberately contrived conservation plans will lower incomes all round.[45]

One particular argument of the conservationists is highly relevant to Hayek's epistemological position. This is the view that central direction of the conservation of natural resources is justified because the government possesses superior knowledge. While it is true, he says, that governments are quite likely to have knowledge of some facts about future developments which will not be known to individual resource owners there will always exist a greater store of knowledge, dispersed throughout the market as a whole, which will be used and which cannot in the nature of things be made available in a concentrated form to centralised authorities.[46] It is true that individual owners will be unaware of forecasts of future technological and economic developments that will affect future prices, but the market will automatically take into account just this sort of information. Furthermore, Hayek is highly critical of one very popular justification for governmental control of scarce resources which rests upon the idea that individual owners do not have the means to invest in processes that conserve scarce resources. He says this view depends solely on the obvious fact that government can use its coercive powers to tax. The advantage of the government follows from the fact that failure in its investment is borne by the taxpayer. It does not in any way prove that governments are more likely in their actions to take a better account of future prospects than are individuals.[47]

No doubt contemporary critics of economic growth would accuse Hayek of undue complacency. He has not discussed the subject in any great detail and his most recent observations have been no more than passing comments. In his Nobel Prize Lecture, delivered in 1975, he suggested that constructivist rationalism and the desire to consciously control the environment was the basis of the anti-growth school.[48] The critics of growth were condemned as scientistic and Hayek quoted respectable scientific authors as having refuted them. However, it must be pointed out that the particular thesis that Hayek claimed had been refuted, that contained in *The Limits to Growth*, the report by the Club of Rome which predicted a catastrophic future for mankind, is the least sophisticated of the anti-growth doctrines.[49] There are some technical problems about the rate at which resources are used up, and the external costs that are imposed on society if growth is relentlessly pursued without government intervention, which seriously strain the doctrine of spontaneous evolution. Given the essentially qualitative nature of Hayek's approach it is very difficult for him to say anything on the question as to whether society suffers an actual welfare loss, through damage to the environment and general deterioration of life-styles in urban areas, when economic growth proceeds at twentieth-century rates. Furthermore, there is the ultimately ethical question, which is now beginning to receive more attention, of inter-generational equity. Is the present generation under any moral obligation to future unknown generations to place limits on its use of the earth's resources?

6. PLANNING

Since Hayek's complete works may be said to consist of a continuing argument with central planning in various forms it may seem odd to include a special section on the subject. But it may be useful for the purposes of exposition to particularise one or two aspects of government planning. One point, although fairly obvious, needs clarification if only to save Hayek from an unfair charge of being irrational. This is that Hayek is not against planning as such but only the various forms of central planning that have emerged in economics and the social sciences in this century (although their intellectual origins go back much further) and which have been associated with the scientistic belief that a social organism can be controlled. This form of planning, he maintains, is self-defeating and ultimately irrational, while the correct form of planning, the decentralised decision-making of individuals, although less ambitious and based upon the limitations of human knowledge, brings about a more rational social order. It is rather unfortunate that the word planning, like so many other words in the vocabulary of the social sciences, has been appropriated by those who often recommend a state of affairs very nearly opposite to it. The believers in planning, especially those who have no background in economics, seem to be of the view that an economic order would not emerge if individuals were left to transact spontaneously. Those who maintain that Hayek's argument that economic science predicts that an order, the market or *catallaxy*, will emerge from the voluntary actions of individuals is rather trivial, may well grasp its true importance when they reflect on the fact that the post-war programmes of almost all the major political parties in the West belie this fundamental truth. It is not just the socialists who are the planners. The truth of the theory that a spontaneous order will emerge is not diminished by a certain dogmatism on Hayek's part and perhaps an exaggerated fear of the consequences of even the mildest of experiments in planning.

One piece of public policy that Hayek attacked in some detail can be used as an almost textbook example of what might be called the unforeseen consequences of planning. This was the scheme, under the 1947 Town and Country Planning Act in Great Britain, by which the owners of land were to be taxed on the increased value their property underwent through a change in use brought about by planning permission.[50] Originally a Central Land Board was set up to administer the scheme, the main features of which were later abandoned. Among Hayek's many objections to the whole plan were his arguments that it not only entailed breaches of the rule of law but also that it actually implied economic planning on a vast scale, which was not intended by its authors. Since the general principles under which the Central Land Board was to work were not contained in the Act but appeared in the Board's *Practice Notes* individuals could not predict how officials would treat them. The 100 per cent charge on the increased value due to a change in use of land was not fixed until after the Act was passed. Further, since the Board was not to be bound by general rules in its responsibility for deciding the future use of development land it would inevitably be subject to political and other pressures in its dealings with individual applications.[51] On the economic side not only would the charges be a disincentive for firms to take risks in extending their operations but also, from the point of view of the Board, when deciding whether particular industrial developments ought to take place or not, it would need an economic plan for the development of the entire country. This was not the intention of the authors of the scheme but since they were proposing to abandon the price mechanism for determining the most efficient use of land centralised planning could be the only alternative. In situations in which a small group of technical specialists succeeds in getting through legislation which itself confers great discretionary powers on officials, democracy can offer little protection for individuals against the extravagance of planners.[52]

However persuasive Hayek's arguments are concerning the unintended consequences of planning, it must be pointed out that there is a subtle mixture of objections on grounds of efficiency and those based on the loss of liberty that planning entails. It is the case that societies can tolerate a fair amount of inefficiency resulting from planning while still keeping intact the structure of freedom. Hayek's thesis that even a small venture into planning must lead to tyranny because the failures of the first plan lead to further extensions of government power in order to correct them, does not, of course, attempt to predict quantitatively how much planning a free society can take. It is difficult to see how it could even be falsified because the presence of some elementary form of planning in a free society is consistent with it. It is a statement of a general pattern that will emerge if a certain kind of central planning is pursued. But a sceptic might well see the explanation as curiously narrow. After all, the historical evidence of this century is not that experiments in planning have led to tyranny but that economic planning has been imposed by tyrannical regimes.

At the end of the day Hayek's case against planning rests on his argument for limited government. Planning involves the investing of great powers in government and it cannot always be assumed that these powers will be used benevolently. The system of democracy was at one time thought to ensure that elected officials would pursue the public interest, but only the most naive of optimists today thinks this is an effective guarantee. Rather than rely on the chance of a benevolent and well-informed planner emerging in a political system Hayek would prefer restraints on the behaviour of any political leader. As I shall show in Chapter 8, this lies at the heart of his objections to the economic theory of Lord Keynes, which in its practical application does depend upon a benevolent and fully-informed economic manager.

7 Hayek's Theory of Justice

I. THE PROBLEM OF JUSTICE

The concept of justice has always been a key word in the vocabulary of political philosophy. No systematic account of political ideas can omit a discussion of this concept whether the interests of the author are in the field of value-free conceptual analysis or in that of the appraisal and recommendation of laws, policies and institutions. Moreover, it has been the practice in traditional political theorising to combine both activities. The earliest and most famous systematic treatise on political philosophy, Plato's *Republic* was significantly both an enquiry into the 'true nature' of justice and a construction of an ideally 'just' state against which existing empirical states could be evaluated.

Yet despite more than two thousand years of subsequent political theorising the concept still has no settled meaning. It is not simply that there are fundamental disputes at the normative level, it is only to be expected that individuals will disagree as to the justice or injustice of particular laws, policies and institutions; it is the fact that there is so little agreement as to what the concept *means* that causes such serious problems.

The confusion as to the meaning of the concept has been exacerbated in recent years by the dominance of *social justice* as a moral and political value. Since the last war progressive social thinkers, alienated from Marxism both by the practical examples of tyrannical communist regimes and by more fruitful intellectual advances in the social sciences, have justified radical social and economic policies by an appeal to social justice within the general framework of western liberal democratic regimes. As a consequence the concept of justice has been perhaps irredeemably associated with problems of the appropriate distribution of wealth and income. The proponents of social justice have therefore been concerned to demonstrate the criteria by which 'social justice' sanctions certain distributive policies. The criteria are usually desert, merit and need, or sometimes merely more equality for its own sake. The emphasis placed on these different, and often conflicting, criteria may vary but the members of the 'school of social justice' are united in their belief in a forward-looking reformist concept of justice. That this view is more than just a declaration of policy or the justification of a substantive set of values but involves the appropriation of the *meaning* of justice to the radical view can be seen in a comment by one of its leading proponents, Brian Barry. In criticising the views of David Hume, the eighteenth-century conservative philosopher who refuted radical and reformist views of justice in defending a traditional rule-based view, Barry said: 'although Hume uses the expression "rules of justice" to cover such things as property rules, "justice" is now analytically tied to "desert" and "need", so that one could quite properly say that some of what Hume calls "rules of justice" were unjust'.[1]

However, traditionally most users of the word justice were not necessarily radical, and nor is the contemporary usage necessarily tied to a reformist moral and political outlook. Those who are sceptical of 'social justice' do not regard themselves as antithetical to what they would regard as a properly articulated conception of justice. In ordinary speech generally we talk of justice and injustice where the words do not refer to the desirability or otherwise of states of affairs or particular income and wealth distributions but to the rules and procedures that characterise social practices and which are applied to the actions of individuals that participate in those practices. In this narrower conception justice is normally seen to be a property of individuals. When in the context of the common law we speak of a breach of the rules of 'natural justice' we are referring to an arbitrariness suffered by an individual in a rule-governed process.

This latter concept has undoubtedly legalistic overtones but it should be sharply distinguished from a purely legalistic concept of justice. Justice is not merely conformity to law and it is certainly permissible to consider a law to be unjust without committing ourselves to the radical view. Hayek is indeed the major exponent of this rule-based view yet we know from his analysis of law that many legal expressions are inconsistent with the ideal of the rule of law while being perfectly valid law in the technical sense.[2] To determine the properties of this concept of justice upon which law properly conceived depends will be the purpose of this chapter.

Before we can proceed with this there are still some more general conceptual difficulties with the concept of justice. The word is part of a family of concepts which are intricately related. The concept most often used in the same context as justice is that of equality, and of the members of this family of concepts it is this with which we will be mostly concerned. While there are clearly uses of justice which do imply equality, we speak of equality before the law and often regard certain forms of inequality as arbitrary and unjust, more often than not there is tension between the concepts. Justice, for example, would not sanction equality of reward to individuals who render widely differing services. Hayek has been associated with the view that the attempt to impose *material* equality on unequal people is destructive of the rule of law and necessitates totalitarianism and consequent injustice towards individuals.

Contemporary discussion of justice has focused on John Rawls's *A Theory of Justice*[3] and no account of the subject would be complete without a reference to this work. The issue is confused by the variety of reactions to Rawls's book. Some critics have interpreted it as a justification of quite radical egalitarianism while others see it as a defence of the justice of traditional liberal, if not conservative, market economics.[4] In fact, as we shall see, while there are some important differences between the two writers, there is a remarkable similarity between the *general approaches* of Rawls and Hayek on the question of the justice of social and political institutions and on the criteria for the justification of the distribution of incomes. On this question, and that of the policy implications that flow from various conceptions of justice we shall reserve discussion until the exegesis of Hayek's theory of justice has been completed.

An understanding of Hayek's theory of justice is impossible without a much more precise delineation of the subject than the general account of the area given above. Three approaches can be isolated. I shall call these extreme legal positivism, procedural justice and end-state justice.

Extreme legal positivism is the doctrine that there is no rational conception of justice outside the positive law. It holds that justice is a creature only of positive law, that there is no 'objective' justice and that all statements of justice that claim to evaluate positive law by an external criterion of morality are inherently subjective and metaphysical. The implication of this extreme view is that justice is a relative concept that only has meaning in connection with particular systems of positive law. This view is dramatically asserted by Hobbes, 'laws are the rules of just and unjust; nothing being reputed unjust, that is not contrary to some law'.[5] This means that the words just and unjust have no meaning outside the law, a law being the command of a sovereign.

Similar views can be found in modern legal positivists, who may not necessarily accept Hobbes's particular explanation of law and sovereignty. A convenient example is Hans Kelsen's famous essay 'What is Justice?'[6] In this essay Kelsen takes the essentially logical positivist's position that meaningful statements are either analytically true (tautologies) or empirical propositions which can be verified by experience, all other statements, including ethical statements, being metaphysical. Since justice, he claims, is about the conflict of values, and since values are subjective, no rational argument can settle conflicts. Absolute justice is an illusion and from the point of view of rational cognition, there are only interests of human beings and hence conflict of interests. Justice in an abstract sense can have no application to such problems since all statements about justice are relative to positive law which is a product of will not reason. In fact, Kelsen argues that justice, and freedom have meaning only as expressions of the majority in a society.

Hayek maintains that this view depends upon the erroneous assumption that there is only one type of law, namely legislation, whereas in Hayek's theory of law, as we have seen, legal systems as systems of general rules exist independently of legislatures. These systems of rules, which have emerged by the process of adaptive evolution, have a validity independent of command. The positivists' answer that they exist only by tacit consent of the sovereign is not sufficient to explain the *content* of such rules. The content of these rules, the rules of just conduct or the rules of private law that govern the relationships between individuals, has been demonstrated beyond doubt by historians of private law and the common law. That such legal systems may be authorised and implemented by officials and legislators does not mean that those officials and legislators determine what the rules shall be. To say this, says Hayek, is to commit the fallacy of 'methodological essentialism', the fallacy of supposing that laws must necessarily be of one type, in this case public law, or the rules of organisations with specific purposes. Once it is shown that there are rules of the evolutionary type in a legal system then it follows that decisions reached in this process are not a product of the unfettered will of a sovereign but are a product of ratiocination within the system. It is the process of reasoning within a system of general rules that constitutes the 'objective' nature of justice. Decisions of judges within a common law system are not policy decisions, or decisions to settle conflicts between interests but are attempts to determine what is implied by the rules of the system.

For those who reject the extreme version of legal positivism, and anybody who wishes to demonstrate a substantive theory of justice has to do so, the most popular type of theory is the end-state or 'patterned' type. These terms have been borrowed from Robert Nozick's important book *Anarchy, State and Utopia* but the general approach is not unique to him. An end-state or patterned theory of justice does not see justice as a property of individual behaviour but as a property of certain 'states of affairs' or 'outcomes' of social processes. Or as a recent writer put it: 'it is impossible to assess the justice of actions without a *prior identification of just states of affairs*[7] (italics added).

The proposed patterns of a just society have taken many forms but they all have one thing in common. That is they all require some form of centralised authority to impose some desirable pattern of distribution, a pattern that is different from the economic and social order that would have been produced by the process of free exchange within general rules of law. It is true that most suggested end-state systems of social justice are radical egalitarian systems but there is no reason in logic why patterns of extreme inequality should not be recommended. Indeed, a patterned distribution which made claims to income and wealth depend solely upon a rigorous version of desert would produce highly inegalitarian outcomes. The point here is that those opposed to end-state or patterned conceptions of justice, especially Nozick and Hayek, are associated thereby with 'right-wing' or Conservative political ideologies. But this is mistaken. The stance is if anything *anti-political*. The main emphasis of Hayek has always been on the possibility of a spontaneous social order which requires very little centralised, political direction.

The most commonly used criteria for interfering with a naturally evolving *cosmos* are desert and need but since we shall be considering these in some detail in the detailed discussion of Hayek's theory of justice we can deal at this stage with a different end-state principle, that of utility. For many reasons utilitarianism is not normally associated with the principle of justice at all. If, in its simplest form, it simply means that the policies are right insofar as they maximise happiness or pleasure in a society then it clearly has no necessary connection with any distributive criteria at all. As has often been pointed out, it would entail the proposition that the worst-off in a society have no claim in justice against the better-off if any redistribution would produce a net loss in total utility. It has even been suggested that slavery would be consistent with utilitarianism if it could be shown that the pleasures of the slave-holders are greater than the pains of the slaves.

Political theorists who regard themselves as 'pluralists', that is, they believe that in any policy judgement a number of possibly conflicting principles will have to be applied and that decisions will depend on how the individual 'weights' each principle, would say, therefore, that utilitarianism is merely one consideration, the aggregative consideration, and may have to be modified by distributive principles such as justice, equality or fairness.[8]

Hayek's criticisms of utilitarianism however, do not take this form. He does not want to merely modify utilitarianism by the principle of justice, as this might well commit him to an end-state view of justice, but to show the doctrine's incoherence. He uses two arguments.[9] Firstly, utilitarianism presupposes that the utilities of each individual can be measured and summed so as to produce a utility function for a whole community. As we have seen, Hayek has maintained that utility is not a common measuring rod, as for example, weight, length and volume are measuring devices, and therefore all *interpersonal* comparisons of utility are illegitimate. If utility is not quantifiable then the well being of one individual cannot be compared with another, hence no policy can be appraised as good or bad, right or wrong on grounds that it produced more, or less, utility than any alternative. This reasoning, which is conventional in economic theory, is not directed only against utilitarianism but against any attempt to derive collective choices (end-state principles for our purposes) from individual preferences.

In addition to these conventional criticisms of utilitarianism Hayek has his own individual complaints against the doctrine, for him it is a clear example of 'constructivist rationalism'—that is, the attempt to impose a set of ends upon a self-generating *cosmos*, these ends being derived from *a priori* reasoning and owing nothing to tradition or experience.

Furthermore, as an example of constructivist rationalism, utilitarianism contains a mistaken view of knowledge. This is clearly demonstrated in the extreme form of utilitarianism, act-utilitarianism. Act-utilitarianism presupposes that an act can be appraised as good or bad solely in terms of its immediate consequences. Thus if an act can be shown to produce 'pleasure' for a community then that act ought to be pursued irrespective of whether it involves the breach of a rule. This would appear to license unlimited acts of intervention by legislators on the assumption that utility is thereby maximised. Traditional moral and political rules, for example rules of promise-keeping, property and justice, are by this doctrine provisional only. They are to be upheld only if they can be seen to be immediately beneficial.

Hayek's objection to this is predictable. The doctrine contains the extravagant presumption that legislators can know the consequences of all actions.[10] But we know that the distinguishing feature of the Great Society is that we can never have that kind of knowledge. The order that the Great Society has is not a product of the will of an omniscient centralised legislator but the product of individuals subjecting their behaviour to the discipline of abstract rules, rules that have no ideological purpose in the utilitarian sense.

However, not all utilitarians are act-utilitarians, and *rule-utilitarianism* developed largely as a result of criticisms not unlike those made by Hayek. The rule-utilitarian would concede that rules themselves are to be judged good or bad and right or wrong, not particular acts. Thus the traditional rules of justice would be then held to be justified because experience has indicated that adherence to them produces beneficial consequences in the long run. This would prohibit particular breaches of rules even though such breaches might be justified on act-utilitarian grounds.

Against this Hayek has fewer objections. He largely follows Hume's view that traditional rules are followed because of the benefits they bring to man. But who could dispute this really innocuous statement? The real point is that an acceptance of rule-utilitarianism implies the rejection of the main thrust of utilitarianism proper, its ideological, purpose-directed interpretation of all human action via the notion of measurable pleasure. In addition, Hayek claims that the approach to rules adopted by utilitarianism is incoherent because even in the rule-utilitarian's own doctrine there will be at least *one* rule in the system which is not followed solely for its consequences.[11] The effects of any rule will depend not only on that rule but also upon the others being followed. It would be impossible for the rules to be taken in isolation and assessed for their consequences. Meaningful action must take some rules, at least one, as given.

In fact, Hayek's position is that we cannot understand the notion of a rule in terms only of ends. It is the characteristic of the Great Society that men cannot agree upon ends but only upon means. It is this agreement about means that produces order in the *cosmos* and enables individuals to pursue a variety of ends. Amongst these means are the rules of justice which individuals need to make their behaviour predictable. The most that we can say about the utility of rules is that in the long run the *whole system of rules* was gradually developed because men found it a convenient means to their individually-determined ends. These considerations apply just as much to non-utilitarian notions of justice and welfare which are similarly presented as ends to be pursued by central authorities.

Procedural justice can be best understood as a contrast to end-state or patterned conceptions of justice. Instead of social situations being compared in terms of such external criteria as merit, desert, need and so on, they are evaluated by reference to rules and procedures; if these rules and procedures are adhered to rigorously then no further comment on the justice or injustice of the outcome is required. This is in essence the 'justice as fairness' approach which limits the application of the concept of justice to 'fair rules'. The content of such rules is normally fairly limited. In social and economic practices they would consist of prohibitions on the use of force or fraud in the making of contracts, and rules and institutions to protect individual property holdings.

The point to stress here is that in their least complicated forms theories of procedural justice are not concerned with social or distributive justice. In fact most theorists of procedural justice would maintain that any attempt to impose a particular pattern of distribution by centralised economic planning, or redistributive taxation, would inevitably involve a breach of the rules guaranteeing procedural justice for individuals. The best examples of procedural justice are in competitions, such as races. A fair race is not one in which the person who won 'deserved' to win but one in which there was no cheating, nobody jumped the gun, and nobody had an unfair advantage through the use of drugs and so on.[12]

This is not meant to imply that theorists of procedural justice see social practices as exactly like running races, or that they are uninterested in social welfare. The fact that one man may break down half-way through the race with a pulled muscle may involve no problems for the fairness of an athletics competition but analogous cases in social affairs of course do present problems for even the most extreme *laissez-faire* economist or political theorist. What a theorist of procedural justice would maintain would be that these problems are not problems of justice. A proper theory of social welfare, it is said, would always be concerned to justify policies to help the least fortunate members of society, those who could not survive within a social practice governed by the rules of fairness, but such policies would not be justified by the principle of justice. Furthermore, nobody's position in the outcome of a social process should in any way depend upon another's opinion of his deservingness or neediness.

One particularly rigorous version of this theory is Nozick's entitlement theory of justice. Here there are only three principles of justice—acquisition, transfer and rectification. This means that an individual is entitled to his property holdings if he acquired them fairly, without force or fraud, or if they are transferred voluntarily by bequests and gifts. The purpose of the principle of rectification is to justify procedures to rectify past injustices in the acquisition and transfer of property. From this Nozick concludes that if each person's holdings are just then the total set (distribution) of holdings is just.[13]

It has been a criticism of the justice as fairness school that it is always possible to say of a social outcome that, although the procedural rules were meticulously followed the outcome was nevertheless unjust. Ordinary language, and 'commonsense' morality, contain words like desert and need precisely to do this job of appraising social outcomes. Brian Barry, for example, concedes only that there is an empirical tendency for fair procedures to produce just results and that all such procedures must ultimately be evaluated by more substantial notions of social justice.[14] This is an important point for, as we shall see, Hayek would not merely object to substantive notions of justice on evaluative grounds but on grounds that such notions are strictly speaking *meaningless*, that no operational meaning can be given to evaluations and end-states based on desert or need.

While most procedural theorists of justice would not take this particular line they would cite something of great significance in favour of procedural justice. Its particular virtue they would claim lies in the fact that there is more likely to be agreement about rules of fairness than about substantive ends. This approach depends upon there being a *minimum of coercion* in social life, and it is maintained that there will be less coercion under the rules system than under the end-state system of justice. Indeed, some go as far as to make unanimity a requirement of a social decision procedure.[15]

But there is a slightly more ambitious version of the procedural justice school. Rawls, for example, is aware of the problem that the outcomes of a justice as fairness procedure may not satisfy the demands of a commonsense notion of justice and has therefore attempted to show that under certain specified conditions, the principles that would be chosen by rational, self-interested individuals to govern social practices are indeed *the* principles of justice revealed by ordinary speech and commonsense morality.[16]

This somewhat detailed diversion into the general theory of justice has been necessary in order to understand Hayek's position. It should be quite clear by now that Hayek is opposed to all end-state or patterned theories of justice, but just what content he places in his procedural rules, and how this theory relates to Rawls's doctrine, still remains to be explained.

2. HAYEK'S THEORY OF JUSTICE

The prevailing theme of Hayek's writing on social philosophy is the belief that to make the distribution of income and wealth in a society correspond to an *a priori* conception of social justice is destructive of a free social order. Indeed, in later years he has made this argument one of the main planks in his critique of the welfare state. The first indications of the critique of social justice are evident in Hayek's first essay in social philosophy, *The Road to Serfdom*, when in a chapter entitled 'Who, Whom' he argued not only that a commitment to distributive justice would entail the determination of incomes by the coercive apparatus of the state but that there would be little likelihood of agreement amongst workers over distributive shares.[17] Since then these points have been elaborated in great detail. In the exposition that follows we shall confine the discussion to Hayek's two major works *The Constitution of Liberty* and *The Mirage of Social Justice*, with additional reference to a small number of essays that deal with the same topic.

As we have suggested earlier, Hayek conceives of justice as a property of individual conduct. The word sometimes used in this context is 'commutative' justice. This is an awkward word to define and is best understood as a concept of justice that indicates what is owed to a person under a general rule, as opposed to distributive justice which indicates a desirable state of affairs. The stress on commutative justice is consistent with Hayek's methodology for as he has said many times the whole notion of social justice is anthropomorphic. There is no person called society who can be called just or unjust, or morally evaluated in any way at all. Since a social order, and a market order, are the unintended consequences of individual actions the words just and unjust have no application to these states of affairs.[18]

An act can only be called unjust if it is a breach of some general rule. The question then is, what are the general rules that make certain forms of conduct obligatory? Clearly, a rule that is general is not a rule of just conduct for that reason alone. One can easily conceive of general rules that are unjust. One can think of less fanciful examples than that suggested by William K. Frankena: 'if a ruler were to boil his subjects in oil, jumping in afterward himself, it would be an injustice, but there would be no inequality of treatment'.[19] J. R. Lucas has suggested that laws of strict liability, while being perfectly general and non-discriminatory, may be unjust on the commutative view as they clearly do not 'give every man his due'.[20]

The rules of just conduct have then to be given some content if they are to function so as to locate unjust and just behaviour. Yet Hayek gives us very little indication of the content of the rules of just conduct. In the *Principles of a Liberal Social Order* he says that the 'injustice to be prevented is the infringement of the protected domain of one's fellow men'.[21] The point is repeated in *The Mirage of Social Justice* and elsewhere in Hayek's writings. The phrase 'protected domain' means, as we have seen, property and the rules of just conduct that protect and preserve property rights. This is, of course, a conception that extends beyond the notion of property as material goods to include personal liberty, freedom of movement and so on.

Beyond this emphasis on a protected domain, and an approving reference to Hume's three fundamental laws of nature ('stability of possession, of its transference by consent, and of the performance of promises'),[22] Hayek does not give us a complete account of what the rules of just conduct should be. There is a suggestion (that seems similar to Nozick's) that there may be a case in justice for 'correcting positions which have been determined by earlier unjust acts or institutions'[23] but he is wary of extending this principle very far since all but the most recent acts of injustice will be difficult to correct.

There is a reason for Hayek's reluctance to elaborate on the substantive content of the rules of just conduct and it lies in his particular methodology. Rules of just conduct emerge through a process of evolution and it is impossible for the human mind to construct all the rules in advance of experience. The only things that can be said about rules relate to existing systems of rules.[24] It would follow from this that the rules of just conduct are known 'negatively'. This means that we are in a better position to say what an injustice is than to say what justice is. A sense of justice can indicate clear breaches of the rules of just conduct but we may not be able to formulate the concept in words.

How do we know which rules are unjust? Hayek recommends the negative test of universalisability.[25] A particular rule can only be shown to be unjust if it cannot be universalised within a general system of rules. Thus the procedure is identical to the method Hayek used to distinguish general rules of law from mere legislation in his account of law in general (see Chapter 5). And the same problems arise here over whether the concept of universalisability can do the job Hayek wants it to do.

The first thing to note is that Hayek is not using the notion in quite the same way as it has been used since its first systematic formulation by Kant. In moral philosophy the method of universalisability is used to demonstrate what moral principles rational individuals would accept if they were ignorant of their present interests. It is suggested by some that the *only* genuine moral principles are those that can be universalised. If 'man' is taken as the appropriate reference group then the universalisability procedure would subject *particular* moral systems and rules to this general criterion, and this may entail a very rationalistic conception of morality.

Now it is clear that Hayek is using a weaker version of universalisability. A rule is to be adjudged just or unjust by the method of 'immanent' criticism,[26] which is a test for its consistency, with the system as a whole. This consistency is not a matter of logic. A judge, for example, in testing a particular rule of the common law is not making a deductive inference from the system as a whole: 'consistency in this connection means that the rules serve the same abstract order of actions and prevent conflict between persons obeying those rules in the kind of circumstances to which they have been adopted'.[27]

While it is true that the reasoning Hayek suggests will produce 'objective' conclusions, conclusions not dictated by particular wills or the outcome of clashes between interest groups, it seems to be the case that Hayek has merely restated the rules of just conduct, derived from his theory of law, as *the principles of justice*. However, most other doctrines of justice that stress the special significance of that concept attempt to show how a particular set of rules may be evaluated by reference to a set of principles of justice. This is how the method of universalisability is normally used. But Hayek's rules of justice may turn out to be, if not as relative as Kelsen's, justice is clearly not the will of the majority or the balance of interest groups, at least not as compelling as some of the traditional natural law conceptions of justice.

Leaving this aside there is still the problem of determining which rules are valid within a given system. Hayek himself concedes that a number of different systems may satisfy the test of negative universalisability but he does not consider seriously enough the possibility of two different rules being equally universalisable within the same system. But this is clearly a possibility if the test for the justice of rules is not one of logical consistency. Furthermore, it may very well be possible to universalise a rule which would be quite unjust by a 'commonsense' view of justice. The procedural rules that Hayek characterises as the rules of justice will need considerably more content if they are to be considered as *the* principles of justice.

Two of the other characteristics of Hayek's rules of justice may be considered before we move on to discuss his rejection of end-state theories. Firstly, the rules of just conduct function typically as prohibitions rather than as positive directions to individuals.[28] Only in rare circumstances can individuals be directed towards specified ends as a consequence of justice. Such circumstances as disasters, famines and catastrophes[29] might entail that an individual perform certain positive duties as a matter of justice but normally the rules of justice, considered both in a moral and legal sense, merely require the individual to refrain from certain courses of action. Secondly, the rules of justice are quite consistent with a wide area of liberty in the sphere of personal morality. This means that the rules of an evolving *cosmos* do not have to embody any particular moral purpose beyond the maintenance of the system itself.

3. THE ATTACK ON DISTRIBUTIVE JUSTICE

The main thrust of Hayek's reasoning on justice has been to refute the ideas of theorists of social justice (we shall use the terms social justice and distributive justice interchangeably). This attack has taken two forms. The first systematic refutation of desert-based distributive justice appeared in *The Constitution of Liberty* where Hayek argued that the attempt to implement social justice would involve the destruction of the market order and the free society. These arguments were repeated in *The Mirage of Social Justice* with the further argument that desert, need, merit or any other ethical end-state criterion have no application to the results of *catallactic* or market process. The phrase 'social justice' is strictly speaking meaningless, it refers to nothing at all, like the word 'witch'.[30]

We normally understand by the word 'desert' that some special property of an individual is worthy of some appropriate reward or punishment. In a liberal society where individuals are considered to be morally responsible for their actions desert is a peculiarly important concept. It locates more or less precisely how actions are to be praised or blamed in accordance with efforts and results. Now while Hayek would accept that in moral contexts outside the sphere of economics words like 'desert' and 'merit' have a perfectly legitimate use, his particularly daring, and some would consider offensive, argument is that in connection with income distribution they have no relevance at all.

It is important to distinguish Hayek's sense of desert or merit (he uses desert and merit interchangeably) from other senses. By merit he means *moral* merit. In matters of income distribution he maintains that the pattern of incomes in a *catallaxy* should not, and indeed in many cases will not, reflect moral merit at all. Some writers, however, mistakenly believe that the only justification for the spread of incomes in a market order lies in the fact that it accords with merit. For Hayek it is an empirical coincidence that this spread may on occasion reflect moral merit in the sense of personal worthiness, effort, skills and so on.[31]

The resulting pattern of incomes in a market order, for Hayek, reflects *value*, and this is quite a different thing from merit in the sense outlined above. The value of a person's services is determined by the impersonal forces of the market and this means that in the *game of catallaxy*[32] earnings may merely reflect luck or ingenuity (for example, in the case of the successful speculator) rather than any semblance of moral merit. In this approach 'material rewards are made to correspond to the value which a person's particular services have to his fellows'.[33] The implication is that no centralised authority can have that intimate knowledge of a person's actions to make them accord to any other value except that determined by the market.

By the same token arguments to the effect that certain people because of the nature of their work should be rewarded at a higher rate than the market are illegitimate. For example, miners are paid high rates because the value of their services to their fellow men is high and not because of the onerous and dangerous nature of their occupation. By the same reasoning other workers who do unpleasant and onerous jobs may be rewarded with relatively low wages because this is, unfortunately for them, the only way they can secure a return for their labour.[34] Furthermore, it may be offensive to popular morality that property speculators and popular singers can gain enormous rewards with apparently little in the way of effort, and therefore moral merit, to recommend them, but there can be no objection to this on *catallactic* grounds.

The point of all this is to show that, for Hayek, no ethical standards of any kind can be applied to situations that are the unintended consequences of human action. Of course, praise and blame can be attached to individuals in the performance of their individual actions, a breach of a general rule is an injustice, but since no one person is responsible for the resulting pattern of incomes in a *catallaxy* this cannot be evaluated by the criterion of social justice. Hayek maintains that if a centralised authority, or one person, were responsible for the resulting distribution of income and wealth then it would be quite likely that terms like 'undeserved' or 'unmerited' could be applied.[35]

It is appropriate to consider here the concept of the marginal productivity of labour as it is clear that Hayek has this, the neoclassical theory of wages, in mind when he talks about income distribution. The marginal productivity of labour theory holds that if, for example, the output of a firm of 100 men is A and the output of the same 100 men plus an additional worker is A plus B, then we can infer that the product of the additional worker is B. In general the theory states that an employer will employ workers up to the point at which the wages of the last man equal his marginal product.

Now it would not be quite correct to interpret Hayek to mean that value, in the context of income distribution, should equal marginal productivity because, as Nozick points out,[36] to make value accord to marginal productivity is to propose a 'patterned' or end-state system of distribution. This is especially important in view of the fact that in complicated productive processes with products emanating from joint and cooperative activities it may be impossible to disentangle precisely the marginal product of one individual. Marginal productivity may then be only one of several, probably unknown, factors that determine the benefits that individuals produce for their fellows. Nevertheless, this will be important as there is a rationale and a purpose to economic activity which is revealed by the market's evaluation of labour.

It should be quite clear now what Hayek's objection to social justice is. First of all, the theorists of social justice presuppose a distinction between production and distribution where none exists. There is not a 'pie' which we can divide up amongst members of society on grounds of merit. A person's earnings merely reflect his contribution to the total output of a *catallaxy* and there is no analytical distinction between production and distribution. The function of a market, therefore, is not to 'distribute' income on grounds of merit or any other criteria but to draw the factors of production into those enterprises where their marginal productivity is highest. As has already been shown it is a signalling device to transmit economic knowledge efficiently and its outcomes are ethically neutral.

Many writers fail to appreciate the inappropriateness of attaching moral value to market processes. J. R. Lucas, for instance, while conceding that social justice has very little application in economic life, and indeed regretting the contemporary obsession with the concept, nevertheless cannot eliminate it from his political vocabulary. He writes that: 'free exchange is not fair exchange' and that although in practice the market price is a 'just' price it is not so in principle because the pursuance of it can lead to a diminution of the collaborative aspect of life.[37] The system of *laissez-faire* (which is not distinguished by Lucas from the market order) is then dismissed as 'unethical'. But the point Hayek is making is not that the resulting distribution is ethical or unethical, it is ethically neutral. Similarly, David Miller, on the one hand asserts that desert means merely what the market distributes but on the other states that: 'the assertion that the economic market accurately rewards desert is quite as vulnerable to empirical refutation as the claim that desert will be rewarded in a "properly organised society"'.[38]

To opt for desert, claims Hayek, is to opt for a system that makes an individual's rewards turn upon the opinion of his fellow men. This can only mean that a society will be turned into a *taxis* with purposes and ends set by centralised authorities. Since there can be no agreement about ends in contrast with means, the result will be an imposed pattern of distribution which will require constant interference with individuals' spontaneous activities in order to maintain the proposed distribution.[39] The market's signalling functions will be obliterated, and if the ends are to be implemented efficiently the direction of labour will be inevitable. It is to be noted that one leading exponent of end-state justice, Brian Barry, implies just this.[40]

Social justice then for Hayek is the justice of the intimate closed society where people's abilities, efforts and merits can be known. In the Great Society, where individuals cannot know more than the immediate consequence of their actions the discipline of the abstract rules of just conduct which apply to an unknown number of future cases, constitute the means which people can agree upon to enable them to pursue their diverse ends.

It is to be noted, however, that Hayek's objections to social justice do in fact turn upon the consequences of the implementation of schemes for social justice and not usually upon the meaninglessness of the doctrine. It may be true or false that the consequences of policies based upon social justice are the direction of labour and ultimately totalitarianism, the evidence so far suggests that a loss of productive efficiency is the most likely outcome, but this does not mean that its adherents are talking nonsense. They may very well accept the loss of efficiency as a price worth paying for the increase in social justice. Furthermore, Hayek himself admits that the concept does have meaning, albeit in the context of a totalitarian society, so that the dispute may not be so much about justice as about 'types' of society.

Furthermore, it is not enough for Hayek to say that people cannot agree upon ends. This may be true but it is also worth pointing out that Hayek's proposition that people can agree upon means is itself an empirical one which may be true or false. The rules of procedural justice may not be regarded by people as *the* principles of justice if they often sanction quite bizarre distributions of income and wealth. Irving Kristol has a point when he suggests that for all Hayek's ingenuity he has not demonstrated that the market order, as he describes it, can generate the system of moral values needed to sustain it.[41] And that Hayek believes that capitalism requires a system of moral values is beyond doubt. He constantly stresses that the notion of individual moral responsibility is essential for a free society,[42] yet his somewhat spartan concept of justice may well serve to undermine that responsibility.

Hayek is naturally interested in the question of why it happens that the radical concept of justice should have such a hold over western intellectual opinion. Its influence is undeniable; people who would not regard themselves as socialists, least of all Marxists, nevertheless often make social justice an object of government policy, on the assumption that it has some content in the way of redistribution by taxation, or the satisfaction of some supposed clearly demonstrable need.

Hayek has put forward a number of explanations for the phenomenal popularity of the concept. The first is envy.[43] While it is true that a lot of talk about social justice may only be a rationalisation for envy it is difficult to imagine all socialist reformers being motivated by envy. In fact, Hayek has repeatedly stressed that his refutation of socialist and other collectivist arguments in no way depends on an assessment of their motives in a moral sense. While it is true that some individuals are genuinely envious in the sense that they would prefer a lower standard of living for the worst-off, provided that there were no substantial differences between rich and poor, to a situation where, although everybody including the worst-off was richer, this situation was characterised by significant inequality, most proponents of social justice seem to believe that a more egalitarian distribution of wealth is consistent with a higher standard of living than is possible under alternative economic and social principles.

Hayek makes very little of envy but concentrates on two more explanations of the popularity of social justice. The first is the argument that the principle of social justice is normally espoused by groups who are descending in the social scale.[44] These groups are likely to seek government aid to protect their positions from the forces of the market under the anodyne principle of social justice. There are plenty of examples of workers whose skills fail to yield the return they once did because of technological innovation; the history of the Industrial Revolution is often written as a tale of social injustices meted out to displaced groups of workers.

Hayek maintains that such outcomes are an inevitable part of the *game of catallaxy*. The market order cannot protect all interests, all it can do is to guarantee the application of the rules of just conduct to all participants, and we cannot predict in advance which particular group will benefit from the market process. Furthermore, Hayek claims disadvantaged groups at particular moments in time have no grounds in justice for complaint since the rules of the market order enabled them at one time to secure the advantages, achieved at the cost of the losses of other groups, they are now about to lose. One cannot, says Hayek, support the market order only when it is in your interests to do so.

It is undoubtedly true that groups on the brink of losing a favoured position because of economic progress do occasionally appeal to the concept of social justice purely to protect their interest. But it is something of a discredit to the concept to link it with this pattern of behaviour. Many exponents of the doctrine may still maintain that there ought to be some aid for groups who lose out through economic progress without invoking the principle of social justice. It seems slightly disingenuous of Hayek to link social justice with the selfish interests of sectional groups.

The second of Hayek's explanations of the rise of social justice is more interesting. He says that the demand for a system of remuneration based upon subjective views of merit is associated with the rise in the number of salaried employees and the consequent decline in the self-employed.[45] Those employed in large-scale organisations are likely to be used to having their salaries determined by merit because of the difficulty of measuring individual contributions to a large collaborative enterprise. However, this merit-based reward will bear a close relationship to market values in the long-run, as these large-scale organisations will be competing with one another, but the participants in the internal operations of the organisation will not have the same experience of the market's evaluation of their services that the self-employed have. The self-employed are, says Hayek, in their daily activities made constantly aware of the impersonal mechanisms of the market in determining the values of particular services.[46]

Now this presents something of a difficulty for Hayek. Undoubtedly, the emergence of the large-scale enterprise is part of the spontaneous evolution of the market order yet it would appear to be accompanied by a set of values which are not merely inimical to the market order but are agents of its destruction. It would seem to be the case that as the market evolves it creates a moral order antithetical to its further evolution in a spontaneous manner. This is the same problem alluded to above, that of generating a value system that sustains and develops the *cosmos* itself. Hayek, on many occasions, laments the apparent passing of the individualist market order but does not really examine adequately the value system needed to sustain it.

4. HAYEK AND RAWLS

We mentioned earlier in this chapter that no discussion of the theory of justice could be regarded as complete without some consideration of John Rawls's *A Theory of Justice*. While in no way endeavouring to add to the already enormous output of critical literature from the Rawls industry a brief description of his ideas is imperative if we are to locate Hayek's place accurately on the contemporary intellectual map. A precise description of the intellectual relationship between Hayek and Rawls is difficult because opinions differ so widely as to the political import of Rawls's ideas. While most critics have identified a basic egalitarianism in the structure of *A Theory of Justice*, for reasons the nature of which we will explore below, others have suggested that the argument is no more than an elegant rationalisation of liberal capitalism. An extreme exponent of this latter interpretation is Brian Barry who claims that Rawls, in his social theory, is a lineal descendant of Herbert Spencer.[47] And Hayek himself regards Rawls's doctrines as not egalitarian at all and suggests they reveal a definite similarity with his own ideas. The difference between Hayek and Barry is that while Hayek approves of the affinity Rawls has with the general capitalist tradition, for Barry this is a reason for serious and sustained criticism.

What follows is then a brief description of Rawls's ideas and a comparison between these and Hayek's views.

Rawls attempts to show that under certain clearly specified conditions rational individuals would choose a particular set of principles to guide and restrain them in their actions. These principles are *the* principles of justice, that is, they are identical with our commonsense notions of justice.

The specified conditions are covered by the suggestion that rational individuals should deliberate upon these principles behind a 'veil of ignorance', this means that individuals are assumed to be ignorant of their special interests and are ignorant of any characteristics and abilities which may be rewarded in any future society. For example, a person will be obviously aware of the fact that he has a white skin but will not know if whites or blacks, or any other race, are to be privileged in any future society. Therefore, it would be rational to choose a *non-discrimination* rule. Such men are capable of following moral rules, they are not pure egoists, but will only choose those rules that maximise their primary goods—liberty, opportunity, income and wealth, and self-respect.[48] Furthermore, they are not envious, they wish to maximise their advantages and are not concerned about the position of the best-off in a future society as long as they can be in a better position than any alternative. They are also risk-averse, this means that they will not, for example, gamble on the possibility of being a slave-holder if that involves them in the slightest chance of being a slave.[49]

From this description of the imaginary 'original position' (his version of the state of nature concept in classical social contract theory) Rawls hopes to demonstrate by deductive reasoning what principles would be chosen to govern behaviour in future social and economic systems. The hypothetical agreement would therefore be unanimous and the principles chosen properly universalisable. The principles chosen, Rawls maintains, are the principles of justice as understood by commonsense morality. Rawls's methodology is therefore a full-fledged piece of 'moral geometry'; the relationship between the conditions of the 'original position' and the principles chosen is a logical one. Questions of justice then turn not upon interests, claims or needs of individuals but on principles that would be adopted by rational individuals to govern their behaviour on the assumption that they are ignorant of these interests, claims and needs. The principles that would be chosen are as follows:

(1) Each person is to have an equal right to the most extensive basic liberty compatible with a similar liberty for others.
(2) Social and economic inequalities are to be arranged so that they are both
     (a) to the greatest benefit of the least advantaged and
     (b) attached to offices and positions open to all under conditions of fair equality of opportunity.[50]

Both principles (1) and (2) and the two principles within principle (2) are arranged in lexical order. If two principles are arranged in lexical order this means that one has an absolute priority over the other. Thus in Rawls's case this means that the equal liberty principle, in practice an individual's fundamental constitutional rights, takes precedence over any economic advantages derived from the second principle. Thus a rational individual would not approve of a system which allowed a constitutional equality to be exchanged for an improvement in the economic wellbeing of the worst-off. By the same reasoning principle (2b) is superior to principle (2a). I follow here Rawls's slightly confusing way of setting out the principles.

Without going into the validity of Rawls's deduction of these principles it is worth making some comments on the nature of them. Like Hayek, Rawls is concerned to refute utilitarianism. The principles chosen would not be utilitarian because no rational individual would opt for a system in which losses of the worst-off individuals could be compensated for by gains of the better-off. Individuals are not interested in maximising a sum of pleasures but in producing principles of justice.

The aspect which has aroused most interest is the principle that says inequalities are only justified if they are to the advantage of the worst-off in a society. Rawls maintains that a 'maximin' strategy[51] on the part of rational individuals produces this principle which he calls the 'difference principle'. Individuals in a state of ignorance, and being risk-averse, would opt for a rule that was to the benefit of the least advantaged just in case they turned out to be in the least advantaged group.

Now it is important to note what is going on here. Rawls presupposes the total assets of a society constitute a common pool which is to be shared according to rational principles. The principles of justice consist of an agreement to regard the distribution of natural talents as a common asset and to share in the benefits of this distribution.[52] It is obvious from this that nobody is *entitled* to their holdings, or even their natural talents, but that these have to be regarded as a common asset and distributed according to the principles of distributive justice. It would appear that Rawls justifies this assumption on the ground that natural assets are valuable insofar as they are parts of collaborative, social enterprises. This would seem to indicate a clear differentiation between production and distribution, a differentiation heavily criticised by Hayek.

But Rawls has another assumption which Hayek has had cause to criticise in other writers. This is the assumption of an hypothetical equality amongst individuals, all departures from which have to be rationally justified. 'All social values—liberty and opportunity, income and wealth, and the bases of self-respect—are to be distributed equally unless an unequal undistribution of any, or all, of these values is to everyone's advantage.'[53] When the phrase 'everyone's advantage' is modified we get the complete Rawlsian *patterned* or end-state principle of justice that social inequalities are justified if and only if they are to the benefit of the *least advantaged*.

If this maximin principle is a patterned, basically egalitarian, principle, why should Hayek say that it is similar to his own *unpatterned* theory? The answer lies in the fact that although maximin looks egalitarian, in practice it is quite likely to produce highly inegalitarian outcomes. For the principle permits any inequality between rich and poor provided that the position of the poorest is better than it would be under an egalitarian system. Furthermore, Rawls accepts the validity of marginal productivity theory so that a market in labour (which Rawls thinks is possible under capitalist and socialist regimes) is required to draw the greatest talents into their most efficient uses.[54] Since Rawls denies the possibility of making interpersonal comparisons based upon cardinal utility (one cannot compare the utilities of different individuals as there is no common, objective measuring-rod) the resulting distribution of incomes can take any form, providing of course that the worst-off gain.

Two other factors point to a basic similarity between Rawls and Hayek. Firstly, they both reject the application of (moral) desert to income distribution. Rawls distinguishes between legitimate expectations (what men are entitled to under the rules of the social practice) and intrinsic worth (or desert). He says that a just scheme answers to what men are entitled to, it satisfies their legitimate expectations as founded upon social institutions, but what they are entitled to is in no way dependent on their worth or merit. This is very much in line with what Hayek has to say about the results of the *game of catallaxy*.

The second factor is that Hayek, both in *The Constitution of Liberty* and in the *Mirage of Social Justice*, does suggest that the justification of capitalism lies in its tendency to raise the incomes of the worst-off. In the former book he says: 'the existence of groups ahead of the rest is clearly to the advantage of those who are behind', and also suggests that as long as the scale is continuous from top to bottom the inequalities therein are bound to raise the position of the worst-off.[55] This, and similar points, are even more emphatically put in the latter book where he suggests that it would be rational to choose a society where one's position was determined by accident or chance but whose general rules provided for anyone, selected at random, to improve his life prospects more than in any alternative; for example, an egalitarian order. And Hayek notes that the tendency of capitalism over the last two hundred years has been to generate the wealth which has tended to raise the income of the lowest groups more than the relatively higher ones.[56]

Yet it is important to stress the differences between Hayek and Rawls. Rawls's theory is a theory of distributive justice which picks out a particular *pattern*, the one that maximises the wellbeing of the worst-off, as *the* just distribution. Apart from saying that capitalism tends to favour the poorer, Hayek, when talking about welfare, says that in a market order those who cannot earn a satisfactory income by the process of free exchange should be paid an additional income to bring them up to a satisfactory level. But it would appear that this has nothing to do with justice—it is not owed to them as a consequence of a general rule of just conduct.

Furthermore, there is something of the constructivist rationalist about Rawls. His approach is essentially that of the 'social contract' school that hoped to deduce political rules from hypothetical contracts made in the absence of law and government; an approach heavily criticised by Hayek in the past. Whereas Rawls seems to think that the fundamental rules of a free society can be determined geometrically Hayek believes that such rules are stumbled upon through experience and, indeed, can never be known in their entirety. Nevertheless, whatever their methodological differences it is undeniably true that a Hayekian society does resemble a Rawlsian society much more closely than any conceivable alternative. The crucial point to stress here is that just as Hayek's rules of just conduct are sets of abstract rules to deal with an *unknown* number of future cases, Rawls's principles of justice are designed for men who do not have knowledge of what abilities will be rewarded and interests satisfied in a future social system, and who therefore will require rules that maximise their advantages in all hypothetical future cases.

5. EQUALITY AND THE WELFARE STATE

We cannot regard our discussion of Hayek's theory of justice as complete without some consideration of his views on the equality principle and on the welfare state.

Whereas the conventional social democratic theory of justice presupposes that equality is the *good*, departures from which are agreed to reluctantly and with elaborate justification, Hayek on occasions proclaims the virtues of inequality itself. In a free society the emergence of inequality is not only inevitable but highly desirable. In regard to this last point Hayek means that the 'spillover effects' from the existence of pockets of private wealth are significant.[57] These private sources of wealth constitute barriers against the ever-encroaching power of the state in social and liberal democracies and function as essential sources of innovation and experiment in science and the arts. Many things now enjoyed as mass consumption products originated as minority tastes. The need for some privileged groups to experiment with different ways of living would be as great in a socialist, planned society as in a Great Society, says Hayek. The virtue of private pockets of wealth in the latter is that their existence makes such experimentation possible independently of political privilege. Hayek even makes the slightly bizarre suggestion that in the absence of such a class there would be some justification for distributing at random large amounts of wealth in order to create one.[58] This suggestion is not explored elsewhere in his writings; indeed it would be unwise for Hayek to do so for it constitutes a kind of inegalitarian's patterned or end-state distribution.

Hayek is not prepared to say how much inequality the spillover effects of private wealth would sanction. There is a problem here that arises out of his methodology of the social sciences because the Austrian, anti-scientistic approach would automatically rule out any possibility of quantifying the effects of inequality. Strictly speaking, therefore, since Hayek is committed to a qualitative judgement on this issue, the level of justifiable inequality is virtually unlimited. This is especially so as any moral judgement to the effect that the demands of liberty may be modified at the margin by an appeal to equality as a substantive principle, the procedure favoured by the political and ethical pluralists, is ruled out by Hayek.

Hayek is on firmer ground with his objections to attempted impositions of equality by law. While he is well-disposed towards the natural, social equality that exists, for example, in America, and might even favour some measures towards equality provided they

involve no loss to liberty, he suggests that the wholesale implementation of *material* equality is destructive of a free society and of the
rule of law. This is because naturally unequal people can only order
their lives by general, impartial and equal laws. The attempt
however to make naturally unequal people equal must entail that
people are treated very differently by the law; for example, the
talented would be treated differently to the less talented, and this
would destroy the generality and predictability of the rules of just
conduct.

Furthermore, if the equality of opportunity doctrine is taken
seriously it would mean the destruction of the family and all other
supposedly 'arbitrary impediments' to the establishment of a fairly
equal starting point in life for everybody.[59] Not only are the
consequences of this doctrine destructive of liberty but the idea is
itself incoherent. A rigorous application of it would produce much
more rigid inequalities than those that exist at present. Hayek adds
here the point that the inequalities produced by the application of
this doctrine would be much more resented, precisely because they
appear so reasonable, than those produced, say, by the accident of
birth.[60]

The welfare state in Britain has been the means whereby social
justice and some equality have been implemented. Now it must not
be supposed that Hayek is opposed to welfare; the thing that
disturbs him is the form that it has taken in Britain and other
western democracies. This has been in the manner of the collective
production and consumption of certain services, for example,
health, housing, and pensions. The semi-articulated principle
behind this approach is the 'need' principle.

It is assumed that people are poor because they lack certain
tangible goods that all individuals ought to have for a satisfactory
life. It is further assumed that these needs can be identified and
measured, and that the state ought, as a matter of justice provide
them. The consequences of this are 'universality' in the distribution
of welfare ('everybody ought to have a certain level of health care'
etc.), greater discretionary power to ministers and officials, inefficiency in that the poorest do not often benefit from the policies,
and high taxation to pay for the system. The main response by
Hayek is that there is no identifiable 'need' in individuals which
ought to be satisfied as a matter of justice. The problems of poverty
are best dealt with by cash transfers rather than collective, uniform
consumption of 'welfare' goods because at the very least this will

allow individuals freedom of choice in expenditure.[61]

One final argument of Hayek on justice and equality must be briefly considered. These principles have been used to sanction the seemingly ineluctable growth of progressive income tax this century. Hayek maintains that this may have been originally introduced as an attempt to make those able to pay more shoulder the burden of taxes, but suggests that its main purpose now is to redistribute wealth between rich and poor.[62] Hayek objects that as well as being in breach of the rule of law such a system confers upon government the right of virtually unlimited appropriation. The principle of progressive income tax offends against the 'equal pay for equal work' principle in that those who produce the most are penalised more than those who produce the least, it enables the majority to dictate to the minority, it misdirects resources into non-productive areas (accountants become specialists in tax avoidance), and by slowing up the formation of capital it prevents newcomers coming into the market.[63]

It is clear that Hayek presents a formidable battery of arguments against the two concepts, social justice and equality, that have dominated western democratic thinking throughout most of this century. Not all of the arguments are of the same type—some centre on a conceptual analysis of the various principles and some centre on an inquiry into the consequences of basing policy on them. On the latter point Hayek is elaborating the basic implications of his general methodology. In many arguments against socialism, for example, he would maintain that he is not disputing these values but merely pointing out that the implementation of socialist methods involves, as a matter of scientific demonstration, certain consequences that would be regarded as unacceptable by socialists themselves. But many countries have followed the principles of social justice and equality and have not experienced totalitarianism or the destruction of the market order, although the effects on efficiency are clearly noticeable. Yet we can be sure that empirical evidence is not crucial, quantification plays only a small role in social science for Hayek, for we can never know in the sense of being able to measure it, what is the precise effect of implementing certain policies. Because so many of Hayek's judgements about the effects of certain policies are qualitative there is room for considerable disagreement over social policy.

8 Economics and Economic Policy

I. HAYEK'S CAREER AS AN ECONOMIST

Up to and during the Second World War Hayek was known only as a technical economist concerned with the rather specialised areas of monetary theory, the theory of the trade cycle and the theory of capital. While some of his work in those fields did have policy implications he was not concerned with economic policy as such, and only after the publication of the polemical *The Road to Serfdom* did he begin the long and arduous task of integrating economic theory and economic policy into a general theory of society. The economic writings of the 1930s are, however, important not only because of their place in Hayek's intellectual system but also because they loom large in the fierce debates over the economy that characterised that era. The Austrian theory of the business cycle, of which Hayek was the leading expositor, was at one time the dominant explanation of the cause of industrial fluctuations and naturally the theory had some policy implications, albeit of a fairly negative kind, as to how such fluctuations might be avoided, or at least their worst effects mitigated. Indeed, Hayek's own university at the time, the London School of Economics, was associated with a particular policy for coping with the Great Depression, from 1929 to 1933, a policy of non-intervention that largely derived from Austrian teaching.

For the purposes of this exposition of Hayek's ideas I shall be concerned primarily with those aspects of Hayek's economic writings that have a bearing on policy and general methodological issues. I shall therefore say very little about Hayek's contribution to *pure* economic theory, which is to be found in his aptly titled *The Pure Theory of Capital*. It might be helpful to explain more fully the various types of economic theorising that Hayek has engaged in over the past forty years to make clear this distinction.

The Pure Theory of Capital belongs to the body of equilibrium theory which is concerned with the nature of economic relationships undisturbed by disequilibriating phenomena, money being one clear example of such phenomena. The analysis of the capital problem therefore assumes away the kind of difficulty posed in the real world by the fact that people wish to *hold* money. Since Hayek's equilibrium position excludes this the analysis is made entirely in terms of the 'real' factors that determine economic relationships; thus the rate of interest will represent not the price of loans—that is determined by the market for loans in a money economy—but will represent the difference between the prices of the factors of production and the expected prices of the products.[1] But although Hayek's equilibrium concept is a purely theoretical construction that is not intended to function as a causal explanation of events in any actual economic world, it must not be confused with the orthodox concept of general equilibrium found in the neoclassical paradigm. The distinction between Hayek's fictitious equilibrium and the conventional notion of a general, stationary equilibrium was made in Chapter 3 and can be elaborated here. The criticism made by the Austrians of the stationary equilibrium was that it removed all incentives to economic change. According to Hayek, the idea of equilibrium as a stationary state is peculiarly inappropriate for the study of capital because capital theory is about economic change. Capital problems are about what kinds of equipment will be used and what kinds of changes will be made in the capital structure, whereas stationary equilibrium theory assumes that the same stock of instruments will be constantly reproduced.[2] Furthermore, the stationary state concept cannot be used to explain the process by which this state was brought about. Also, the notion of savings and investment implies that individuals will be doing different things in the future from what they are doing in the present.

It is for these reasons that Hayek speaks of a non-stationary, but nevertheless fictitious, equilibrium which accounts for the way that individuals adjust their plans through time, not because they continue to do the same things they have done in the past but because they correctly foresee changes in the actions of others. The means by which all the various actions are harmonised is, of course, the market process. This coordinates the dispersed knowledge of individuals *as if* the arrangement were the product of a single, directing mind. One further observation needs to be made, which connects Hayek's theory of capital with his general methodology, and that is his emphasis on capital *not* as an homogeneous mass which can be observed and quantified but as an arrangement of complementary goods that reveals an order. It is an arrangement or order of non-permanent resources which contributes to the maintenance of income at a particular level. Needless to say, this order is a mental reconstruction and not a measurable physical entity.

The other main branch of economic theory that has concerned Hayek is that which explains departures from this fictitious equilibrium, and this is the theory of the trade cycle. The phenomenon of the trade cycle, the regular and seemingly ineluctable ups and downs of business activity, poses a particular problem for economists who stress the automatic, self-adjusting mechanism of a *catallaxy*. This is not merely a theoretical problem but also one that has crucial policy implications, for the proponents of a *dirigiste* form of economic organisation have frequently pointed to the existence of the business cycle as evidence of a deeper, inherent instability within the capitalist system. In fact, Hayek's unshakeable, indeed *a priori*, faith in the market system has survived two highly significant threats to its stability, the Great Depression of the 1930s and the inflation of the 1970s (there have been other threats if the great inflation in Europe in the 1920s is included). The causes of these disturbances have been for Hayek the influences of money or government, or more precisely, the combined effects of government and money. It would not be too much of an exaggeration to say that Hayek's contribution to the theory of economic policy has been solely to demonstrate that it is possible to construct a rational economic order which minimises the maladjustments caused by monetary and governmental institutions. Money and government are things that civilised man cannot live without, yet living with them can be a painful business, as experience of the past few decades has clearly shown. The problem of limiting the influence of government will be discussed in the final chapter, while the problem of money, and related economic policy areas, will be the primary concern of this chapter.

It would be true to say that Hayek's ideas on the problem of money have undergone a dramatic change in the last three or four years. While throughout the 1930s he stressed the disequilibriating influence of money, and warned of the dangers that might result from the government's control of the monetary instrument, he never denied the necessity of a government monopoly of money. He was mainly concerned with suggestions as to how the adverse effects of this essential monopoly might be mitigated. There were some economists who did believe that the institution of money could be left to the market but as late as 1960 he insisted that the spontaneous forces of the *catallaxy* could not generate a satisfactory form of money.[3] He gave three reasons for this view: firstly, that money at all times is the most important factor affecting prices and production; secondly, that modern monetary systems pose special problems because they are based on credit; and thirdly, the post-war rise in public expenditure has greatly increased the influence of government on the monetary system. In an illuminating phrase Hayek described money as a kind of 'loose joint',[4] in an otherwise self-adjusting market system, which requires some kind of regulation if business fluctuations are to be ironed out. Yet as recently as 1976 Hayek, after a life time's study of the most efficient ways of regulating money, has concluded that such regulation is impossible by governments and claimed that only the forces of self-interest operating through the market can now provide financial stability. In the area of money, at least, Hayek has despaired of the possibility of binding political authorities by strict rules. It is important, therefore, to trace the evolution of Hayek's ideas towards this dramatic conclusion.[5]

2. THE AUSTRIAN THEORY OF THE TRADE CYCLE

Hayek's first published work in English on the theory of the trade cycle was *Prices and Production*, published in 1931. This was followed in 1933 by the publication of *Monetary Theory and the Trade Cycle*,[6] a translation of some earlier articles originally written in German. It is important to stress the immediate economic background to these early theoretical writings. The western liberal democracies were in the throes of the Great Depression in which a catastrophic drop in output, prices and employment threatened not just the economic stability of these countries but also the whole social fabric. It must be remembered that this was not just a recession following inevitably upon the boom of the late 1920s, but a quite different type of economic phenomenon in that it seemed highly unlikely that the recovery would come from the normal processes of adjustment. In retrospect it seems unfortunate that Hayek's theoretical work should appear at this time since the explanation he was propounding seems more appropriate for less dramatic circumstances, and critics have always said that the policy implications that followed from his explanation could not have succeeded. Nevertheless, Hayek himself thought that his theory was relevant to the situation and, indeed, emphasised that it was designed to explain why the normal processes of adjustment were failing to work. Furthermore, the London School of Economics, where he was Tooke Professor of Economic Science and Statistics, became, in a sense, the head-quarters of the Austrian theory of the trade cycle, and was associ-ated with a policy of general non-intervention by government in the economy. It was rivalled to some extent by Cambridge where, under the influence of Keynes, more radical theories of active government involvement in the form of contra-cyclical economic policies were being formulated.[7]

In fact it was at this time that Hayek's intellectual controversy with Keynes was at its most fierce and *not* after the publication in 1936 of the latter's *General Theory of Employment, Interest and Money*,[8] as is commonly thought (although Hayek has been a prominent opponent of the post-war Keynesian economic policies). The reason for this is rather curious. Hayek had devoted considerable time and effort on two articles in criticism of Keynes's *A Treatise on Money*, published in 1930,[9] only to be informed by Keynes that he had since abandoned the views expressed in that two-volume work.[10] Hayek says that at the time of the publication of the *General Theory* he did not subject it to a critical review because he fully expected its author to retract the bulk of its content just as he had done with *A Treatise on Money*. Hence Hayek's critical comments on the *General Theory* are scattered among a number of his works and are nowhere systemati-cally presented. Although Keynes was concerned with similar problems in *A Treatise on Money*, indeed both he and Hayek started from foundations laid by Wicksell, he reached very different conclusions. But I shall not be much concerned with the differences in this area, since they are of historical interest only, and will concentrate on the exposition of Hayek's views.

There are a number of theories which attempt to explain the trade cycle but they can, for convenience, be divided into theories that say that cyclical patterns are caused by 'real' factors in the economy, for example, new inventions, changes in investment and consumption habits, or sudden waves of optimism or pessimism on the part of businessmen, and those that maintain that monetary factors, changes in the supply of credit, bring these about. The

Austrian theory, first developed by Mises, is a monetary theory, though of a special kind. While monetary disturbances *cause* the movement away from equilibrium, and prevent an automatic adjustment, real factors *constitute* the trade cycle.[11] This means that the course of the cycle is characterised by important changes in the structure of production, changes brought about initially by monetary influences. It is the fact of money that makes formal general equilibrium analysis inappropriate for the study of the cycle because in this analysis money plays no causal role in the determination of economic phenomena. Nevertheless, Hayek's theory is a deductive, *a priori* theory which involves the following through of the logical implications of the one causal factor, money, in the disequilibriating process; and he is especially critical of the merely quantitative studies of business cycle phenomena which provide no theoretical explanation.

Hayek starts his analysis from an equilibrium position with the assumptions of full employment, no unused resources and completely flexible prices. This procedure in itself invited criticism since the experience of the trade cycle belied these assumptions, but he maintained that it was necessary for the analysis to take this form in order to explain the deviations from this initial position. In fact, a later work, *Profits, Interest and Investment*,[12] presented a not-dissimilar analysis from rather different assumptions. In the earlier versions, however, the emphasis is on the way that money causes changes in relative prices that could not occur in a situation of static equilibrium. These changes consist of disproportionalities in the prices of consumers' goods and producers' goods.

It is changes in relative prices that are crucial, and which, says Hayek, are concealed by the traditional quantity theory of money. This theory has always been concerned only with changes in price levels that are brought about by changes in the supply of money. All prices are assumed to move uniformly up or down in accordance with increases or decreases of the supply of money. Money is assumed to be neutral in its effect on the structure of production. While Hayek has insisted on the basic truth of the elementary quantity theory,[13] and has blamed recurring inflations on the neglect of it, he has always argued that money cannot be neutral in the understanding of the trade cycle. It is, he says, quite false to suggest that money affects prices and production only if the general price level changes.

His criticism here entails the rejection of price stabilisation as a policy aim. If, for example, in a growing economy prices are to be kept stable there will have to be an increase in the supply of money, but it is argued that this increase will not affect all prices uniformly but will bring about relative price changes. This is because the important issue is that of the particular point at which the additional money is injected into the system. This will determine the relative demand for consumers' goods and producers' goods. One example should make this general point clear. The boom in the American economy in the 1920s was thought to be especially beneficial for future economic progress precisely because it was characterised by a stable price level. Indeed most economists thought that America had embarked upon a course of virtually assured prosperity.[14] But Hayek at the time suggested that this had been brought about by an increase in investment that could not be sustained in the long run. The stability of the general price level had concealed the underlying disequilibrium.[15]

It should also be noted at this point that Hayek's criticism of what he calls the naive quantity theory is an example of his general, methodologically-based distrust of macroeconomic variables. From his earliest days as an economist he was sceptical of the usefulness of regarding magnitudes like the general price level as determinants of economic behaviour. It is not these absolute totals that influence individuals. The causal factors that influence people are always relative prices of goods and services and it is these that cannot be so easily observed and quantified. Therefore, in trade cycle theory it is misleading to direct attention to the *value* of money as such. What is important, however, is to study the role of the price mechanism in determining the production of consumers' goods and producers' goods and here it is always relative prices and values that are crucial.

Hayek's monetary theory of the trade cycle builds on the distinction made by Wicksell between the natural rate of interest, or equilibrium rate as it is sometimes called, and the market or money rate of interest. The natural rate of interest acts so as to secure an equilibrium between the production of consumers' goods and producers' goods. In the absence of monetary disturbances the amount individuals *save* will constitute the supply of loanable funds available for entrepreneurs to invest, and the price paid by entrepreneurs for the use of these funds is the rate of interest. The rate of interest in an economy is ultimately determined by the time preferences of individual economic agents. The idea of time preference expresses the relationship between consumption and saving for individuals. A high time preference means that an individual prefers present consumption to the future rewards of saving, while a low time preference indicates that an individual is prepared to defer present consumption and save. The time preferences of all individuals determine the natural rate of interest which reflects exactly the consumption-savings ratio of the public. Savings and investment are identical because there will always be a rate of interest which will equate the demand for loanable funds by entrepreneurs with the supply of savings made available by the public. If the natural rate of interest falls this means that time preferences have changed, the public are saving more therefore more funds are available for capital investment, and conversely, if it rises this means that less savings are available for investment. The natural rate of interest will also change in response to changes in demand by entrepreneurs. The problem is that the banking system, by increasing credit, lowers the market rate of interest on loans below the natural rate, thus making a greater supply of funds available for investment than is actually warranted by the voluntary savings of individuals. This greater diversion of extra funds towards investment than would occur in the absence of monetary disturbances is known as 'forced saving'.[16]

While recognising the crucial importance of the distinction between the natural rate of interest and the market rate the Austrian analysis went beyond that of Wicksell. Hayek claimed that Wicksell was mistaken in thinking that if the rate of interest equated the demand and supply of voluntary savings, if the market rate were not allowed to diverge from the natural rate, money would be neutral towards prices. According to this theory the banks ought not to increase the amount of money in circulation because this would bring about a divergence in the two rates of interest. Unfortunately, if the price level is to be stabilised in circumstances of increasing productivity then the supply of money must be increased to prevent a fall in prices. Thus, against Wicksell, Hayek argued that the banks could either keep the demand for investment funds in line with the supply of savings or they could stabilise the price level, but they could not do both at once.[17] If the supply of money is increased to stabilise the price level this is bound to have some effect on the structure of production because the doctrine of 'forced saving' entails that more funds will be directed towards investment goods than would occur in the moneyless economy of the static general equilibrium. It is this that causes the maladjustments that constitute the real factors in the Austrian theory of the trade cycle. Before the effect of the maladjustment can be fully understood, however, it is necessary to say something on the Austrian theory of the structure of production.

This theory explains the working of the capitalist economy in terms of the length of the production process. The structure of production is divided into stages with consumers' goods at the nearest stage of consumption and producers' goods at much further stages away from consumption. As an economy becomes more capitalistic it employs more 'roundabout'[18] methods of production. The roundabout methods take longer to bring goods to the point of consumption but will yield ultimately a greater quantity of consumers' goods. As the production process is lengthened a greater amount of consumers' goods will be available. But there will also be intermediate goods; these come in between final consumption goods and the factors of production (land, labour and capital). Now to sustain a continuous output of a given supply of consumers' goods the amount of intermediate goods must grow with the length of the roundabout processes of production.

The transition to more capitalistic methods of production will occur if the total demand for producers' goods increases relatively to the demand for consumers' goods. This transition can come about in two ways, by an increase in voluntary saving, that is, if individuals' time preferences change so that less is consumed, or if more funds are made available by the banking system to finance the lengthening of the production process. If there is an increase in voluntary saving then the longer processes can be sustained precisely because there will not be an increase in consumption at the nearer stages; there will have been a change in the distribution of demand between consumers' goods and producers' goods.

In the second case, however, where the transition to more capitalistic methods has been brought about by an increase in credit from the banking system, the longer processes cannot be sustained. This is because time preferences will not have changed and the increased incomes earned in the longer processes will be spent on consumers' goods and because, in the transition to roundabout methods, there will be proportionately less consumers' goods available. There will be therefore a switch back to the shorter methods to meet the increased consumers' demand. But the use of a larger proportion of the original means of production for the production of the intermediate goods which are required in the roundabout methods of production requires a retrenchment of consumers' demand. The crisis comes when the injection of additional credit ends, and the longer processes cannot be financed.

The crisis will result in unemployment as the economy has to adjust to the sudden switch to shorter methods of production. There will therefore be processes that will have to be written off because they are no longer profitable. A superficial view of the crisis would be that it is characterised by a surplus of capital equipment but the reverse would be the truer picture. There is, in fact, a scarcity of capital because the investments in the longer processes are normally highly specific, they can only be used for a limited range of activities, and the non-specific goods have been switched back to the shorter methods. Further, it will no longer be profitable to produce the intermediate goods required to complement the longer investments to maintain output. The existence of unused capital does not therefore imply an abundance of capital. Capital cannot easily be switched from one use to another because the production process is a system of complementary goods and if vital intermediate goods are not available, as they will not be in a depression, then plant and equipment at the higher stages will lie idle.

From this it follows that the problem of depression in the economy is not under-consumption, or lack of effective demand, which was, and still is, a popular interpretation of periods of prolonged recession, but the very reverse, over-consumption. An over-consumption brought about by the injection of credit into the system leading to an over-extension of the production process which could not be sustained given the present ratio of consumption to saving. What would be required to effect a normal adjustment would be an increase in saving which would make available enough investible funds to bring the higher stage processes back into use. It is, of course, clear that the expansion of credit, which lowers the market rate of interest below the natural rate, cannot be continued indefinitely. It will be considerably shortened if a country is on the gold standard or has some other device for maintaining the value of the currency. Nevertheless, the expansion of credit that can be effected is, for Hayek, entirely responsible for the distortions and malinvestments that occur in a slump and which could not occur in the moneyless world of static equilibrium. The time to start worrying about the business cycle is in the boom itself, not the depression, which is when action is usually taken. The course of the trade cycle hampers the spontaneous operation of the price mechanism in its determination of the way the various producers' goods will be used along the stages of production.

The policy implications of this analysis must now be considered. If the belief in the self-regulating properties of the *catallaxy* is to be sustained then it is to be expected that Hayek's view would be that very little that can be done in the way of government action to iron out industrial fluctuations. In general, his view is that the malinvestments ought to be liquidated through the normal market process and central intervention to prevent this is to be eschewed. The worst possible policy would be to stimulate consumer demand by monetary methods, since it was excess consumer demand that precipitated the crisis and made inevitable the shortening of the production process. He considers the possibility that, since it was a scarcity of capital that constituted the depression, banks might be encouraged to grant credit for producers' goods, since the shrinkage of the capital structure may have gone further than was necessary, but doubts that the banks could keep the expansion within the necessary limits.[19] There is very little that monetary policy can do to mitigate a depression which will not at the same time sow the seeds of future maladjustment; and Hayek maintains that, although the root of the problem is the modern system of banking, attempts to manage the currency would be self-defeating and he recommends no change. He obviously has in mind here stabilisation policies that aim to prevent a fall in prices during a depression. In fact, he sees a price fall as not only harmless but essential if the price mechanism is to play its full role in allocating resources. Of course, Hayek's model presupposed that all prices were flexible whereas in the real world one price, that of labour, has always been notoriously inflexible and Hayek was well aware that the rigidity of wages was the major obstacle to a spontaneous adjustment from disequilibria to equilibria during the course of the trade cycle.

Many writers on the trade cycle have spent some considerable time on the question of whether disturbances away from equilibria are *exogenously* or *endogenously* generated. The distinction between exogenous and endogenous explanations is not absolutely clear-cut but, for analytical convenience, exogenous theories can be treated as explanations that locate some phenomena external to the economic system, such as government policy or climatic changes as being responsible for economic fluctuations, while endogenous theories claim that some aspect of the internal working of the economic system itself is the cause of departures from equilibrium; that is to say, the private enterprise, market economy is inherently unstable. Now one would expect Hayek's theory to be an exogenous theory, an explanation that pinpointed some extra-economic phenomenon, such as the government's control of the money supply, as the main cause of disturbance in an otherwise self-regulating *catallaxy*. But in his writings of the 1930s Hayek says that his theory is endogenous; that 'loose joint' in the economy, money, and the working of the modern banking system, are both necessary elements in a market economy but also generate its disturbances.[20] Indeed, he says that there is little that a government can do to regulate the volume of credit that banks issue throughout the course of the trade cycle, and that to attempt to 'manage' the currency may involve worse consequences, such as runaway inflation or uncontrollable deflation, than a policy of benign neglect. The policy of benign neglect does, however, depend upon some ultimate and automatic guarantee of stability, such as the gold standard. This view, that trade cycles are endogenously generated, is not a necessary feature of traditional Austrian theory which did regard the cycle as exogenously generated by the government's monopoly of money and its control of the banking system through a central bank. For these reasons the system of 'free banking', in which the government does not have a monopoly in money and competition between banks is expected to prevent disequilibriating expansions and contractions in the supply of money, has always found some advocates among liberal political economists. It is to this idea that Hayek is returning in his most recent pronouncements on money, which will be considered in a later section of this chapter.

A few more comments on the nature of the banking system may be helpful in the understanding of why Hayek's original formulation of the theory of the trade cycle stressed its endogenous properties. The system of banking that capitalist countries have developed is the fractional-reserve system, that is, of all the money in circulation only a small fraction consists of cash reserves, the rest is credit, deposits created by banks in their normal lending operations. Banks are, in a sense, inherently bankrupt in that at any moment in time they obviously could not pay out cash to all those who have a legal claim to it. The system rests entirely on confidence.

It is the elasticity of credit, a feature of the normal operations of the banking system, that brings about the divergence between the natural rate of interest and the market rate and which causes business fluctuations. It is not extravagant lending, or exogenous disturbances, but routine banking practice that is therefore at the heart of the trade cycle. It is the banking system as a whole that has developed in this way and must continue to do so, for obviously the process of competition between banks means that it would not be in the interests of any one bank to refrain from lending out in excess of cash reserves in the upswing of the boom. In the boom excessive supplies of credit must inevitably occur, and in depressions, contractions in money take place as banks call in loans in a bid to re-establish cash reserves to forestall runs. Hayek said in the 1930s that the system had developed spontaneously, and this is in full agreement with the methodological position he was to develop systematically much later, therefore fluctuations were an inevitable part of the economic system. For another reason banks could not be blamed for causing fluctuations. A change could be initiated without them actually increasing the rate of credit expansion; if, for example, the natural rate of interest rose, then issuing the same credit as before will lower the market rate below the natural rate and bring about an expansion of production not warranted by the level of voluntary saving. It must also be remembered that the natural rate of interest is not an observable economic phenomenon.

This spontaneous development of the practice of banking made Hayek doubtful of the efficacy of some of the suggested reforms in the 1930s. One radical scheme involved the abolition of fractional-reserve banking and its replacement by a 100 per cent reserve system, which would put an end to 'forced saving'. On the whole he thought that the banking system that had grown up was so much a part of the market economy that it would be likely to reappear in other forms even if it were to be outlawed.[21] It also might very well appear in forms more difficult to control than the present system. Money substitutes would no doubt appear in some form or other, and Hayek emphasises here that a clear distinction between money and near-money cannot be drawn and that other things than normal money may satisfy the demand for liquid reserves. Hayek is also critical of the view, associated with Mises, that the trade cycle is exogenously generated because of the establishment of central banks, supposedly designed to regulate the supply of money. Mises had argued that central banks were infected with the 'inflationist ideology' and could not be prevented from trying to get the market rate of interest below the natural rate. While Hayek thought that this was probably true he still maintained, in his trade cycle theories of the 1930s, that credit created by banks was nevertheless an independent, and endogenous, cause of industrial fluctuations.[22]

The question must now be asked of the truth of Hayek's theory in relation to the Great Depression of 1929–1933, which was at its deepest during the writing of *Prices and Production* and the articles that were to make up *Monetary Theory and the Trade Cycle*. One point must not be forgotten, the Great Depression was not simply an inevitable recession following upon the previous boom but an extraordinary and unprecedented drop in economic activity. It is something that has haunted economic theory and policy ever since, and the doubts about the self-adjusting properties of the market economy that accompanied it gave rise to a 'revolution' in economic theory, the Keynesian system of macroeconomics. The consensus of opinion about Hayek's work on the trade cycle is that it appeared out of its time. A theory that characterised the crisis in terms of over-consumption could have little appeal in the circumstances of the fall in effective demand in the early years of the 1930s. Furthermore, Hayek's theory depended upon two conditions, the full employment of all resources and price flexibility—conditions which were not met in that era. Sir John Hicks has suggested that Hayek's theory of the trade cycle may be more appropriate for the world of inflationary slumps where the price of labour will have to come down if there is to be a proper adjustment in the economy rather than the mass unemployment and under-utilisation of all resources of the Great Depression.[23]

At the time Hayek's view did not depart very much from the orthodox view which held that if any market failed to clear the price must be too high, and since the labour market failed to clear this must be because wages were kept artifically high by trade union pressure. Hayek's view was that the normal process of adjustment must take place and that to stimulate consumer demand so as to stimulate employment would prevent the necessary liquidation of malinvestments. There would be some temporary unemployment as a consequence of higher stages of investment being written off but this tends to be prolonged by trade union monopoly of the supply of labour. Of course, it is now known that the Great Depression was caused by a fall in demand occasioned by the collapse of the world monetary system. It has been established that the American Depression could have been mitigated by orthodox monetary policies but what happened was that the Federal Reserve Board allowed a massive contraction of credit to take place which turned a mild recession into a deep depression. Furthermore, the case of Britain's sustained unemployment has now been explained by the return to the gold standard in 1925 at the pre-war parity, when the value of the currency had depreciated considerably.

Hayek has himself made the important distinction between an ordinary mild depression following the boom and a 'secondary depression', a genuine deflation where the supply of money actually contracts.[24] The fall in demand that the monetary contraction entails generates a further contraction which causes a downward spiral. The implication is that different policies apply in the two situations, although it is not easy to disentangle them in Hayek's writings, especially the books and papers written before the last war. He has since denied that he ever recommended that a genuine deflation be allowed to proceed so as to liquidate the malinvestments.[25] He also criticised the return to the gold standard at the pre-1914 parity as being deflationary, and pointed out that it was not at all required by classical economic doctrine. Nevertheless, he certainly hoped that the deflation following the return to gold would break the rigidity of wages, although he now regards deflationary policy as politically impossible and thinks it should not be attempted in future recessions. But it would be wrong to associate Hayek with those who always recommend general wage cuts as a solution to unemployment. Only in exceptional circumstances is unemployment caused by the general wage level being too high. What is normally required is a change in the relative prices of labour, some wages going up and others going down so as to bring about an equilibrium between the distribution of demand and the distribution of labour in the various parts of the economy. There must, then, be flexibility of wages if the distortions occasioned by the trade cycle are to be eliminated.

While Hayek now says that he would recommend action to be taken to prevent a secondary depression there is not much evidence for this view in the 1930s. He does speak of desperate situations, in *Profits, Interest and Investment*, which may justify policies to boost spending.[26] He also speaks of the possibility of temporary public works to relieve unemployment in the same book, although earlier in the decade the London School of Economics was in opposition to Cambridge economists over the latter's recommendation of public works.[27] Hayek may deny that he sees deflation as some necessary curative process of the business cycle but it is not clear that this is consistent with Austrian orthodoxy. After all, the doctrine tells us that depressions are a *necessary* consequence of an over-expansion; a salutary reminder that if expansion is not a product of genuine saving malinvestment will take place which must then be liquidated. Government policy must not therefore be directed to alleviating a depression, which is a necessary process of readjustment. Now if that should lead to a deflation the same process must still be gone through, although it will be more painful, and, as there is less money in circulation, all prices, including that of labour, must eventually come down. There is nothing, of course, the Austrians object to in the possibility of prices gently falling in the long run. The price of labour would fall but at a lower rate than that of consumers' goods because of the use of more roundabout methods of production. This doctrine maintained that prosperity was compatible with a gentle fall in prices.

Hayek did present a new version of his theory of business fluctuations in the already-mentioned *Profits, Interest and Investment*, and in this he attempted to meet the major objection to his theory that he had assumed full utilisation of resources and complete price flexibility. He argues that the thesis defended in *Prices and Production* is correct but that the later work approaches the same subject from a different angle. The main purpose of the work is to refute the underconsumptionist thesis that an increase in demand for consumers' goods will always lead to an increase in demand for investment goods. That this will not always happen is because of the operation of what Hayek calls the 'Ricardo Effect'.[28] The Ricardo Effect holds that a rise in wages will encourage capitalists to substitute machinery for labour and, conversely, a fall in wages will encourage them to substitute labour for machinery. In the upswing of the boom the prices of consumers' goods will rise and real wages will fall so leading to entrepreneurs investing more in labour than in capital goods, thus eventuating in the shortening of the process of production and the use of less capitalistic methods. In the depression real wages will be high and this will lead to the substitution of machinery for labour and the eventual revival in investment. Most of the issues discussed in *Profits, Interest and Investment* are perhaps of historical interest only now but some familiar Hayekian themes are elaborated. Notable is the systematic critique of the attempt to create full employment by stimulating demand, the underconsumptionist argument. As long as there is still a maldistribution of labour in the various industries, as there will be because of previous booms, full employment policies will eventually lead to inflation. Hayek admits that in a situation of unused resources an expansion of credit need not be inflationary and that investment in the longer production processes may not lead to a rise in consumer prices. But this cannot last for long and overall Hayek's, at the time, uncongenial message was that net investment had to be matched by net saving if distortions were to be prevented. The general point is that the price mechanism must be allowed to operate freely, and the most important instance of this is Hayek's argument that monetary policy must not be used to keep the rate of interest down. This policy is the enemy of stability.

Since the Keynesian 'revolution' the Austrian theory of the trade cycle has suffered almost a complete eclipse. Indeed, the problems associated with the trade cycle have fallen into the background and there seems to be general agreement amongst economists that, while the ups and downs of the business cycle will continue, there is no likelihood of a general depression occurring again.[29] Keynesians would maintain that correct demand management policies will avert a slump while monetarists argue that correct stabilisation policies by central banks will prevent a repeat of the catastrophic fall in output which occurred in the 1930s. Also, various techniques have been devised to prevent a collapse of the banking system.[30] Most of Hayek's early work on the trade cycle was in criticism of the stabilisation policies associated with the exponents of the quantity theory of money yet Hayek is popularly known for his opposition to the ideas of Keynes, and it is to this important topic that I now turn.

3. HAYEK AND KEYNES

It has been pointed out earlier in this chapter that the most fierce intellectual dispute between Hayek and Keynes occurred in the early 1930s over the theory of money and the theory of the trade cycle rather than over Keynes's much more famous later work. Yet the publication of *The General Theory of Employment, Interest and Money* brought about a revolution in economic theory which for a period of perhaps thirty years completely dominated a large part of economics. Its main achievement was to establish macroeconomic theory, the theory that explains the behaviour of large-scale variables such as the level of employment, national income, investment and so on. It is true that there was an aggregative strand in the traditional model but this was not separated from the bulk of general theory, indeed it was a special claim of neoclassicism that the theory of employment was integrated completely into formal analysis. Keynes, however, claimed to demonstrate that the existence of widespread unemployment could not be explained by the traditional tools of neoclassical (which he called, confusingly, 'classical') analysis. While there are clear differences between the orthodox neoclassical theory and the Austrian approach there was sufficient agreement on the fundamental features of the market as a self-equilibriating device to make Keynes's new under-employment equilibrium theories a threat to both of them.

If the Keynesian argument that there is no necessity for an unhampered market economy to equilibrate at the full employment of all resources were valid then this would make Hayek's system redundant, much of conventional economics irrelevant, and would open the door to considerable state intervention. Of course, Keynes himself argued that his rejection of orthodoxy applied only to its macro aspect; he accepted traditional teaching on value and distribution but thought that the classical theory came into its own only when a full employment equilibrium had been established by interventionist methods. Furthermore, Keynes also emphasised the fact that his theories were designed to save the free market private enterprise economy from collectivists and Marxists, for whom he had little respect. Nevertheless, Hayek has always regarded Keynesianism as a major threat to the workings of a free society, and certainly a more insidious one than the crude collectivist economic philosophies that have in fact succeeded in supplanting capitalism.

The case for self-adjusting properties of the market in the traditional theory rested upon the assumption that the price mechanism would ensure that all markets are cleared. An increase in the supply of labour would not result in unemployment but in lower real wages and a higher labour–capital ratio throughout the economy. Similarly, an increase in saving does not indicate a fall in aggregate demand but a shift in demand from consumers' goods to producers' goods; the latter being required to provide for the future consumption of current savers. In an automatically-adjusting economy, then, only relative prices are defined at equilibrium and money is demanded only to finance transactions. The quantity of money is therefore irrelevant to everything except the determi-nation of the absolute price level.

The Austrians did not, as we have seen, accept that money was neutral, as the above statement implies, and they were less interested in general equilibrium models. But nevertheless, their belief in the tendency towards equilibrium depended upon the self-adjusting properties of the market and this required that the rate of interest should function as the delicate mechanism for equilibriating savings and investment, as in the above argument; and it was one of the main claims of Keynes that this just does not happen. In rejecting a long-run tendency towards equilibrium via the price mechanism Keynes attempted to show how a short period equilibrium could be established by interventionist methods. It would be impossible even to summarise Keynes's arguments here, especially, as the nature of the 'Keynesian revolution' still provokes considerable debate in the economics literature. However, the main features that affected Hayek's political economy can be picked out.

The most important general point is that Keynes started from the assumption of the under-utilisation of all resources and tried to show that this was not a temporary phenomenon caused by, for example, one particular rigid price, but a quite likely occurrence. For Keynes the demand for money did not comprise simply a transactions demand, as the neoclassical theorists had maintained, but also included a speculative demand—that is, a demand for money to be held as an asset in preference to interest-bearing bonds on which a capital loss might be made if interest rates rose. It was this speculative demand for money that accounted for the quite different function that money played in the Keynesian system. For Keynes the demand for money varied inversely with the interest rate and the latter's role was that of equating the demand for money with the available stock. This, Keynes believed, meant that the rate of interest could not be the delicate instrument by which the investment of full employment savings is secured.

In fact, regardless of the rate of interest, Keynes believed that the investment intentions of entrepreneurs were influenced by quite different factors than those supposed by classical doctrine. Keynes regarded businessmen as responding to irrational waves of optimism and pessimism rather than fine changes in interest rates. Hence any attempt by the monetary authorities to get the rate of interest down may not succeed in inducing them to make the additional investment required for full employment. In a mature economy the marginal efficiency of capital, his name for the traditional notion of the rate of profit, would decline. In the long run Keynes envisaged the possibility of the exhaustion of all investment opportunities. Since then full employment investment demand could not be guaranteed and since consumption varied with income (as income rises consumption rises but as a diminishing proportion), there could be no assurance that investment and consumption would generally sum to full employment income.

While Keynes did not preclude the use of monetary policies in such circumstances to bring down the rate of interest, these will not be effective if liquidity-preference is high. And to the classical argument that unemployment was caused by wages being above their market-clearing price, he said that to cut wages would further reduce demand, thereby increasing unemployment. In a depression the only way to raise employment is to raise spending, and if private spending is inadequate then only increased public expenditure, through budget deficits, can fill the gap.

In short, an increase in demand during depressions would increase expenditure throughout the economy. National income would rise and employment would increase. The respective roles of the rate of interest in determining the volume of investment and the market price of labour guaranteeing employment for all willing labour, both related aspects of the price mechanism, were replaced by government raising aggregate demand in order to raise national income and therefore employment.

As has been mentioned earlier in this chapter, Hayek never systematically analysed Keynes's *General Theory* as he had his earlier work. There is a fairly detailed criticism of the rate of interest as a purely monetary phenomenon in *The Pure Theory of Capital*[31] and some observations on the dangers of increasing spending even during depressions in *Profits, Interest and Investment*, but the bulk of Hayek's criticisms have taken the form of general methodological strictures and attacks on the post-war Keynesian economic policies. Nowhere does he consider the particular arguments and theories contained in the *General Theory*. Nevertheless, it is possible to single out a number of key areas for discussion.

First of all, Hayek always denied that it was a general theory and claimed that it was no more than a tract for the times.[32] It had been known, he said, for a long time in economic theory that in a situation of substantial unemployment of all resources an increase in spending brought about by monetary injection would increase economic activity, but only for a short while. Sooner or later monetary injection would lead only to inflation. Continued monetary injection would, furthermore, bring about distortions in the structure of production, since according to the Austrian theory, money is not neutral. It does not affect all prices uniformly and the relative prices of goods and services change according to the point at which extra spending is injected into the economy. While in the early 1930s Hayek's criticisms were addressed to those economists who sought to ensure stability by monetary methods, they apply equally to Keynes's arguments that increases in employment could in the main be brought about by fiscal methods, for example, by running government deficits during depressions. Both techniques involve a type of demand management which implicitly casts doubt upon the self-adjusting properties of the market, although this is less true of the purely monetary devices.

Keynes had used the *special circumstances* of the Great Depression to construct a supposedly general theory of employment. The events of the 1930s could be more accurately explained by an extraordinary monetary contraction and the special problem of the rigidity of wages. In general, argued Hayek, unemployment was not caused by demand deficiency but by distortions in the labour market and the structure of demand brought about by previous booms based on expansions of credit.[33] Such unemployment would only be prolonged if government interference prevented the movement back towards equilibrium. This takes some time and must be contrasted with Keynes's aim of establishing a short-period full employment equilibrium by manipulating macroeconomic variables.

The most important question, perhaps, is that of wages. Keynes accepted the wage rate set by unions as a kind of historical constant, which could not come down in monetary terms. Yet he knew that real wages would have to come down eventually if all willing labour was to be employed in a normally functioning economy, and thought that this could be achieved by mild inflation. In fact, it seems to be the case that Hayek regarded the whole Keynesian doctrine as rather an elaborate, and indeed unnecessary, theoretical structure designed to cope with the problem of the downward rigidity of wages. A lot has been written recently about 'money illusion', the idea that workers would not realise that real wages will be cut if money wages are inflated, and the general consensus is that if it ever did operate it no longer does, and that unions now include inflationary expectations in their wage demands. In fact as long ago as 1937 Hayek pointed out that workers would not be deceived for very long by 'money illusion'.[34] He has constantly stressed the fact that if wages are accepted as constant, and any consequent unemployment eliminated by boosting aggregate demand, then this could only result in never-ending inflation and the handing over of the economy to the unions. The particular Keynesian response to this, although it was not Keynes's, is to institute prices and incomes policies. Hayek has always opposed these as they take the determination of wages out of the market place, suspend therefore the operation of the price mechanism and lead to further distortions in the structure of production. Hayek claims too, that they have a longer-term political effect; they lead to the direction of labour with all the trappings of a command economy.[35] This last point is not really economic, and requires an additional premise about the traditional commitment to liberty in a community to substantiate it, but nevertheless serves as an important warning to those extreme Keynesians who seem intent on politicising all aspects of the economy.

Hayek concedes that previous theories of employment were deficient in that they did start from a position of full employment of all resources and complete flexibility of all prices but argues that Keynes, in effect, committed the same error in reverse.[36] And he says that at least the traditional approach fully entails the commitment to the price mechanism as the most important, indeed only, allocative device. In contrast, Keynes's emphasis on macroeconomic variables completely masks the causal role played by relative prices in the process of economic adjustment. The persuasiveness of these macroeconomic magnitudes rests entirely on the fact that they are amenable to objectification and quantification, a point which was considered in Chapter 2. The causes of unemployment, says Hayek, must always be sought in the microeconomic structure of an economy, that is, in the maladjustments in the labour market occasioned by changes in the structure of production and prolonged by the effect of union monopoly and the relative immobility of labour.

It may be useful to conclude this discussion of the Hayek–Keynes dispute by some account of their personalities: not because Hayek has ever personally attacked Keynes, or any other intellectual opponents, as Schumpeter said, even his most passionate adversaries were convicted of 'intellectual error only', but because the intellectual difference between Hayek and Keynes reflected important differences in their personal social philosophies.

Hayek is fond of quoting an extract from Keynes's *Two Memoirs* (London, 1949) where the author described the views he and his friends, held in the early years of this century.

We entirely repudiated a personal liability on us to obey general rules. We claimed the right to judge every individual case on its merits, and the wisdom, experience and self-control to do so successfully . . . We repudiated entirely customary morals, conventions and traditional wisdom.[37]

There could not be a clearer contrast between this extravagant act-utilitarianism, and personalised, anthropomorphic view of the world, and Hayek's cautious rule-utilitarianism, with its almost metaphysical belief in the accumulated, but undemonstrable, wisdom of traditional, impersonal rules of behaviour. This is not merely a psychological but a philosophical distinction: a difference between the self-confident rationalist of Edwardian Cambridge who saw no limits to knowledge, and a more modest, but equally scientific, man who saw a large part of social life as simply not explicable in terms of a simple dichotomy between the true and the false that physical science provides.

Keynes always thought that knowledge was more important than rules and that the application of economic knowledge to policy matters was hampered by archaic rules which seemed to fulfil no immediate purpose but to ensure the survival of outmoded ways of thinking. He led perhaps the most active public life of all the great economists, and never missed an opportunity to try out the latest piece of economic gadgetry on men of influence and power. His fashionable aphorism, that 'in the long run we are all dead' was not merely an economic proposition. Not only does it reveal a refusal to believe that the ultimate determinants of economic behaviour may be long-term factors, but also it is a 'social philosophy of impatience'. Hayek has in turn rejected the fashionable aphorism as an antiliberal statement.[38] That, too, may be a little extreme but does indicate that the obsession with the 'immediate' may indeed be no more than a way of postponing future painful events.

A further general point is Keynes's failure to provide us with a theory of politics. Despite the obvious presence of a Keynesian social philosophy, albeit somewhat primitive and unsystematic, and Keynes's own political activities, he never systematically integrated his proposed system of economic management with an explanation of the political process. This is crucial in an age of liberal democracy where schemes of demand management have to be constantly trimmed to suit the exigencies of the moment, the clamourings of pressure groups, and the electoral timetable. The economic theory of democracy has now reached some sophistication, and there is nothing in it that is at all inconsistent with what Hayek has been maintaining for the last thirty years.[39]

Keynes always proceeded from the assumption of the instability of liberal capitalism. It is, of course, true that the market system of his age was characterised by crisis, slump and boom. But whereas Hayek has always maintained that there is a limit to what can be done about this, and that governments should restrict themselves to cultivating the mechanism, Keynes seemed to believe that the right advice and the appropriate piece of knowledge, would enable a potentially stable government to direct the machine towards some desired end. The possibility that government, even a well-informed and knowledgeable government, might itself be a destabilising force, and even wreck the mechanism itself, may have been known to Keynes, but he was, according to Hayek, supremely confident of his ability to persuade governments and public opinion.[40] Keynes was unquestionably an elitist, a philosopher-king, who did not have an *a priori* faith in the self-adjusting properties of the market, or in the kind of decentralised knowledge that that system embodies. His contempt for businessmen was ill-concealed, and his followers at Cambridge, as Harry Johnson has shown, have built on this to produce a system of economics which systematically downgrades the entrepreneur and elevates the role of interventionists and planners in the determination of economic events.[41] However, it may be true that it is the ideas of the Keynesians, rather than those of Keynes himself, that have been influential in post-war economic policy, especially in Britain, and this general topic requires a section in itself.

4. POST-WAR ECONOMIC POLICY

Hayek's main contribution to economics since the last war has been in the field of policy rather than pure theory. More specifically, he has endeavoured to integrate economics into a general social and political philosophy. He has often said that a knowledge of economics alone is not enough for a comprehensive understanding of social affairs and has claimed that an economist who knows only economics is likely to be more of a hindrance than a help in matters of policy. Whatever may be the merits of Keynes's *General Theory* as a general theory of economics it was certainly no general theory of society.

The past thirty years have seen the dominance of Keynesian demand management policies in many western capitalist countries, especially in Britain, but it is only in the last five years that Hayek's long-standing criticisms of this approach have begun to get any kind of a hearing. There is, of course, the perennial question of whether the Keynesian techniques for creating full employment are really those that would have been advocated by Keynes. It is true that in the last few years of his life Keynes was as much concerned about inflation as he had been previously concerned with unemployment, and that the particular targets of employment which he regarded as feasible were much more modest than those of his acolytes.[42] Hayek, himself, agrees that were Keynes alive today he would be leading the struggle against inflation, but nevertheless, the impression is clear that he regards Keynes as being intellectually responsible for Keynesianism. He does not distinguish the doctrines of Keynes from Keynesianism and seems to imply that had Keynes been faced with the problems of today he would simply have written a new 'general theory'. Furthermore, as we have just noted, Hayek says that Keynes always believed he could use his personal powers of persuasion to bring back the political managers to the path of economic rectitude. This is obviously completely at variance with Hayek's argument that stability is only possible in the context of depersonalised general rules.

The Keynesian demand management policies did seem to produce an era of prosperity and economic stability which lasted longer than Hayek expected; but the main problems have come from the attempt to prolong that prosperity longer than was economically feasible.[43] The crisis in Keynesian economics has come in the form of rising inflation *and* rising unemployment. According to the doctrine, inflation should only begin to emerge as full employment is reached, and this is the rationale that lies behind incomes policies. These are designed to cope with the dangers of cost-push inflation which is said to be a consequence of union monopoly power in the context of rising employment. Hayek has always maintained that the really damaging effect of Keynesian policies is that the injection of spending power into the economy to create jobs can only bring about temporary improvements in employment. Such jobs can only remain if the extra spending power is maintained, and if it is not the jobs will disappear. Yet if the

inflation is increased this will only cause further economic dislo-
cation and greater unemployment in the long term. The real causes
of unemployment are therefore to be found in the structure of
industry and the various impediments to the free movement of
labour, and these cannot be solved by raising aggregate demand. In
his articles and monographs of the 1960s and 1970s Hayek has
repeated his argument of the 1930s that there must be wage
flexibility. in the labour market if employment is to be increased.
While in that era he thought that the downward rigidity of wages
could be broken he now thinks that, for obvious practical reasons,
this is impossible but nevertheless insists that some method must be
found to restore the price mechanism in the labour market.[44] Just
how this can be done is not really explained; obviously he cannot
recommend the method of inflation in which the real wage of one
group of workers is brought down by inflating the wages of others.
He also would recommend that action should be taken by monetary
authorities to prevent a deflation, a genuine contraction in the
supply of money.[45] But it is difficult to see how flexibility in prices
can be achieved without some policies which will inevitably hurt
some politically significant groups.

The causes of the post-war tendency towards inflation can, in
fact, be seen in the context of Hayek's general philosophy. What has
happened over the past few decades has been the removal of
traditional restraints on the behaviour of monetary authorities. The
rise of constructivist rationalism in economics and the belief that all
economic knowledge could be centralised so that planning, either of
a direct kind in collectivised economies or of an indirect kind in
managed capitalist or mixed economies, could be made more
effective has entailed the destruction of those rules that men have
developed to cope with their necessary ignorance.[46] The rules that
Hayek refers to are the gold standard and its replacement, the
regime of fixed exchange rates between currencies. Once these limits
were removed there was virtually no limit to the extent to which
monetary authorities could inflate the currency in the pursuit of
impossible economic policies. While, for technical reasons, Hayek
now thinks the gold standard could not be re-imposed, his support
for fixed exchange rates dates back to 1937. He believed then, and
now, that the system of floating currencies would be used as a device
for reducing the international value of the currency in order to get
over the problem of the rigidity of prices at home.[47] It is a device
that enables politicians to evade their responsibilities.

It is only recently, however, that Hayek has faced up squarely to the problem of money, that loose joint in an otherwise self-adjusting *catallaxy*, which has perplexed him since his earliest days as a professional economist. Having considered all the possible ways of restraining governments in their control of the supply of money he has now cut the Gordian knot and argued that money should be taken out of the hands of the politicians and put back into the markets. In two recent pamphlets for the *Institute of Economic Affairs*[48] he has made the daring suggestion that government should lose its monopoly of the supply of money and that notes issued by banks, and foreign currencies, should be allowed to circulate along with the government's money.

In at least one area of social and economic life, then, Hayek has despaired of the possibility of rules being effective and ordinary self-interest is called upon to deliver the good of financial stability. In effect, Hayek has solved the problem of monetary policy by simply ending the possibility of monetary policy. The technical details of the scheme cannot be gone into here but the main principles are clear enough. Banks would issue notes, backed by a 'basket of commodities' to ensure a stable value, and individuals would be allowed to use any money they wished to conduct their transactions. The forces of competition would prevent a bank over-issuing its notes and consumers could easily be informed of the day-to-day value of the various currencies by regular bulletins. If a government wished to maintain the value of its currency, as it surely must, this would happen by the normal process of the market. And this would mean that public expenditure would have to be financed by taxation and genuine borrowing rather than by inflation. One likely misunderstanding, however, must be immediately cleared up. It is commonly held that a free market in currency would not work because of the operation of Gresham's Law, which holds that bad money drives out good. In fact, Hayek dealt with this problem in an earlier article.[49] Gresham's Law only holds if two currencies are both exchangeable at the same given rate, in which case the sound currency will disappear. If this condition does not hold, and it would not in Hayek's scheme, then the reverse is true.

Some general methodological comments may be made about Hayek's scheme. Firstly, it illustrates very well how economic theory can be useful in the absence of empirical evidence. A state of affairs is constructed imaginatively and certain consequences deduced, and these conclusions are invaluable even though the

truth of them is independent of experience. Secondly, the problem
of whether trade cycles are endogenously or exogenously generated
can now be seen in a new light. The implication of the new scheme,
although Hayek does not discuss this, is that economic disturbances
must be exogenously caused, as Mises always maintained. For if
stability is now to be ensured by a free market in money, the
historical fluctuations must have been due to the absence of this free
market caused by government monopoly and influences of central
banks over the supply of credit. The loose joint appears to be loose
only because of government interference.[50] Whatever the technical
merits of the scheme it does cast doubt upon the efficacy of rules, the
backbone of Hayek's social philosophy. If governments cannot be
bound by rules over monetary matters, can they be bound by any
rules at all? The optimism that lies behind the scheme for a free
market in money may very well mark an even more disturbing
problem, the problem of controlling government in those areas
where its monopoly cannot be removed.

  Before we leave this section a brief comment would be in order on
the differences between Hayek and his fellow warrior against
inflation, Milton Friedman. While Hayek has always stressed the
elementary truth of the quantity theory of money he has never said
that money is neutral. And Friedman's monetary rule, that the
supply of money should only be increased in line with increases in
productivity, would imply that money is ultimately neutral in
respect of the structure of production.[51] Indeed, Hayek was
attacking not dissimilar stabilisation policies in the 1930s. Furthermore, Friedman's criticism of Keynes largely turned upon his
refutation on empirical grounds of the crucial Keynesian hypotheses, and of his quantitative work on American monetary
history which showed that the Great Depression was caused by a
massive contraction in the supply of money brought about by the
mistaken monetary policies of the Federal Reserve Board.[52] An orthodox Austrian approach would hold that concentrating on the
supply of money is not that much different from Keynesian demand
management policies in that they both ignore the importance of
relative prices in causing changes in the structure of production. A
really extreme Austrian answer to the problem of a deflation would
be to say that in a monetary contraction prices should be allowed to
adjust downwards. Furthermore, the emphasis that Friedman
places on observable magnitudes would certainly make his methodology scientistic by the strict praxeological standards.[53]

Nevertheless, it may be unwise to emphasise too much the differences between Hayek and Friedman. Hayek does himself depart occasionally from these strict Austrian standards and Friedman is as much concerned to stress the limitations of monetary policy as he is its positive virtues.[54] Friedman's monetary rule is not a method of eliminating cyclical fluctuations of the normal type, although it can prevent severe depressions. And certainly Friedman does not think that it is possible to eliminate unemployment by manipulating the monetary variables as this is normally caused by microeconomic factors.[55] A monetary rule is no more than an indispensable guideline to give the necessary predictability for the actors in the free market economy.

Hayek and Friedman also agree that trade unions do not cause inflation. For both, inflation is caused by increases in the supply of money which, in modern society, stem from government action. However, Hayek does stress that constant trade union pressure on wages does have an effect on governments' monetary policies. As long as unemployment is regarded as a consequence of deficient demand, rather than of trade unions pricing workers out of jobs through the exercise of their monopoly power, there will be a tendency for governments to try to cure unemployment through inflation.

5. SOCIALISM

Since a large part of Hayek's general social philosophy can be described, not inaccurately, as a radical critique of socialism and collectivism, I shall confine myself here to some general comments on the economics of socialism. It is surprising that, for all the emphasis that socialists put on economic factors, there is not a great deal of socialist economics literature. This is especially true of Marx who deliberately eschewed any detailed discussion of the economic organisation of the future socialist commonwealth, the implication being that capitalism had eliminated the economic problem and bequeathed to socialism a world of infinite abundance. However, there was a period, in the 1930s, when socialist economics was part of the mainstream of orthodox economics. It was during this period that socialist economists tried to demonstrate that there was a socialist solution to the problem of the efficient use of scarce resources, the universal problem of economics, which was consistent with the neoclassical paradigm.

The great debate over the possibilities of a technically efficient socialist economy was really started by Mises who, in a famous essay first published in 1920,[56] had claimed that a socialist economy without money and the price mechanism could not be organised rationally. He nearly went as far as to claim that a socialist economy was an impossibility. His argument was that if resources are to be used efficiently there must be some index of scarcity, and the only way to establish this is to allow exchanges to take place on the market so that the relative prices of productive resources can be established. A socialist planned economy would have no way of establishing the value of resources if a market were not allowed.

In three important papers in the 1930s Hayek took up this theme and the replies to Mises that were made by socialist economists.[57] Hayek did not go so far as to say that a socialist economy was impossible, that obviously would be false, but tried to show that it would operate at a low level of efficiency if it abandoned the market mechanism. Of course, not all socialist economists abandoned the market mechanism and, for analytical convenience, the socialists can be divided into two groups: collectivists proper, and the theorists of competitive, market socialism.

If economic problems arise when differing purposes compete for the use of scarce resources, and if the market, which determines the value of the resources, is rejected, then collectivists must have some alternative device to calculate the values of wages, interest and rent which would be required for rational planning. If the economic problem were merely the engineering one of getting the best use of labour and equipment to maximise a given purpose the problem could be evaded, but once a variety of purposes are admitted this involves the problem of *cost*. This is an economic problem, not an engineering one, because economic cost is understood subjectively as the forgone value produced by alternative uses of a resource. Collectivists either got round this by arbitrarily assigning value, as occurs in a purely command economy, which is irrational, or by trying to determine economic value non-arbitrarily by centralising all knowledge of productive resources and consumer tastes so as to achieve an optimal output of goods and services without the use of the price mechanism.[58] While the latter approach has the advantage that it might be logically possible to plan an economy, and at the same time maintain free choice in consumption and occupation, it would involve immense practical difficulties. These difficulties would follow from Hayek's account of economic knowledge. Knowledge is not a given whole but is ever-changing and exists in a decentralised form, and to deny individuals the opportunity to take advantage of the knowledge of time and place, as must be the case in a system of centralised management, would mean that society as a whole would not be able to make the best use of its knowledge. Furthermore, the maintenance of free choice in occupation and consumption in the absence of a market would require constant monitoring by a centralised authority.

The system of socialism, however, that Hayek thought much more intellectually respectable was the competitive model suggested by, among others, Oskar Lange.[59] This was because it attempted to make socialist economics consistent with traditional economic theory. Implicit in the neoclassical general equilibrium model was the logical possibility that if knowledge of resources and consumer tastes were available then an optimal economic solution to the problem of an efficient allocation could be calculated mathematically; but, in fact, Lange thought that the market system would itself produce that efficient outcome if it were designed so as to eliminate imperfections caused by private ownership of productive resources, and undesirable inequalities in income and wealth. In essence Lange's competitive model would entail the creation of perfect competition in which he thought prices would more adquately act as signalling devices to allocate resources more efficiently than under capitalist ownership.

This system, although it would *not* have private ownership of the means of production, would have the equivalent of entrepreneurial activity by socialist managers, there would be a small private sector, and there would be free choice in consumption and occupation. Wages and the prices of consumer goods would be determined by the market but the prices of all other goods would be determined by a central authority. The central authority would gradually change the prices of these goods by trial and error.

While Hayek takes this model seriously as an alternative to bureaucratic tyranny he has many objections. These mainly centre on the problem of investment in the absence of a capital market. He does not think that the process of experimentation in fixing the prices of investment goods would be as efficient as the market, and entrepreneurs would have to use political and other methods of persuasion to convince the central authority of the economic desirability of their proposals. This would be because the absence of private ownership of capital means that decisions about the ratio between consumption and investment would ultimately have to be taken by the state.

Nevertheless, Hayek seems to think that competitive socialism is not logically impossible but does insist that any advantages it does have come from its similarity with general economic theory rather than its consistency with orthodox socialism. However, he thought the practical problems raised by the absence of a capital market and private property, and the influence of political factors, would dissipate the advantages secured by competition. Certainly the experiments, either in planning by the use of computers or decentralised management without private ownership, that have been tried in Eastern Europe have been thwarted by the existence of one-party states. What is disturbing about contemporary socialists is that they seem to reject both centralised planning and the market mechanism yet suggest no alternative that meets the minimum demands of economic rationality.[60]

In recent years Hayek's main purpose has been to refute the argument that disputes between socialists and non-socialists depend upon value differences which cannot be settled by rational argument. While he does dispute some of the values of socialists he is emphatic that the issue is not really about these values but whether the means suggested by socialists can bring about their desired ends.[61] Hayek is on very strong ground here. One example is often used to illustrate the general case. Most socialists seem to think that trade union activity helps the working class; yet if trade unions act so as to keep the price of labour above its market-clearing price then fewer workers will be employed.[62] In fact, trade union practices of the kind tolerated in capitalist countries would have no place in the market socialism model of Lange. Furthermore, socialists, being archetypal constructivist rationalists, take very little account of the unintended consequences of their policies. They fail also to see the intimate connection between liberty and the market and blithely assume that the abolition of the exchange process poses no threat to freedom. Sometimes the impression is given that socialists believe that the mere declaration of belief in the *value* of liberty absolves them from even considering the deleterious effect the socialist *method* may have on it. To accuse Hayek of having a different value-system is really an excuse to avoid this kind of intellectual argument.

9 Conclusion

There are two purposes in this final chapter and both involve the tying together of the various elements in Hayek's philosophy. The first is to discuss the chain of reasoning which in Hayek's thought culminates in what might be called 'the road to serfdom thesis'. This idea was first suggested in 1944, although glimmerings of it are visible in Hayek's earlier writings on economics which touched upon policy, but has been more systematically presented in the last few years in a particularly sophisticated interdisciplinary form. The second is to give a more general account of Hayek's political 'ideology' and to try and place it on the intellectual map. In particular I shall be concerned to trace the similarities and differences between it and the more familiar doctrines of liberalism and conservatism. In exploring both these purposes the aim will be to present Hayek's social philosophy as a systematic whole in which, although there are differences of emphasis and even changes of mind, the component parts show a remarkable consistency over an extremely long period of time. In the first two sections I shall be concerned only with the road to serfdom thesis.

The thesis put forward in *The Road to Serfdom* is well-known and a brief summary should suffice to elucidate the main points. The main import of Hayek's notorious book held that there really was very little intellectual difference between communism and fascism and that both doctrines had their roots in a collectivist, anti-individualist mentality. He laid great stress on the similarities between the German socialists and some aspects of Nazism, especially the fact that both showed contempt for market economics and traditional liberalism, and thought he had detected similar tendencies in British socialism.[1] But also, he seemed to cast doubt on whether there was a difference between social democracy and extreme collectivism in practice by suggesting that even mild planning, perhaps in the form of demand management or the establishment of a minimum welfare state, would produce unforeseen consequences not desired by the planners. A road to serfdom would appear to occur because even the slightest interference with the spontaneous evolution of society would set in motion processes that would ultimately destroy that spontaneity. It must be stressed that Hayek did not oppose all of the ends of the planners, some aspects of welfare he approved of, but was sceptical of the means to bring them about which were proposed. In fact, he thought that minor adjustments in the general rules of law would have been sufficient to realise most of the welfare aims of the socialists. However, he has always objected to the entrenchment of a bureaucracy operating through a system of administrative regulations to bring about these ends. It is these methods that are likely to turn, almost accidentally, mild planning into totalitarianism.

It was thought at one time that Hayek's grim prognosis had been disproved by events and evidence was produced of the existence of welfare states, considerable economic planning *and* the survival of fundamental liberties. However, Hayek's thesis is enjoying something of a revival now as there is evidence that three decades of welfare-oriented social democracy, and one can include nominally conservative governments in the welfarist category, have not only produced economic inefficiency but also a loss of liberty. Britain is most frequently cited as a confirmation of Hayek's view.

It is important, however, to be clear what Hayek was saying in the simple road to serfdom thesis. He was not predicting that a totalitarian society would necessarily follow from the smallest steps in the direction of planning but rather than the adoption of certain collectivist principles, which are alien to spontaneous evolution, may produce a totalitarian order which in most cases will not have been desired by the planners.[2] In other words he was not detecting an observable historical trend from which he was, inductively, making a kind of prophecy about the likely course of events, but rather moving within the traditional Austrian methodology. That is, the road to serfdom thesis was an inference not an empirical observation. A totalitarian order could be mentally reconstructed by inferring what would happen if there were certain departures from the principles of spontaneous evolution.

It would follow from this, then, that the thesis would not be refuted by the coexistence of the welfare state and freedom in the 1950s and 1960s or confirmed by the evidence of recent years in

Britain. Hayek's concern was not to make a prediction but really to show how welfarist policies implemented in the wrong way would produce a psychological change of attitude in people which would undermine the spirit of liberty which is required for the continuation of a spontaneous order. Evidence for this might in fact be relevant, and Hayek produces some, but it is of a rather anecdotal kind and not all that convincing.[3]

The real defect of this early thesis was not its consistency or otherwise with the evidence but the more fundamental point that it was not a really satisfactory theory. It was no more than the sketch or outline of a theory that was to be developed later. The simple claim that economic planning would lead to totalitarianism does not really tell us anything at all about the explanation of why certain political and legal systems seem more vulnerable than others to planning, or why, under certain circumstances, the operation of majority-rule democracy can produce outcomes which are not in fact desired by the majority, and are usually inimical to the continuance of the market order. As Hayek was aware at the time, a socialist regime may come about by accident, and be legitimate in a technical sense, yet in 1944 there was no real theoretical explanation of this.

The interest in democracy shown by economists over the last twenty years, and especially the treatment of the political system of liberal democracy as a kind of market with the actors regarded as utility-maximising agents, has produced a body of knowledge which is of the greatest importance in the understanding of non-communist politics. Some normative inferences from this body of knowledge are especially critical of the majority-rule principle in democracies and this criticism stems from the comparisons that are made between political markets and economic markets. Economic markets have built-in stabilising forces which prevent their collapse, while in political markets the stabilising forces are less effective, especially in regimes characterised by sovereignty in which there are no limits on what an elected government may do. The real defect of the political market is that it aggregates individual preferences into collective choices, and where the aggregation rule is a bare majority a large part of the public may be hurt by collective decisions. Furthermore, it is not difficult to concoct majorities out of minorities by suitable tactics and this majority will probably not represent the genuine public interest. Economic markets, however, permit intensity of individual preferences to be expressed through the price mechanism; no individual can be outvoted in an economic market. Furthermore, each individual actor in an economic market acts under a budget constraint whereas in most majority-rule democracies politicians are not under a similar restraint, or rather, they are but the effect is not immediate but long-term and remote.

Much of what Hayek has to say about democracy proceeds along parallel lines to this reasoning, but he has added a number of other factors which, he claims, are contributory to the slow erosion of the market order and the emergence of collectivism. These are: the increasing tendency for law to be cast in the form of commands rather than general rules of just conduct because of the fact that the responsibility for making both types of law lies in the same institution; the commitment of western democracies to distributive justice; and the use of Keynesian demand management policies which disturb the self-regulating processes of the market. Since these policies have to some extent been hastened by majority-rule democracy it would be helpful to look at Hayek's views on this in a little more detail.

2. HAYEK'S CRITIQUE OF DEMOCRACY

It is a little misleading to title this section Hayek's 'critique' of democracy since his main aim in this area has not been to doubt the value of the ideals and institutions of traditional democracy but to point out the perversions of the democratic ideal. Undoubtedly, the main threats to the continued evolution of the *cosmos*—the transformation of private into public law, the obsession with social justice and the pursuit of rationalistic planning—have been aided by the extension of the democratic decision-making procedure, but Hayek is not convinced that the withdrawal from the pursuit of these mistaken policies entails the destruction of democracy. The basic aims of democracy can be achieved, if some major adjustments are made to the democratic machinery.

It is not, then, democracy that Hayek objects to but unlimited government of any kind. The difference between democracy and traditional liberalism is that the former is defined in terms of who is to wield power and authority while the latter is a doctrine about the limitations that must be imposed on whoever it is that wields power and authority.[4] Democracy is a doctrine that locates legitimacy in the will of the people, that is the source of law, while liberalism sees legitimacy in the general opinion that a law meets certain characteristics whatever its source. From this it follows that the opposite of democracy is authoritarianism and the opposite of liberalism is totalitarianism. It would also follow that it is possible that an authoritarian regime could maintain the conditions for a considerable measure of individual liberty while a democratic regime may impose severe restrictions on liberty while maintaining the formal political machinery of democracy.[5] And, of course, some regimes have done this. But Hayek would still say that if strict rules are maintained on the activity of government then majority rule procedures are likely to be the least harmful of all the possibilities, and he does agree with Popper that democracy has the distinguishing virtue of allowing political change without violence.

What has gone wrong, then, with democracy? The fundamental problem is in the nature of politics itself. In economics we can speak of a kind of 'invisible hand' that guides the self-interested actions of individuals towards a social optimum that was no part of their intention. This is still true even when account is taken of externalities. But this is not true of political action in a democracy, and there is no inherent tendency for vote-maximising in a democracy to bring about the public interest. And there is such a thing as the public interest; there are some public actions which it is in the interests of each individual that they should be performed but which it may not be in the interests of each individual to voluntarily perform. The whole system of rules which enables the market to operate, and which requires enforcement by the laws of organisation, is in the interests of each individual as a member of the public, but it would be in the interests of each individual as an individual not to pay the taxes that finance it. There are other such public goods and the rationale of government action from the liberal point of view has permitted the production of public goods, which are required for genuine collective interests. The aim is to limit government action to the promotion of genuine collective interests, and majority-rule procedures are perfectly acceptable if governments are so limited.[6]

According to Hayek, and this is now a commonplace argument amongst political economists, the tendency is for group interests to masquerade as public interests. Just because a collective interest binds a particular group it does not follow that that interest is a collective interest for society as a whole.[7] And it is certainly not the case that the public interest is a sum of all the group interests. Each

group interest is likely to be at variance with the public interest
because group activities in their public aspect nearly always involve
the seeking of privileges for the group—privileges which impose
higher costs on other members of society.

The tendency for group and not public interests to be advanced
in a democracy is a consequence of the vote-maximising strategy
that the system encourages. It is obviously to the advantage of the
political entrepreneur to offer policies favourable to groups because
they are immediate and beneficial rather than promote the genuine
public interest because the benefits from this are longer-term and
remote. Thus it is more likely that party programmes will consist of
policies such as financial aid to declining industries, tax concessions
to mortgagees, and setting of council rents below the market level,
rather than policies of no inflation or the ending of subsidies to
privileged groups. While the latter are clearly in the interest of the
public the benefits of pursuing them are too thinly spread to have
much electoral appeal.

The pluralist argument that the multiplicity of conflicting groups
ensures the emergence of sound policies fails because the majority-
rule procedure requires only that the political entrepreneur puts
together a coalition of interests in order to get elected. The
traditional democratic assumption of voter rationality also fails
because it is in the rational self-interest of each voter to spend his
single vote on that package of policies most favourable to him; he
cannot, rationally, be expected to take account of the public
interest. The problem is that while in a market economy the
economic optimum is the unintended beneficial outcome of self-
interested economic agents, in a political democracy, in which
constraints analogous to the budget restraint in economics do not
exist, an outcome not beneficial to individuals and obviously not
intended by them, may nevertheless emerge from their actions.

Most of the modern commentators on the economic theory of
democracy have concentrated on the fact that vote-maximising
strategies of political entrepreneurs are likely to create the conditions which cause inflationary monetary policies and increase
public spending. Hayek does not dispute this but relates the effects
of unlimited democracy to the structure of the legal system. It is not
just the volume of government activity that is disturbing, it is the
means that are used to implement government policy. It has been
suggested on a number of occasions that Hayek's fear is that a *cosmos*
will be turned into a *taxis* as law is turned from a system of purpose-

independent rules into a system of policy-oriented commands. What has happened is that democracies have developed in such a manner that the institution, the legislature, which makes the orders by which government activity proceeds, also makes the rules of just conduct. This requires a little elaboration.

The real problem behind this is whether the traditional doctrine of the separation of powers, whereby liberty is said to be protected if the legislature, executive and judiciary are in separate hands so that there is no concentration of power at one point in a constitutional system, is adequate for the survival of the *cosmos*. In fact, Hayek thinks that the traditional doctrine is inadequate because it has failed to prevent one institution, the legislature, from enacting both types of law.[8] Therefore, a real separation of powers would entail a division not just between the institutions of government, executive and legislature, but between the two law-making functions of the legislature.[9] If the latter were achieved the question of the division between legislature and executive would not be so important. It is vital to stress here that Hayek is making a qualitative point about the increase in government activity that unlimited democracy is likely to generate, not merely a quantitative one. He is not, for example, saying that if government expenditure exceeds 60 per cent of GNP the market economy is likely to come under great strain, but rather that if government action in the form of specific commands gradually replaces individual action guided by rules, then a *catallaxy* is likely to be transformed into a centrally-directed economy and a *cosmos* into a *taxis*.

One of the major deficiencies of traditional normative democratic theory is that a clear distinction between will as a source of authority and procedural rules as a criterion of rightfulness was not properly articulated. At the time that democratic political theory was first taken seriously, in the first half of the last century, it seemed natural to suppose that the replacement of the single will of an absolute monarch by the collective will of the people would improve the prospects for liberty since the absence of liberty was obviously associated with minority regimes.[10] But what was not fully appreciated was the possibility that personalised collective decision-making might be just as oppressive as the dictatorship of a single person. What is worse, democracy has an aura of legitimacy about it which other forms of government do not, at least in the contemporary world. This makes rational argument about democracy which involves a consideration of its defects unpopular. For these reasons

Hayek attaches supreme importance to procedural rules as the source of legitimacy, since their acceptance entails the negation of any form of unlimited sovereignty.

3. THE RECONSTRUCTION OF THE LIBERAL STATE

In a number of articles in recent years Hayek has explored the possibilities of fundamental reforms which might prove effective in saving the order of the *cosmos*, and its associated economic order, the *catallaxy*, from the unintended consequences of unlimited democracy. For the problem, he says, is not that private enterprise does not secure large support in democratic societies, but that the operation of the majority-rule system does not maximise this public support, since private groups clearly gain when strict rules and rigid free market principles are relaxed in their favour. The aim is to secure a division of powers between the authorities that make the two types of law. The results of these explorations seem startlingly radical for a writer who has so frequently and effectively stressed the importance of the slow growth of institutions.

Hayek suggests that in the case of a parliamentary system the two parts of the legislature should be strictly divided, charged with different functions, and their composition determined by different procedures.[11] One part should be concerned with the making of the rules of just conduct, those general rules that have no specific purpose, and the other with the laws and regulations that are required for the despatch of government business. While there is no limit on what governments actually do, what they do must be done in accordance with the rules of just conduct. As one would expect from Hayek's jurisprudence, the emphasis lies not on the content of laws but on the form that they should take. The part of the legislature concerned with the making of government policy in this way would be democratically elected under familiar procedures and would be in a sense 'sovereign'.

To illustrate this proposal the example of the government's budget is very helpful.[12] According to Hayek's scheme the decisions about public expenditure and the economic policies that are to be pursued are matters for the democratically-elected part of the legislature, but the raising of the revenue is a matter for the second, or upper, chamber. It is very important what form the tax laws should take and Hayek obviously has in mind a point he has made frequently, that progressive income tax is in breach of the rule of law because it is discriminatory, whereas proportionate income tax is consistent with the rule of law as the same rule applies to everyone. The upper chamber, which is concerned with the making of the general rules of just conduct, would, Hayek hopes, design tax rules that meet the standards of the meta-legal doctrine of the rule of law. Hayek seems to think also that the particular tax rule should be fixed so that a government would know in advance how much revenue was available and would adjust its expenditure to this. This would prevent the vice, to which democratic governments are particularly prone, of initially determining government expenditure and then finding the revenue to pay for it.[13] In the proposed scheme, however, there would be no limit on what the democratic government may do within the rules of just conduct.

What guarantees are there that the second chamber would pass laws in the form of rules of just conduct? To answer this question Hayek suggests a form of composition that must sound slightly odd to modern ears. It should be composed of people who would be both independent of party or factional interest and who would be guaranteed some permanence in the assembly. Thus he suggests that it should consist of those between their forty-fifth and sixtieth year (though he has also said the age span might be forty to fifty-five), and elected for fifteen years. Each member would be elected by those members of the electorate who reach their forty-fifth birthday and would be ineligible for re-election. This means that as voters would vote only once, when they reached forty-five, and some members would retire every year, the composition of the assembly would be constantly changing.

Hayek hopes that such provisions might ensure that the second chamber, which, to repeat, would be charged only with the responsibility of making rules of just conduct, would be immune from the vote-maximising motivations, and the desire to promote group interests, that characterise the democratic assembly proper. He hopes therefore that the properly-constituted second chamber might develop a genuine concern for the public interest, where this concept represents *not* a sum of group interests but those interests that an individual has as a member of the public.[14] These genuine public interests include the maintenance of the whole system of rules which an individual as a member of a group may wish to see relaxed in his particular case.

One example might illustrate the logic of Hayek's proposed

system. While mortgagees in Britain as group members benefit from the income tax concessions they get, this relaxation of the discipline of the market produces misallocations in the economy from which in the long run everybody suffers, and it also involves a breach of the rules of just conduct in relation to tax law. If the second chamber members were above party interest they would, presumably, create perfectly general tax rules which would not contain special exemptions for politically privileged groups. The whole of Hayek's argument in this area can be interpreted as an attack on the claims made on behalf of the advocates of pressure group politics who believe that somehow a social harmony will emerge if the various groups in society are given an influence in politics proportionate to their strengths.

It should be stressed that Hayek is making quite a different interpretation of the separation of powers from that traditionally made. It is not the simple separation between legislature, executive and judiciary, which he thinks is inadequate in an age of majoritarian democracy, but a complex one between the two bodies that make the two types of law. The problem of limiting government is then not the quantitative one of restricting the volume of economic activity by the government but the qualitative one of enforcing the adherence by government to the rules of just conduct in whatever it is that the government does—a problem that was discussed in Chapter 6. The question to be asked is whether the qualitative approach is superior.

Is it really true that government can be limited by perfectly general rules alone? As we have seen in discussing law in general we are entitled to be a little sceptical of Hayek's claims, since the mere generality of a law may not be sufficient for Hayek's purposes. In the example of tax relief on mortgages, it might be possible to couch a tax law in such a form as to pass Hayek's test of generality yet which picks out the favoured group for exemption, as the examples given in Chapter 5 indicated. Furthermore, even under Hayek's rigorous rules for the composition of the second chamber, can we be sure that it will be independent of factions? The economic theorists of democracy seem to be saying that because of the universality of the vote-maximising motivation in a democracy there ought to be some formal limit on what a legislature does, *whatever form it takes*. Thus when Tullock suggests replacing majority voting by a two-thirds rule in democratic legislatures he is not making any judgement about the type of legislation passed.[15] This may be as effective as

Hayek's separation of the law-making authorities, since if Hayek's second chamber did become politicised there is nothing in his ideal 'constitution' to prevent it subtly passing laws favourable to groups in the name of rules of just conduct.

In some ways the technical solution to the problem of democracy is easier than Hayek thinks. The problem in a democracy like Britain's is that the costs of political activity are relatively low, so that political entrepreneurs do not normally have to appeal to a very wide group in order to achieve political power. The absence of proportional representation means that seats are normally won with less even than a majority vote, with the consequence that parties overall can win an election with a relatively narrow base of support; and the absence of a written constitution means that there are no formal limits on what elected governments can do. The simplest solution to the problems of democracy that Hayek accurately portrays is to raise the costs of political activity. This could be done with changes which would not only be minor in comparison with Hayek's elaborate and utopian scheme but which would be more consistent with the process of evolution.

Also, Hayek has written of the problems of British democracy as if they were the problems of democracy as such. While the vote-maximising feature is common to all democracies its particular manifestations will vary considerably from country to country; and it is clear that its effects are different, for example, in America, which has the traditional separation of powers, from those in Britain, which has no formal safeguards against the power of electorally-contrived majorities. Yet Hayek's epistemology, which understands political and social phenomena in terms of general orders drives him to make the following quite misleading statement: 'All democracy that we know today in the west is more or less unlimited democracy'.[16] But this is only even roughly true if we accept Hayek's account of the separation of powers as a separation between the two law-making bodies; if it is viewed any other way then clearly there are many varying ways of limiting elected majorities in liberal democracies, and more efficient limitations can be devised which are within the tradition of an evolving rule-governed political democracy. Against the proposed solution, that ways be found of raising the costs of political activity so that political entrepreneurs are forced to widen the base of their support, Hayek would reply, no doubt, that this takes no account of the qualitative distinction between the two types of law, even severely limited democratic assemblies might still make perverted rules of just conduct on behalf of particular interests. But if it is logically possible that this may happen even under Hayek's utopian scheme can that scheme be said to be any better? Even minor adjustments which might make substantial improvements, such as the introduction of proportional representation, are dismissed rather lightly by Hayek.[17]

There is, then, good theoretical and empirical evidence that the process of democracy can lead a community along the road to serfdom, and Hayek's fears of this, although they have not yet been fulfilled, sound more plausible when put in the context of modern theories of democracy. But unlike the major exponents of these theories his argument is not primarily about the volume of government activity that occurs under a democracy, although this obviously concerns him, but its character and form. Therefore he does not resort to quantitative arguments, either about the appropriate level of public expenditure or the mix of public and private goods which will maximise social welfare, in his discussion of democracy and capitalism, but makes only qualitative propositions about the transformation of rule-based societies into command-based organisations that is likely to occur as the unintended consequence of unlimited majoritarian democracy. It is because of this that his reform proposals appear rather utopian and impracticable in comparison with those of writers who have been concerned with the quantitative increase in government activity.[18]

4. LIBERALISM AND CONSERVATISM

It should be clear that Hayek's social and economic philosophy can be seen as a system of ideas in which epistemological and methodological arguments underlie both the theoretical propositions in economics, law and politics and the policy conclusions that follow. But what kind of system is it? The policy conclusions are normally associated with conservatism, or perhaps what is sometimes called the 'radical right', or old-fashioned *laissez-faire* liberalism, but it would be wise to eschew these terms when they have only a political connotation. This is not merely because Hayek has frequently denied that he is a conservative, and rejected the label *laissez-faire*, but because his whole stance is fundamentally anti-political where politics refers to the use of coercion to bring about states of affairs that would not have resulted from free exchange within general rules of just conduct. Political action is appropriate, however, in the enforcing of general rules, and even in their creation, but such action must not be used to direct a *cosmos* towards any particular destination. What Hayek is offering is a kind of algebraic utopia which is characterised by a set of general rules which allow a plurality of ends and purposes to be pursued. It is also a pessimistic utopia in that Hayek doubts that there will ever be agreement about fundamental ends and does not trust politicians to do anything but impose their conception of the good life on others. It is here that the importance Hayek's study of economics has for his political philosophy can be seen, for the economist's conception of the market is of a kind of utopia in that theoretically it allows all tastes to be satisfied, it is impersonal and end-independent. It is politics that is disequilibriating: it replaces exchange by coercion and puts 'social ends' over individual purposes. But Hayek is no anarchist, we cannot do without a monopoly of coercion as we can do without a monopoly of money.

This really has little to do with orthodox conservatism and Hayek has always dissociated himself from political conservatism.[19] Conservatives tend to value tradition for its own sake whereas Hayek approaches tradition, as Popper does, from the point of view of the critical rationalist. In fact, he really is interested in only one tradition, the tradition of spontaneous evolution, celebrated by the eighteenth-century writers Smith, Hume and Ferguson and restated by Menger, precisely because it embodies the value of freedom and his special conception of rationality. Tradition is not a god to be revered, but is to be understood with the help of our critical faculties. This is why Hayek has always distrusted those appeals to mysticism and intuition that so often emanate from conservatives. Although he stresses very much the limitations of our knowledge and understanding this argument is itself an intellectual one; it is the true, or critical, rationalist who is most aware of the limits of human reason. Too much of conservative thinking is deliberately anti-intellectual.

But the real difference between Hayek and orthodox conservatism lies in his emphatic rejection of pragmatism. Conservatives, in general, distrust arguments from principle, pour scorn on comprehensive systems of ideas, and in politics stress expediency and compromise. It is one of Hayek's main arguments that the obsession with the immediate, and with what is 'politically possible', is likely to bring a free society further down the road to serfdom. Furthermore, conservatives like to make a virtue of flexibility, and of judging every case on its merits, an attitude which Hayek has shown, in the case of freedom especially, to be destructive of progress in a rule-governed social order. If every case of liberty were to be judged on its merits there would be very little freedom left. The commitment to liberty, he says, must be dogmatic and inflexible precisely because the advantages it brings are unpredictable. Conservative flexibility, indeed opportunism, can be seen in the attitude of conservatives towards the free market. This is not really understood by conservatives who tend to support a market allocation only when it coincides with their approval which has been reached on other grounds. Conservatives are often, for example, associated with the idea that wages should accord with desert or worthiness and are as eager as socialists to denigrate the 'unmerited' earnings of film stars or property speculators.

An important difference, too, is that conservatives normally have certain views on what a society should be like; their's is not an algebraic conception of a social order. Sometimes it is no more than a mild belief that a society's purposes should reflect the importance of the family, limited patriotism and perhaps an undemanding religious belief; but even this approach may become as collectivist as the socialist equivalents. Metaphysical conceptions of 'community' and 'state' that one finds in conservative political literature can be as oppressive to individuality, when translated into political terms, as the notion of 'class' is in socialist creeds. Furthermore, conservatives are often paternal in their attitude towards consumer choice. For the liberal, with his stress on the private world, what a person does with his money, within general rules, is not a fit subject for central authority. This, taken literally, would entail a degree of permissiveness in personal consumption habits which might well be unacceptable to conservatives, who often have an elevated view of the purpose of society that extends beyond individual choice.

Conservatives are fond of illustrating their differences from liberals by quoting a famous remark of Professor Michael Oakeshott, Britain's leading conservative thinker, on Hayek's *The Road to Serfdom*. Of this book Oakeshott wrote: 'A plan to resist all planning may be better than its opposite, but it belongs to the same style of politics';[20] so condemning the work as rationalist. This comment, plus Oakeshott's distrust of all political ideology, and overt faith in hunch and intuition, would seem to put the two in opposite camps.

Yet this would be too premature a judgement. Hayek's anti-rationalism, his anti-scientism and theory of knowledge are not greatly different from Oakeshott's ideas and he has on occasion quoted Oakeshott's distinction between *nomocracy* and *teleocracy* as being equivalent to that between *cosmos* and *taxis*. Also, it would be highly misleading to categorise Oakeshott as an orthodox conservative.

The term that Hayek has always favoured to describe his social and political views is 'Old Whig'. Because the term liberal has been appropriated by interventionists and egalitarians he thinks that this term best captures the ideas of evolution, the rule of law, limited government and individualism that characterised the eighteenth-century, anti-rationalist school of political economy. The expression certainly differentiates, for Hayek, true liberalism from the false liberalism that developed from the constructivist rationalism of utilitarianism. The connection between Hayek's ideas and conservatism really lies only in the fact that, historically, conservatives have absorbed many Old Whig ideas on society. This has usually been a case of intellectual opportunism. Conservatives use those ideas that they find convenient. They rarely accept the whole structure with all its implications.

The term Old Whig also serves to mark off Hayek's rather cautious liberalism from the more rationalistic variety of libertarianism practised by the followers of Mises, mainly in America. We have already seen in Chapter 2 the differences between Mises and Hayek over methodology and there are other differences, too. Mises was undoubtedly a rationalist. He was much less influenced by Adam Smith and the doctrine of spontaneous evolution of rules and institutions, and sought to find a set of criteria to demarcate the respective spheres of the state and the individual on rationalistic, even utilitarian grounds. While, of course, on many issues Mises and Hayek are in agreement, the former displays an almost Cartesian certainty not only in the truth of his fundamental economic axioms but also in his discussion of the extent of political authority. The followers of Mises, notably Murray N. Rothbard, are associated with a certain kind of sophisticated libertarian anarchism.[21]

5. SCIENCE AND VALUES

From the outset, this enquiry into Hayek's social philosophy has been concerned with the relationship between science and values. While he believes that ultimately ethical values are not amenable to scientific investigation, he does believe that many disputes, for example, between socialists and non-socialists, can be settled without reference to values. This is, as we have seen, easy to show in certain areas, such as the effect of the monopoly power of trade unions, which, when exercised in wage negotiations cannot advance the interests of the working class as a whole; yet support is given to trade unions by socialist intellectuals. This would be agreed with by economists who may not share Hayek's particular methodological position.

This may not be so clear, however, if a socialist were to take a rather different line. He might concede that socialism was incompatible with trade union privilege and also accept that free exchange was the only way to maximise both economic efficiency and freedom. But he might also add that the terms under which people exchanged, the distribution of wealth, need not be taken as given but is alterable, and that such alteration could be achieved, presumably by an egalitarian tax policy, without affecting the process of exchange. In other words, the socialist would say that free exchange does lead to a more complex and efficient economic order but that he is not thereby committed to the given distribution of resources under which exchange takes place, and that Hayek, by opposing any egalitarian tax changes is not simply demonstrating the scientific superiority of decentralised markets over planning but is also revealing a moral acceptance of the *existing* distribution of resources. Since an efficient allocation can emerge from any distribution, is the present distribution beyond criticism?

This is a common objection to Hayek's way of thinking and there are perhaps two answers implicit in his work. Firstly, there is the argument for the positive virtues, in terms of sources of independent power against the state and the external benefits from the existence of private pockets of wealth, of inequality. Since this argument is quasi-moral it is difficult to refute and there is no indication of just how much quantitative inequality Hayek would regard as acceptable. The second answer, Hayek claims, is scientific. This holds that the investing in centralised authority the power of altering the distribution of wealth must lead to consequences not intended by

affairs, largely through the painful experience of regular disappoint-
ment of expectations, the times may be more propitious for Hayek's
reminder that only through the following of abstract rules can we
cope with our necessary ignorance.

But it is a reminder that is not likely to be congenial to many
people. A doctrine that tells us more of the limitations on our ability
to manage social affairs than of the possibilities of controlling the
course of social and economic development is not likely to be
popular in an age of scientism. Hayek's constant, even depressing,
reminder is that so much of our knowledge in economics and social
science has to be learnt anew by each generation. And, furthermore,
it is not normally the intellectual virtues of the liberal system that
guarantee its occasional successes but the practical failure of
socialist and collectivist doctrines to deliver much of what they
promise.

the authors of the scheme. This seems only plausible in relation to
wages where egalitarian taxation not only leads to inefficiency but
could result in the direction of labour if the market signals were
deliberately suppressed; but even here the plausibility of the thesis
depends crucially upon the acceptability of the Austrian methodology. It would be impossible to refute Hayek's thesis by pointing
to examples of highly egalitarian tax policies that had not produced
the direction of labour.

A market socialist, however, could accept the outcomes of an
impersonal market but still say there was room for considerable
political action in the removal of private sector monopoly and the
implementing, perhaps, of a wealth tax to make *access* to the market
more equal. The inequalities that resulted, for example, in wages
would then be acceptable. That such intervention would lead to
totalitarian conclusions cannot be scientifically demonstrated; and
it is true that Hayek himself favours some role for political action in
establishing the conditions for the emergence of a *cosmos*. But it is
also true that collectivists' political programmes rarely exhibit the
end-independent features of the market socialists' model. It is
because of this that Hayek thinks that an individual's starting point
in life should be left to chance rather than conscious planning.

A most important consideration is the connection between
Hayek's methodological position and his liberal values. While he
would want to maintain that it is not possible to logically derive a set
of political and moral values from methodological premises alone,
he would certainly maintain that the values of freedom and
spontaneity were perfectly consistent with his epistemology and
general philosophical position. If one believed in the necessary
limitations of knowledge, the impossibility of constructing theories
that predict particular events, and denied that society was like a
piece of physical phenomenon that could be understood, observed
and directed towards predetermined goals, then it would follow that
freedom and spontaneity would be valued as instrumental devices
to make the best use of existing knowledge and to produce a more
complex social order. But it is also true that some social scientists,
especially economists, have similar moral and political beliefs but
have a rather different methodological position. I am thinking of
those who have a more quantitative approach to social science.
They might also refute socialist arguments, perhaps by stressing the
measurable aspects of certain socialist policies rather than detecting, qualitatively, certain unintended consequences, which is

Hayek's general procedure; but they might be wary of making too strong a connection between methodology and values.

Nor is it clear how Hayek could demonstrate that virtually all social progress does come from spontaneous evolution as compared with conscious direction and control. While obviously Hayek does not think that all evolutionary processes lead to desirable consequences, he nevertheless does believe that central direction and planning would make things worse. But it is very difficult to disentangle which elements in a given complex order are the result of spontaneous evolution and which are the result of political control. There is, furthermore, in Britain at least one political institution, the sovereign parliament, which is the result of spontaneous evolution and yet which on Hayek's own admission is partly the cause of the gradual transition of that country from a free to a collectivist society. It may only be possible to change this by an act of political *will*. It is this vagueness about what the course of evolution implies that enables Hayek to present quite radical schemes of reform, in political institutions and the monetary system, in the context of a generally quietist social philosophy. It is only quietist in the sense that it is very nearly silent on the direction a society should take. Given that so many governments in the West have tried to push their societies in a particular direction then the doctrine does seem highly radical.

Ultimately, the whole of Hayek's system does depend upon agreement about fundamental values. He is convinced that what has gone wrong with liberal democracy is not that values have changed but that certain connections between law, government and economic institutions and the variety of ends that people may want to pursue have been forgotten. Instead of improving those delicate mechanisms that service a free society, removing privileges and opening up access to the market, political leaders have tried to steer the *cosmos* in particular directions but in doing so have created new privileges and new impediments to the free movement of individuals. But can we be so sure that there is not a disagreement about values and merely an argument about policy which can be scientifically resolved? In other words, it is possible that there are fundamental disagreements about values which the doctrine of spontaneous evolution is powerless to resolve. While I would agree with Hayek that there is more agreement about values than people often suppose, the agreement may not be as great as he suggests.

The discipline of abstract rules and the logic of the market order

set very high standards which, although it would be in the interests of individuals to submit themselves to them, may prove too demanding. Tribal affiliations and the collective impulse may well triumph over individualism and the rule of law. It is noticeable that Mises was openly contemptuous of the masses for their inability to see their own interests,[22] and Hayek, for all his criticism of the political realists, has to modify on occasions the logic of abstract principles in the light of political reality. One example worth mentioning is that of the movement of labour across national frontiers. In *The Mirage of Social Justice* he says that the free movement of labour is an ideal which it is impossible to realise in practice and that restrictions on immigration have to be accepted simply because people of different cultures find it difficult to live under the same rules.[23] We know that Hayek's rules of just conduct are perhaps not quite as abstract as some natural law systems from looking at the process of validation. A rule is valid if it can be universalised within an ongoing system of rules, and this means that all rules are to some extent relative, including moral rules as well as legal rules. This does not make them arbitrary or merely conventional. That which is not a product of nature, as rules clearly are not, can still be in a special sense 'natural'. The moral rules that have developed are a product of individuals but they cannot be changed according to individual wills without great damage being done to the *cosmos*. Thus, while Hayek is insistent on the radical distinction between fact and value, and that therefore moral rules cannot be derived from factual premises alone, he would say that some rules are essential if the ends and values of the parties to the *cosmos* are to be served. But we can only know what these are by reference to some particular ongoing system of rules. This reference distinguishes Hayek most clearly from the libertarian rationalist who would subject existing rules to more universal tests.

It was perhaps unfortunate that Hayek's social philosophy should have been formulated during the heyday of dirigiste interventionism when public affairs were dominated by political leaders and social scientists who had little respect and an over-exaggerated faith in social engineering. There are, inevitably, items in Hayek's social philosophy that will be disputed, undoubtedly his great achievement has been to establish the importance of rules both for the smooth functioning of society and for the moral end of preserving freedom. If men are slowly learning the limitations of ou

Notes

In the notes I have used the following abbreviations

The Constitution of Liberty	*CL*
The Counter-Revolution of Science	*CRS*
Individualism and Economic Order	*IEO*
The Mirage of Social Justice	*MSJ*
New Studies in Philosophy, Politics, Economics	
and the History of Ideas	*NS*
The Pure Theory of Capital	*PTC*
Rules and Order	*RO*
The Road to Serfdom	*RS*
The Sensory Order	*SO*
Studies in Philosophy, Politics and Economics	*SPPE*

Publication details of these titles are given in the Select Bibliography.

I have not indicated all the sources of particular references, as many ideas appear frequently throughout Hayek's published works, but have confined myself to the most important.

Notes

CHAPTER I: INTRODUCTION AND PHILOSOPHICAL BACKGROUND

1. This approach is exemplified in T. D. Weldon, *The Vocabulary of Politics*, London, 1953.
2. Apart from Hayek the most rigorous and consistent exponent of this view is probably Milton Friedman; see his *Capitalism and Freedom*, Chicago, 1962.
3. *Political Philosophy*, Oxford, 1967.
4. The theme was celebrated in D. Bell, *The End of Ideology*, New York, 1962.
5. *RS*.
6. *CL*, p. 410.
7. Throughout this book I shall use the word 'liberalism' in its traditional sense where it describes the market economy and its associated political and legal framework. Unfortunately, in America especially, liberalism is more often represented by the very nearly opposite doctrines of economic interventionism and social welfare. I stick to the original usage but shall occasionally speak of libertarianism to mean the same thing.
8. Preface to *CL*.
9. *RO*, p. 6.
10. *MSJ*, p. 136.
11. Translated as *Principles of Economics*, edited by James Dingwall and Bert F. Hoselitz, Glencoe, Ill., 1950.
12. See 'Individualism: True and False', in *IEO*, p. 7.
13. *RO*, pp. 26–9.
14. Hayek's important British Academy Lecture 'Dr Bernard Mandeville', delivered in 1966, is reprinted in *NS*.
15. *NS*, p. 261.
16. *NS*, pp. 253–4.
17. This is a prevailing theme in Hayek's writings. The first, and most complete, systematic refutation of scientism is in *CRS*.
18. 'Individualism: True and False', in *IEO*, pp. 10–13. Also, see *CL*, Chapter IV.
19. Menger's methodological work, first published in 1883, has been translated as *Problems of Economics and Sociology*. Translation by F. J. Nock, edited by Louis Schneider, Urbana, Illinois, 1963.
20. 'Individualism: True and False', in *IEO*, p. 14.
21. Ibid.
22. This argument appears in many versions throughout Hayek's writings. Especially important expositions can be found in *CL*, Chapter II and *RO*, Chapter I.
23. See 'Degrees of Explanation' and 'The Theory of Complex Phenomena', Chapters I and II of *SPPE*.

24. 'The Theory of Complex Phenomena', in *SPPE*, p. 35.
25. *CL*, p. 26.
26. *CL*, pp. 22–5, and *CRS*, p. 97.
27. *CRS*, p. 98.
28. 'Economics and Knowledge', in *IEO*, pp. 50–1.
29. *RO*, p. 14.
30. *CL*, p. 64.
31. London, 1952.
32. *SO*, p. 23.
33. *SO*, pp. 107–112.
34. *SO*, Chapter VIII.
35. *SO*, p. 194.
36. *SO*, pp. 184–90. Also, see 'Rules, Perception and Intelligibility', in *SPPE*, pp. 60–3.
37. *RO*, pp. 8–15.
38. H. L. A. Hart, *The Concept of Law*, Oxford, 1961, pp. 92–3.
39. *CL*, pp. 69–70.
40. See Chapter III of *RO*, and 'Rules, Perception and Intelligibility', in *SPPE*.

CHAPTER 2: THE METHODOLOGY OF THE SOCIAL SCIENCES

1. Although *CRS* was first published in book form in 1952, the bulk of it was published in article form between 1941 and 1944.
2. London, 1967.
3. First published in Hayek's Institute of Economic Affairs paper, *Full Employment At Any Price?*, 1975; this has now been reprinted in *NS*.
4. K. R. Popper, *The Poverty of Historicism*, London, 1957, pp. 130–43.
5. Adam Smith, *The Wealth of Nations*.
6. See Murray N. Rothbard 'In Defence of "Extreme A Priorism"', *Southern Economic Journal*, January, 1957. Rothbard is the leading exponent of the ideas of Mises. The most complete statement made by Mises of his economic and philosophical position is his *Human Action*, Yale, 1963.
7. *Human Action*, p. 124.
8. *Problems of Economics and Sociology*, Urbana, Illinois, 1963, p. 69.
9. *CRS*, p. 28.
10. *CRS*, Chapter II.
11. *CRS*, p. 25.
12. Ibid.
13. *CRS*, pp. 30–1.
14. Chicago, 1953.
15. Ibid., p. 4.
16. This is not Hayek's example but he gives similar ones in *CRS*, Chapter III.
17. *CRS*, pp. 30–2.
18. *CRS*, p. 28; see also 'The Facts of the Social Sciences', in *IEO*.
19. *Methodology of Positive Economics*, pp. 16–23.
20. 'The Facts of the Social Sciences', in *IEO*, pp. 72–3.
21. 'In Defence of "Extreme A Priorism"', p. 315.
22. First formulated by P. A. Samuelson: 'A Note on the Pure Theory of

Consumer's Behaviour', *Economica*, 5 (1938).

23. 'The Place of Menger's *Grundsätze* in the History of Economic Thought', in *NS*, p. 277.

24. This is the criticism made by Murray N. Rothbard in *Toward a Reconstruction of Utility and Welfare Economics*, New York, 1977. This was originally published in 1956 in a *Festschrift* in honour of Mises.

25. *The Concept of Law*, Oxford, 1961, Chapters IV and V.

26. 'Ideal Types and Historical Explanation', in A. Ryan (ed.), *The Philosophy of Social Explanation*, Oxford, 1973, pp. 100–1.

27. *SPPE*, p. viii.

28. 'Degrees of Explanation', in *SPPE*, p. 8.

29. 'The Pretence of Knowledge', in *NS*, p. 28.

30. 'The Theory of Complex Phenomena', in *SPPE*, pp. 28–9.

31. Ibid.

32. Ibid., p. 35.

33. 'The Pretence of Knowledge', in *NS*, p. 32.

34. 'The Economy, Science and Politics', in *SPPE*, p. 262.

35. 'Degrees of Explanation', in *SPPE*, p. 11.

36. Ibid., p. 12.

37. Ibid., p. 17.

38. 'The Theory of Complex Phenomena', in *SPPE*, p. 29.

39. Ibid., p. 31.

40. Ibid., pp. 32–3.

41. Ibid., p. 32.

42. 'Degrees of Explanation', in *SPPE*, p. 17.

43. 'The Theory of Complex Phenomena', in *SPPE*, p. 29.

44. L. von Mises, *The Ultimate Foundations of Economic Science*, New York, 1962, p. 69.

45. *CRS*, p. 32.

46. 'Degrees of Explanation', in *SPPE*, pp. 17–18.

47. 'The Pretence of Knowledge', in *NS*, pp. 33–4.

48. Reprinted in *Economica*, 13 (1933).

49. *CRS*, pp. 73–4.

50. *CRS*, p. 75.

51. This is the famous *Methodenstreit* (dispute over methods) that followed the publication of Menger's methodological work.

52. *CRS*, pp. 37–8.

53. *CRS*, p. 53.

54. *CRS*, p. 39.

55. 'The Theory of Complex Phenomena', in *SPPE*, pp. 34–5.

56. See Hayek's introduction to *The Collected Works of Carl Menger*, London, 1934, p. xxx.

57. Cf. K. R. Popper, *The Open Society and Its Enemies*, London, 1945, Vol. II.

58. Cf. E. Nagel, *The Structure of Science*, New York, 1961, pp. 484–5.

59. This is the economic theory of democracy in which the traditional tools of economic analysis are applied to political behaviour. It will be discussed in more detail in Chapter 9.

60. 'The Pretence of Knowledge', in *NS*, p. 24.

61. Ibid., p. 25.

62. Austrian economists have persistently criticised those monetarists who believe that measurable changes in the price level are the only important effects of changes in the supply of money.
63. Although in the literature Popper is often mistakenly interpreted as a positivist.
64. *Conjectures and Refutations*, London, 1963, p. 217.
65. Ibid., p. 219.
66. *The Poverty of Historicism*, p. 35.
67. Ibid., p. 138.
68. *Conjectures and Refutations*, pp. 223–4.
69. *The Poverty of Historicism*, p. 65.
70. Reprinted in *IEO*.
71. Ibid., p. 55.

CHAPTER 3: THE MARKET ORDER AND COMPETITION

1. For an extremely perceptive discussion of this point see J. Buchanan, 'Is Economics the Science of Choice?', in *Roads to Freedom: Essays in Honour of Friedrich A. von Hayek*, edited by E. Streissler, London, 1969.
2. L. C. Robbins, *The Nature and Limits of Economic Science*, London, 1932, is the standard exposition of this view. While Austrian economists like to differentiate their methodology from that of Robbins it would be wise not to exaggerate the difference as there are many important points on which there is substantial agreement between the two approaches.
3. 'Economics and Knowledge', in *IEO*, p. 36.
4. See *PTC*, Chapter II, for a good account of Hayek's special concept of equilibrium.
5. 'Economics and Knowledge', in *IEO*, pp. 35–6.
6. Ibid., p. 39.
7. Ibid., pp. 40–1.
8. 'Socialist Calculation II', in *IEO*, pp. 152–8.
9. Ibid., p. 54.
10. Ibid., p. 153.
11. *The Confusion of Language in Political Thought*, London, 1968; reprinted in *NS*, p. 90.
12. 'The Principles of a Liberal Social Order', in *SPPE*, p. 164.
13. For a complete description of the idea of a *catallaxy* see *MSJ*, Chapter X.
14. *MSJ*, pp. 109–110.
15. 'Economics and Knowledge', in *IEO*, *passim*.
16. Ibid., p. 53; see also 'Principles of a Liberal Social Order', in *SPPE*, pp. 173–4.
17. *MSJ*, pp. 112–115.
18. Reprinted in *IEO*.
19. 'The Use of Knowledge in Society', in *IEO*, p. 87.
20. See, for example, K. Minogue's review of *MSJ* in *The Times Higher Education Supplement*, December 10, 1976.
21. *Competition and Entrepreneurship*, Chicago, 1973.
22. 'The Meaning of Competition', in *IEO*, p. 100.
23. This is the implication of Kirzner's analysis.

24. Cf. Milton Friedman, *The Methodology of Positive Economics*, Chicago, 1953, pp. 16–23.
25. *CL*, Chapter XVIII.
26. *CL*, Chapter XVIII.
27. *CL*, pp. 327–8.
28. *RS*, pp. 32–5.
29. *RS*, p. 36.
30. See 'The Corporation in a Democratic Society', in *SPPE*.
31. *CL*, p. 265.
32. *CL*, p. 266.
33. *CL*, p. 265.
34. *CL*, p. 266.
35. *Human Action*, Yale, 1963, pp. 388–90.
36. 'Free Enterprise and the Competitive Order', in *IEO*, p. 107.
37. Ibid., p. 111.
38. *MSJ*, Chapter XI.

CHAPTER 4: LIBERTY AND COERCION

1. *RO*, p. 58.
2. 'The Theory of Complex Phenomena', in *SPPE*.
3. 'Socialist Calculation II', in *IEO*, p. 163.
4. *CL*, p. 6.
5. 'The Moral Element in Free Enterprise', in *SPPE*, p. 230.
6. *CL*, Chapter V.
7. See 'The Moral Element in Free Enterprise', in *SPPE*.
8. Cf. Sir Isaiah Berlin, *Two Concepts of Liberty*, Oxford, 1958, and M. Cranston, *Freedom: A New Analysis*, London, 1953.
9. *CL*, p. 11.
10. *RO*, pp. 55–6.
11. *CL*, p. 13.
12. *CL*, pp. 13–15.
13. 'Freedom as Politics', in B. Crick, *Political Theory and Political Practice*, London, 1971.
14. *CL*, p. 14.
15. *CL*, pp. 19–20.
16. 'Hayek on Liberty', in *Politics and Economics*, London, 1963. A detailed and important review of *CL*.
17. *CL*, pp. 18–19.
18. *CL*, p. 18.
19. *CL*, p. 16.
20. *CL*, p. 17.
21. *CL*, pp. 15–16.
22. See especially Berlin, pp. 29–39.
23. This concept appears in many of Hayek's writings, a particularly lucid account can be found in *RO*, pp. 106–110.
24. *RO*, p. 108.
25. *CL*, p. 141.

26. *CL*, p. 140.
27. *RS*, Chapter VIII. Hayek says that this may not be the intention of socialists but they will be driven inexorably to it.
28. H. L. A. Hart, *The Concept of Law*, Oxford, 1961, p. 192.
29. *CL*, p. 35.
30. *CL*, Chapter IV.
31. Cf. R. Harrod, 'Professor Hayek on Individualism', *Economic Journal*, vi, 1946.
32. *CL*, pp. 30–1.
33. *CL*, p. 60.
34. Ibid.
35. See especially J. Buchanan, *The Limits of Liberty*, Chicago, 1975.
36. R. Nozick, *Anarchy, State and Utopia*, Oxford: Blackwell, 1974, Part I.
37. *CL*, p. 14.
38. *CL*, p. 15.
39. 'The Moral Element in Free Enterprise', in *SPPE*, pp. 235–6.
40. *Anarchy, State and Utopia*, Chapter X.
41. *CL*, pp. 39–42.
42. *CL*, p. 29.
43. *CL*, pp. 37–8.
44. *CRS*, p. 88. Also, see *CL*, p. 23.
45. See *CRS*, Chapter X, where Hayek gives a very succinct account of the engineering type of mind which exemplifies the constructivist rationalist epistemology.
46. *RS*, p. 36.
47. *CL*, pp. 46–7.
48. '"Free" Enterprise and the Competitive Order', in *IEO*, pp. 113–114.
49. *CL*, p. 31.
50. 'The Principles of a Liberal Social Order', in *SPPE*, pp. 161–2.
51. *RO*, p. 60.
52. B. Barry, *Political Argument*, London, 1965, Chapter I.
53. *CL*, p. 133.
54. Ibid.
55. *CL*, p. 142.
56. *CL*, p. 143.
57. *CL*, pp. 150–1.
58. *CL*, pp. 135–6.
59. *CL*, p. 136.
60. 'Freedom and Coercion', in *SPPE*, p. 348. This was a reply to R. Hamowy's review of *The Constitution of Liberty* in *New Individualist Review*, April 1961.
61. *CL*, pp. 278–9.
62. Ibid.
63. Milton Friedman, in *Capitalism and Freedom*, Chicago, 1962, argues that, in principle, legal prohibitions of closed-shop agreements are as illiberal as laws enforcing non-discrimination practices.

CHAPTER 5: THE THEORY OF LAW

1. 'Legal Positivism and the Separation of Law and Morals', *Harvard Law Review*, lxxi (1958).

2. *RO*, pp. 91–3; *MSJ*, 12–14.
3. See the quotation at the head of Chapter II of *CL*.
4. Cf. G. Ryle, *The Concept of Mind*, London, 1949, Chapter II.
5. 'Rules, Perception and Intelligibility', in *SPPE*, p. 53.
6. Ibid., p. 51.
7. Ibid., pp. 58–60.
8. Ibid., p. 47.
9. This distinction, which is fundamental to Hayek's jurisprudence, appears frequently in his social philosophy. Good descriptions of it can be found in 'The Confusion of Language in Political Thought', reprinted in *NS*; also, see *RO*, pp. 74–81.
10. *RO*, pp. 105–6.
11. 'Rules, Perception and Intelligibility', in *SPPE*, p. 45.
12. *RO*, p. 165.
13. *MSJ*, pp. 144–52.
14. *RO*, pp. 43–6; 'Notes on the Evolution of Systems of Rules of Conduct', in *SPPE*, pp. 66–70.
15. 'Notes on the Evolution of Systems of Rules of Conduct', in *RO*, pp. 70–1.
16. *RO*, pp. 43–4.
17. 'Notes on the Evolution of Systems of Rules of Conduct', in *SPPE*, p. 74.
18. *RO*, p. 44.
19. *RO*, p. 99.
20. *CL*, p. 149.
21. *CL*, p. 148.
22. *RO*, p. 77.
23. *CL*, pp. 142–3.
24. *RO*, Chapter V.
25. *CL*, p. 153; *RO*, pp. 98–100.
26. *CL*, p. 205.
27. *RO*, Chapter II.
28. *RO*, Chapter V.
29. *RO*, Chapter II.
30. *RO*, Chapter VI.
31. *RO*, p. 132.
32. Ibid.
33. Since the publication of *The Political Ideal of the Rule of Law*, Cairo, 1952, the first full statement of his legal theory, Hayek has repeated the point made there that the English common law has long since departed from the ideal of the rule of law.
34. See Hart, *The Concept of Law*, Oxford, 1961, Chapters II, III and IV for a description and penetrating critique of the Command school.
35. *MSJ*, pp. 45–6.
36. *RO*, p. 100.
37. *RO*, pp. 86–7.
38. *CL*, p. 158.
39. See *The Concept of Law*, especially Chapters I and VII.
40. The American Realist school of jurisprudence, in its extreme form, regards law as no more than a series of predictions of what judges will decide in particular cases. It is summed up in Holmes's famous phrase, 'the prophecies of what the

courts will do . . . are what I mean by the law'. This view almost completely disregards the importance of the obligatory nature of rules.

41. *CL*, p. 208.
42. Compare the comments on codified law in *CL*, p. 198 with those in *RO*, pp. 116–17.
43. *RO*, p. 89. This admission does make Hayek's argument for common law in preference to codified law sound less than completely convincing.
44. *RO*, pp. 124–6.
45. *RO*, pp. 129–31.
46. *RO*, p. 133.
47. *CL*, p. 207; *RO*, p. 90.
48. See especially Chapter VII, *CL*; Chapter VI, *RO*; and *Economic Freedom and Representative Government*, London, 1973, reprinted in *NS*.
49. *RO*, pp. 65–71.
50. For descriptions of these ideas see *CL*, Chapters XII and XIII.
51. *CL*, Chapter XIV.
52. *CL*, p. 206.
53. Ibid.
54. See, *The Concept of Law*, pp. 189–95.
55. *CL*, p. 154.
56. J. W. N. Watkins, 'Philosophy', in A. Seldon (ed.), *Agenda for a Free Society*, London, 1961, p. 40. Watkins also described Hayek's system as an 'algebraic utopia'.
57. S. Brittan, *Capitalism and the Permissive Society*, London, 1973, p. 94.
58. *RO*, pp. 91–3.
59. See, for example, Sir Leslie Scarman, *English Law—The New Dimension*, London, 1974.
60. *CL*, pp. 212–17.
61. *The Concept of Law*, Chapter IV.
62. Ibid., pp. 203–7.
63. *MSJ*, p. 56.
64. 'When I say that the object of laws is always general, I mean that law considers subjects *en masse* and actions in the abstract, and never a particular person or action', in *The Social Contract*, G. D. H. Cole's translation, London, 1913, p. 30.
65. *Taking Rights Seriously*, London, 1977.
66. Ibid., pp. 24–6.
67. Ibid., p. 82.
68. *RO*, p. 159.
69. Also, Dworkin does not regard the right to liberty as central to his argument in favour of rights. See especially Chapter XII of *Taking Rights Seriously*.
70. *The Concept of Law*, pp. 94–6.
71. *MSJ*, pp. 50–1.
72. *RO*, p. 135.
73. *RO*, p. 134.
74. *CL*, pp. 236–9; *MSJ*, pp. 55–6.
75. Watkins, op. cit., p. 39.
76. *CL*, p. 155.
77. Robbins, *Politics and Economics*, London, 1963, p. 95.
78. pp. 101–2.

CHAPTER 6: THE AGENDA OF GOVERNMENT

1. The minority of liberals have continued the argument against collectivism through the publications of The Institute of Economic Affairs, an institution that has published some of Hayek's important papers over the last twenty years. For a discussion of welfare from a market point of view, see A. J. Culyer, *The Economics of Social Policy*, London, 1973.

2. For an excellent summary of this approach to political economy, see G. Tullock, *The Vote Motive*, Institute of Economic Affairs, London, 1976.

3. *RO*, pp. 45–6.

4. *CL*, p. 220. This anti-quantitative approach to the evaluation of government activity is, of course, quite consistent with Hayek's methodology.

5. See especially, *RO*, pp. 56–9.

6. 'The Principles of a Liberal Social Order', in *SPPE*, p. 173.

7. Ibid., pp. 173–4.

8. Ibid., p. 173.

9. *CL*, p. 221.

10. *CL*, pp. 222–4.

11. *CL*, p. 222.

12. G. Tullock *Private Wants, Public Means*, New York, 1970, pp. 53–4.

13. *RS*, Chapter III.

14. *CL*, pp. 227–8.

15. *CL*, p. 227.

16. *CL*, pp. 223–6.

17. *CL*, p. 264. Needless to say, most subsidies in social democracies have a quite different object in mind, that of preserving the jobs of politically important groups which would otherwise be eliminated by competition.

18. *CL*, p. 259.

19. *CL*, p. 144.

20. *RS*, pp. 44–5.

21. See Tullock, *Private Wants, Public Means*, pp. 42–7, for a good discussion of this whole area.

22. Most of the discussion by economists is of external 'bads'.

23. E. J. Mishan, 'The Economics of Sex Pollution', in *Making the World Safe for Pornography*, London, 1973.

24. *CL*, pp. 341–2.

25. His brief critical comment on A. C. Pigou, who did pioneering work in the field of welfare economics, centres on this very point. See 'The Economy, Science and Politics', in *SPEE*, p. 264.

26. *CL*, p. 365. Libertarian political economists are only just beginning to work out a solution to the externality problem which excludes state intervention. An extreme view holds that all cases of pollution can be treated as cases of invasions of property rights and therefore what is required is a development of the legal order so that new forms of individualistically-based property rights can be enforced. This view explicitly rejects the argument that there are any such things as 'public goods'. For a discussion of these problems see Murray N. Rothbard, *For a New Liberty*, New York, 1973, pp. 269–78.

27. *CL*, p. 263.

28. *CL*, pp. 324–5.

29. The idea is argued in two Institute of Economic Affairs pamphlets, *Choice in Currency*, 1976 (reprinted in *NS*), and *The Denationalisation of Money*, 1976.
30. This commitment to a basic level of welfare is mentioned in all the major statements of Hayek's political philosophy, although it is nowhere discussed in detail. There is certainly no quantitative indication of what it might be.
31. *CL*, p. 259.
32. *CL*, pp. 258–9.
33. *CL*, p. 296.
34. *CL*, p. 290.
35. *CL*, p. 304.
36. *CL*, p. 291.
37. *CL*, pp. 298–9.
38. This is the main objection raised today by liberal economists against socialised medicine, although it is not explicitly discussed by Hayek.
39. *CL*, pp. 311–12.
40. *CL*, p. 292.
41. *CL*, p. 293.
42. *CL*, p. 343.
43. See N. P. Barry, 'A Political Economy of Housing', in *CBI Review*, Summer, 1977.
44. *CL*, pp. 369–70.
45. *CL*, p. 374.
46. *CL*, p. 371.
47. *CL*, pp. 370–1. Strict libertarians maintain that collective ownership of natural resources has led to much greater waste than private ownership and that there can be no argument for increased state activity because of the problem of conservation. See Rothbard, *For a New Liberty*, New York, 1973, pp. 259–68.
48. 'The Pretence of Knowledge', reprinted in *NS*, p. 31.
49. Ibid.
50. See 'The Economics of Development Charges', in *SPPE*, Chapter XXV.
51. Ibid., pp. 328–9.
52. Ibid., p. 328.

CHAPTER 7: HAYEK'S THEORY OF JUSTICE

1. Brian Barry, 'Justice and the Common Good', in A. Quinton (ed.), *Political Philosophy*, Oxford, 1967, p. 193.
2. *RO*, Chapter IV.
3. Oxford, 1972.
4. For the latter see Brian Barry, *The Liberal Theory of Justice*, Oxford, 1973.
5. T. Hobbes, *Leviathan* (ed. C. B. Macpherson), London, 1968, p. 312.
6. In *What is Justice?*, Berkeley, 1960.
7. David Miller, *Social Justice*, Oxford, 1976, p. 17.
8. Brian Barry, *Political Argument*, London, 1965, Chapter 1.
9. *RO*, pp. 17–23.
10. *RO*, p. 20.
11. *RO*, p. 20. The basic moral rule, that all subordinate rules are justified to the

extent that they promote utility in the long run, would have to be taken as given.

12. Brian Barry, *Political Argument*, p. 97.

13. *Anarchy, State and Utopia*, Oxford: Blackwell, 1974, pp. 151–3.

14. Brian Barry, 'On Social Justice', *The Oxford Review*, 5, 1967.

15. J. Buchanan and G. Tullock, *The Calculus of Consent*, Ann Arbor, 1962.

16. *A Theory of Justice*, Oxford, 1972, section 1.

17. *RS*, Chapter VIII.

18. *MSJ*, pp. 31–2.

19. 'The Concept of Social Justice', in R. Brandt (ed.), *Social Justice*, Englewood Cliffs, New Jeresy, 1962, p. 17.

20. 'Justice', in *Philosophy*, 47, 1972, pp. 230–1.

21. *SPPE*, p. 166.

22. *MSJ*, p. 80.

23. *MSJ*, p. 31.

24. *MSJ*, p. 5.

25. *MSJ*, pp. 35–44.

26. *MSJ*, p. 24.

27. Ibid.

28. *MSJ*, p. 36.

29. Ibid.

30. *MSJ*, p. xii.

31. *CL*, pp. 94–5.

32. *MSJ*, Chapter X.

33. *CL*, p. 96.

34. *MSJ*, pp. 92–3.

35. *MSJ*, p. 64.

36. *Anarchy, State and Utopia*, p. 188.

37. 'Justice', pp. 243–5.

38. *Social Justice*, p. 309.

39. *MSJ*, p. 142.

40. *The Liberal Theory of Justice*, p. 164., where he suggests that we should 'spread the nastiest jobs around by requiring everyone, before entering higher education or entering a profession, to do, say three years of work wherever he or she was directed'.

41. 'When Virtue Loses All Her Loveliness', in I. Kristol and D. Bell (eds.), *Capitalism Today*, New York, 1972.

42. See 'The Moral Element in Free Enterprises', in *SPPE*, where Hayek says that a free enterprise society requires the belief in the ethic of individual responsibility for actions and also the belief that merit should be irrelevant to reward. He never considers the possibility that the one might undermine the other. Elsewhere, however, Hayek has explicitly attacked the ethics of collectivism, and those of the social justice school, on the ground that by trying to extend the sphere of moral obligation beyond immediate relationships they are attempting something that is impossible, yet the attempt has the effect of destroying morality where it is possible, that is, in close personal relationships (see 'What is "Social"?—What Does it Mean?' in *SPPE*).

43. *CL*, p. 93.

44. *MSJ*, p. 93.

45. *MSJ*, p. 81.
46. *CL*, pp. 121–3.
47. *The Liberal Theory of Justice*, p. 162.
48. *A Theory of Justice*, pp. 90–95.
49. Ibid., p. 158; also p. 258.
50. Ibid., p. 302.
51. Ibid., pp. 152–7.
52. Ibid., p. 101.
53. Ibid., p. 62.
54. Ibid., pp. 278–9.
55. *CL*, p. 46.
56. *MSJ*, p. 131.
57. *CL*, pp. 31–5.
58. *CL*, Chapter III.
59. *CL*, pp. 91–2.
60. *CL*, p. 93.
61. *CL*, p. 93.
62. *CL*, Chapter XX.
63. *CL*, pp. 320–1.

CHAPTER 8: ECONOMICS AND ECONOMIC POLICY

1. *PTC*, pp. 37–8.
2. *PTC*, pp. 22–4.
3. *CL*, pp. 324–5.
4. *CL*, p. 325. The phrase first appeared in *PTC*, p. 408.
5. While the economic crises of the 1930s and the 1970s are obviously very different in their external manifestations they are caused by similar disequilibriating phenomena. Therefore his dramatic solution, the abolition of the government's monopoly of money, is aimed at preventing both inflation and deflation.
6. One of the translators was Nicholas Kaldor, now Lord Kaldor, who has come to be associated with a very different economic theory and philosophy.
7. See D. Winch, *Economics and Economic Policy*, London, 1969, pp. 199–207.
8. London, 1936.
9. See 'Reflections on the Pure Theory of Money of Mr. J. M. Keynes', *Economica*, 11 (1931) and 12 (1932).
10. 'Personal Recollections of Keynes and the Keynesian Revolution', *NS*, pp. 283–4.
11. The following exposition of the Austrian theory of the trade cycle is taken mainly, but not entirely, from Hayek's *Prices and Production*, 2nd Revised Edition, London, 1935, and *Monetary Theory and the Trade Cycle*, London, 1933.
12. London, 1939.
13. Hayek wrote in 1931: 'it would be one of the worst things which would befall us if the general public should ever again cease to believe in the elementary propositions of the quantity theory'. He has repeated the same message throughout the 1970s.
14. Irving Fisher, the leading quantity theorist, said that the American economy

was on a 'permanently high plateau'. Quoted in R. Heilbroner *The Worldly Philosophers*, London, 1969.

15. *Prices and Production*, pp. 160–2.
16. Ibid., p. 18; also, 'A Note on the Development of the Doctrine of Forced Saving', in *Profits, Interest and Investment*, London, 1939.
17. Ibid., p. 27.
18. This word, and the Austrian theory of capital, is derived from Böhm-Bawerk.
19. *Prices and Production*, pp. 97–8.
20. *Monetary Theory and the Trade Cycle*, pp. 143–4.
21. *Monetary Nationalism and International Stability*, London, 1937, pp. 81–8.
22. *Monetary Theory and the Trade Cycle*, p. 150.
23. 'The Hayek Story', in J. R. Hicks, *Critical Essays in Monetary Theory*, Oxford, 1967.
24. This first appeared in an article published in 1933, translated as 'The Present State and Immediate Prospects of the Study of Industrial Fluctuations', in *Profits, Interest and Investment*, see especially pp. 176–7. Also, see The Campaign Against Keynesian Inflation', in *NS*, p. 206.
25. 'The Campaign Against Keynesian Inflation', in *NS*, p. 210.
26. pp. 63–4.
27. Winch, op. cit., is particularly critical of the style of economics practised at the London School of Economics between the wars. See especially, pp. 158–61.
28. *Profits, Interest and Investment, passim.* But see also 'The Ricardo Effect', in *IEO*, and 'Three Elucidations of the Ricardo Effect', in *NS*.
29. See G. Haberler, *Prosperity and Depression*, London, 1964, p. vii.
30. Ibid., pp. xi–xii for details of anti-depression devices.
31. pp. 356–68.
32. *PTC*, pp. 373–4; 'Personal Recollections of Keynes and the Keynesian Revolution', in *NS*, p. 284.
33. 'The Campaign Against Keynesian Inflation', in *NS*, pp. 194–5.
34. *Monetary Nationalism and International Stability*, pp. 52–3.
35. *CL*, p. 282; 'The Campaign Against Keynesian Inflation,' in *NS*, p. 193.
36. 'Personal Recollections of Keynes and the Keynesian Revolution', in *NS*, p. 286.
37. *RO*, p. 26. There is no clearer example of Keynes's failure to understand the importance of rules than in his reaction to Hayek's *Road to Serfdom*. In a letter to Hayek, Keynes lavished great praise on the book but completely missed the point about planning. He said that what was wanted was not less planning but more: 'But the planning should take place in a community in which as many people as possible, both leaders and followers, wholly share your moral position'. Quoted in R. Harrod, *The Life of John Maynard Keynes*, London, 1951, pp. 436–7. Hayek's position is that we need more rules and less planning precisely because we cannot rely on human nature.
38. *CL*, p. 333.
39. Even if it were true that the economic system was not inherently stable it is difficult to see how Keynesian demand-management policies could be reconciled with the democratic process when that is understood as a vote-maximising process. Elected economic managers are far more likely to respond to the demands of electoral politics than the demands of Keynesian economic rationality. In the last thirty years theoretical and empirical investigations

have suggested that it is the *catallaxy* that is inherently stable, if it can be protected from political interference, and the political system of democracy that has a tendency towards instability.

40. Hayek has reported a personal conversation with Keynes in which the latter revealed supreme confidence in his own ability to change public opinion should the use that some individuals made of his ideas ever become dangerous. See Hayek's review of Harrod's life of Keynes in *SPPE*, p. 348.

41. See H. G. Johnson, *On Economics and Society*, London, 1975, Chapter VIII.

42. For a general discussion of these issues, see T. W. Hutchison, *Keynes v the 'Keynesians'* . . .? Institute of Economic Affairs, London, 1977.

43. Hayek, of course, maintains that the post-war economic prosperity was a consequence of adopting free market policies rather than Keynesian demand management policies.

44. 'The Campaign Against Keynesian Inflation', in *NS*, p. 210.

45. Ibid., pp. 211–12, where Hayek says that temporary public works measures may be justified in order to prevent a serious drop in consumer demand.

46. Ibid., p. 214.

47. *Monetary Nationalism and International Stability*, pp. 52–3.

48. *Choice in Currency* and *The Denationalisation of Money*, both published by the Institute of Economic Affairs, London 1976.

49. 'The Uses of "Gresham's Law" as an Illustration of "Historical Theory"', in *SPPE*, pp. 318–21.

50. Hayek claims perhaps too much originality for his scheme. Although he has presented it in some considerable detail, the argument for a free market in money has a long history in liberal political economy. See Mises, *Human Action*, Yale, 1963, pp. 440–1.

51. Accounts of Friedman's monetary doctrines can be found in the following Institute of Economic Affairs publications; *The Counter-Revolution in Monetary Theory*, 1970; *Unemployment versus Inflation*, 1975; *Inflation and Unemployment*, 1977.

52. M. Friedman and Anna J. Schwartz, *A Monetary History of the United States, 1867–1960*, Princeton, 1963.

53. In fact, Friedman's statistical and theoretical work in monetary economics is a natural outcome of his positivist methodology.

54. Although it should be mentioned that before Hayek advocated a free market in money he was a firm opponent of floating exchange rates. Friedman has always believed that currencies should find their own level in the money markets while Hayek believed that the requirement of maintaining a fixed exchange rate would at least constitute a check on government. Hayek also regarded Friedman's own check on government, the monetary rule, as impracticable, see 'The Campaign Against Keynesian Inflation', in *NS*, pp. 207–8.

55. Friedman has coined the phrase 'the natural rate of unemployment' to describe that level of unemployment caused by microeconomic factors, which the monetary authorities ought not to try and bring down by monetary methods because to do so will only cause inflation. Interestingly enough, in view of his positivism, the natural rate of unemployment, like the natural rate of interest from which the name derives, is conceded by Friedman not to be an easily observable phenomenon. See M. Friedman, *Unemployment and Inflation*, Institute of Economic Affairs, London, 1977.

56. Mises's article appeared in an English translation in F. A. von Hayek (ed.) *Collectivist Economic Planning*, London, 1935, as 'Economic Calculation in the Socialist Commonwealth'.
57. Reprinted in *IEO* under the title, 'Socialist Calculation'.
58. It was claimed by socialists familiar with the general equilibrium system that the economic mechanism that determines relative prices could be put in the form of a series of simultaneous equations without the need of private property and decentralised market exchanges. Hayek's objection in the 1930s centred on the impossibility of solving the millions of equations that would be involved but I think he would now stress the impossibility of centralising the knowledge that would be required to fill in the blanks in these equations.
59. See 'Socialist Calculation III: The Competitive "Solution"', in *IEO*.
60. For a discussion of contemporary socialist economics, see Assar Lindbeck, *The Political Economy of the New Left*, London, 1971.
61. See 'Socialism and Science', in *NS*, pp. 295–308.
62. 'The Economy, Science and Politics', in *SPPE*, p. 255.

CHAPTER 9: CONCLUSION

1. *RS*, Chapters II, III and XII.
2. See '*The Road to Serfdom* after Twelve Years', in *SPPE*, pp. 223–4.
3. Ibid., pp. 224–5.
4. *CL*, Chapter VII.
5. *CL*, p. 103.
6. Good discussions of the problem of majority-rule democracy can be found in 'Economic Freedom and Representative Government', Institute of Economic Affairs, London, 1973, reprinted in *NS*; and 'The Miscarriage of the Democratic Ideal', in *Encounter*, March 1978.
7. *MSJ*, pp. 6–8.
8. See especially *RO*, pp. 141–4.
9. See 'The Constitution of a Liberal State', in *NS*.
10. See 'Whither Democracy', in *NS*, pp. 152–4.
11. Descriptions of the proposed system can be found in 'The Constitution of a Liberal State' and 'Economic Freedom and Representative Government'. Hayek has invented the term *demarchy* to describe his system of limited democracy.
12. See *RO*, pp. 136–7.
13. Ibid.
14. 'The Constitution of a Liberal State', in *NS*, p. 103.
15. *The Vote Motive*, Institute of Economic Affairs, London, 1976, p. 55.
16. 'Whither Democracy', in *NS*, p. 153.
17. Ibid., p. 161.
18. Hayek has also considered the possibility of limiting governments by written declarations of fundamental rights. Though he agrees with this in principle, he feels that the rights protected might be limited merely to those enumerated in formal documents, while an evolutionary approach might lead to rights emerging which go beyond these. What Hayek is completely opposed to is the current fashion of treating 'economic' rights as logically equivalent to

traditional negative rights, see *MSJ*, pp. 101–6.

19. See the postscript to *CL*, 'Why I am not a Conservative', pp. 397–408
20. *Rationalism in Politics*, London, 1962, p. 21.
21. A recent complete statement of this is Murray N. Rothbard, *Power and Market*, Institute for Humane Studies, California, 1970.
22. See, for example, *Human Action*, p. 359, where Mises states: 'the immense majority of our contemporaries are mentally and intellectually not adjusted to life in the market society although they themselves and their fathers have unwittingly created this society by their actions'.
23. *MSJ*, p. 58. If the market order is interpreted as a purely abstract order then there cannot be a justification for politically-imposed impediments to the free movement of labour across national frontiers; such laws would be condemned as pragmatic. It was indeed one of the arguments of the libertarians against the welfare state that if this guaranteed individuals a level of income that they could not earn in the market then it would lead inevitably to illiberal immigration laws.

Select Bibliography

I have listed below only a brief selection of Hayek's works, and have confined those to English sources. A complete bibliography can be found in *Essays on Hayek*, edited by Fritz Machlup, London, 1977. An abbreviated title at the end of an entry indicates where the item has been reprinted. A list of the abbreviation is given in the Notes, p. 203.

BOOKS AND PAMPHLETS

Prices and Production, London, 1931, 2nd revised and enlarged edition, London, 1935.

Monetary Theory and the Trade Cycle, London, 1933.

Monetary Nationalism and International Stability, Geneva, 1937.

Profits, Interest and Investment, London, 1939.

The Pure Theory of Capital, London, 1941.

The Road to Serfdom, London, 1944.

Individualism and Economic Order, London, 1948.

John Stuart Mill and Harriet Taylor, London and Chicago, 1951.

The Counter-Revolution of Science, Glencoe, Ill., 1952.

The Sensory Order, London and Chicago, 1952.

The Political Ideal of the Rule of Law, Cairo, 1955.

The Constitution of Liberty, London and Chicago, 1960.

Studies in Philosophy, Politics and Economics, London and Chicago, 1967.

Law, Legislation and Liberty, Vol. I, *Rules and Order*, London, 1973. Vol., II, *The Mirage of Social Justice*, London, 1976.

New Studies in Philosophy, Politics, Economics and the History of Ideas, London, 1978.

Individualism? True and False, Dublin, 1946.

The Confusion of Language in Political Thought, with some Suggestions for Remedying it, Institute of Economic Affairs, London, 1968, *NS*.

A Tiger by the Tail, edited by Sudha R. Shenoy, Institute of Economic Affairs, London, 1972.

Full Employment at any Price? Institute of Economic Affairs, London, 1975.

Choice in Currency, Institute of Economic Affairs, London, 1976.

The Denationalisation of Money, Institute of Economic Affairs, London, 1976.

Economic Freedom and Representative Government. Fourth Wincott memorial lecture delivered at the Royal Society of Arts, 31 October 1973, Institute of Economic Affairs, London, 1973, *NS*.

Collectivist Economic Planning, London, 1935, edited with introductory and concluding chapters by F. A. Hayek.

The Collected Works of Carl Menger, 4 vols., London, 1934–1936. Edited and introduced by F. A. Hayek.

Thornton, Henry, *An Enquiry into the Nature and Effects of the Paper Credit of Great Britain*, 1802, London, 1939. Edited with an Introduction by F. A. Hayek.

Capitalism and the Historians, London and Chicago, 1954. Edited with an Introduction by F. A. Hayek.

ARTICLES

'Reflections on the Pure Theory of Money of Mr. J. M. Keynes', *Economica*, 11, 1931, and 12, 1932.

'The Pure Theory of Money: A Rejoiner to Mr. Keynes', *Economica*, 11, 1931.

'Money and Capital: A Reply to Mr. Sraffa', *Economic Journal*, 42, 1932.

'The Trend of Economic Thinking', *Economica*, 13, 1933.

'Economics and Knowledge', *Economica*, 4, 1937, *IEO*.

'Socialist Calculation: The Competitive "Solution"', *Economica*, 7, 1940, *IEO*.

'The Counter-Revolution of Science', Pts I–III, *Economica*, 8, 1941, *CRS*.

'The Ricardo Effect', *Economica*, 2, 1942.

'Scientism and the Study of Society', Part I, *Economica*, 9, 1942; Part II, *Economica*, 10, 1943; Part III, *Economica*, 11, 1944.

'A Commodity Reserve Currency', *Economic Journal*, 53, 1943, *IEO*.

'The Facts of the Social Sciences', *Ethics*, 54, 1943, *IEO*.

'The Use of Knowledge in Society', *American Economic Review*, 35, 1945, *IEO*.

'The Intellectuals and Socialism', *The University of Chicago Law*

Review, 16, 1949, *SPPE*.

'Full Employment, Planning and Inflation', *Institute of Public Affairs Review*, Melbourne, Australia, 4, 1950, *SPPE*.

'Degrees of Explanation', *The British Journal for the Philosophy of Science*, VI, 1955, *SPPE*.

'Reconsideration of Progressive Taxation', in Mary Sennholz (ed.), *On Freedom and Free Enterprise. Essays in Honour of Ludwig von Mises*, Princeton, 1956.

'The Dilemma of Specialization', in Leonard D. White (ed.), *The State of the Social Sciences*, Chicago, 1956, *SPPE*.

'Inflation Resulting from the Downward Inflexibility of Wages', in Committee for Economic Development (ed.), *Problems of United States Economic Development*, Vol. I, New York, 1958, *SPPE*.

'Freedom, Reason, and Tradition', *Ethics*, 68, 1958.

'Unions, Inflation and Profits' in Philip D. Bradley (ed.), *The Public Stake in Union Power*, Charlottesville, Va., 1959, *SPPE*.

'The Non Sequitur of the "Dependence Effect"', *The Southern Economic Journal*, 27, 1961, *SPPE*.

'The Moral Element in Free Enterprise' in National Association of Manufacturers (ed.), *The Spiritual and Moral Element in Free Enterprise*, New York, 1962, *SPPE*.

'Rules, Perception and Intelligibility', *Proceedings of the British Academy*, 48, 1962, *SPPE*.

'The Legal and Political Philosophy of David Hume', *Il Politico*, 28, 1963, *SPPE*.

'The Theory of Complex Phenomena' in Mario Bunge (ed.), *The Critical Approach to Science and Philosophy. Essays in Honor of Karl R. Popper*, Glencoe, Ill., 1964, *SPPE*.

'Kinds of Rationalism', *The Economic Studies Quarterly* (Tokyo), 15, 1965, *SPPE*.

'Personal Recollections of Keynes and the "Keynesian Revolution"', *The Oriental Economist*, 34, 1966, *NS*.

'The Misconception of Human Rights as Positive Claims', *Farmand*, Anniversary Issue, 1966.

'The Principles of a Liberal Social Order', *Il Politico*, 31, 1966, *SPPE*.

'Dr Bernard Mandeville', *Proceedings of the British Academy*, 62, 1966, *NS*.

'The Constitution of a Liberal State', *Il Politico*, 32, 1967, *NS*.

'A Self-Generating Order for Society' in John Nef (ed.), *Towards World Community*, The Hague, 1968.

'Economic Thought, VI: Austrian School', *International Encyclopaedia of the Social Sciences*, Vol. IV, New York, 1968.

'Carl Menger', *International Encyclopaedia of the Social Sciences*, Vol. X, New York, 1968.

'Three Elucidations of the "Ricardo-Effect"', *Journal of Political Economy*, 77, 1969, *NS*.

'The Primacy of the Abstract', in Arthur Koestler and J. R. Smythies, (eds), *Beyond Reductionism*, London, 1969, *NS*.

'The Place of Menger's *Grundsätze* in the History of Economic Thought', in J. R. Hicks and W. Weber (eds), *Carl Menger and the Austrian School of Economics*, Oxford, 1973, *NS*.

'The New Confusion About Planning', *Morgan Guaranty Trust*, New York, January 1976, *NS*.

'The Miscarriage of the Democratic Ideal', *Encounter*, March 1978.

Index